Reflections
ON LIVING WITH
Children
VOLUME THREE

TAKEN FROM THE
IN RESIDENCE
COLUMNS OF
THE THERAPEUTIC CARE JOURNAL

Dr. Keith J. White

WTL PUBLICATIONS

Published by
WTL Publications,
10 Crescent Road,
South Woodford,
London E18 1JB, UK

Printed and bound in the UK
by Lightning Source UK Ltd

Introduction

Donald Winnicott remarked to the residential child care role model and pioneer David Wills, "In this work the important thing is not so much to do it as to keep on doing it". Mill Grove have been doing what they do for over a century.

Mill Grove is a home. The name Mill Grove is to deliberately avoid any labelling. It is a place called home by people who have lived there and people who have experienced it. Visiting, even for a short while, and you will know this too. One young person described it as "A place for Us", a quote from *West Side Story*. Mill Grove in East London is an East Side Story. A place in a smaller world, a place in a bigger world

The book is not a primer, or a textbook, though there is a lot of learning on these pages. For me reading about Mill Grove is as a story that unfolds as it folds you into its embrace.

Reading this book is to become part of the story. It is inevitable. It is an immersive experience. The learning in this book is integrated. To read it is to absorb it. The learning it offers reaches in to connect to your own experiences. It is a learning experience rather than teaching. We take the learning and creatively adapt it for our use. We are not asked to apply correctly a manualised method for our fidelity to be known. If you choose you can approach its contents as an apprentice or a role model.

There are no obvious methods being proclaimed beyond two primary frameworks, psycho-social and theological. Here are many descriptive responses to the question, "What sort of environment best nurtures the seeds of love?", and in this age of outcomes Mill Grove has one: "How has Love grown?"

Many training and qualification courses focus on something particular; current at the time of writing is trauma, before that safeguarding. The idea is to prove your competence by attendance. What they do not always do is make it part of everything, all the time.

You can read this book at the start of your residential life; you will probably want to return to it after a while and reading it again you will see new things. Others of us will come to it after some while of working with children. This group might find their learning thus far affirmed ("So someone else has thought or experienced this too"), or maybe we will be reminded ("I remember that" and usually the name of the child too), refreshed ("Of course!") redirected ("So you mean it can be like that?"). This book encourages a reflective voice. It accompanies your reading.

You can read it as an individual. I find it best to read a piece at a time, sometimes one a day. Sometimes using the index to find things that will accompany me in my search as to what to do in the here and now.

You can read it as a group. One per month reading by a group I think useful, for reflective discussion at a staff meeting or study session (other reading is useful too!).

There are many ways to describe a residential life. George Lyward described Finchden Manor as "a place of hospitality", the more one thinks about that the more connections can be made: generosity, gratitude, forgiveness, toleration, openness, reassurance, all emerge from within having been part of an environment where they are present continuously and consistently. There is a continuity. We find what has been prepared before.

Every group of people has a culture. To read this book is to discern the Mill Grove particular culture. Pierre Bourdieu describes a "habitus" as a subjective but not individual system of internalised structures, schemes of perception, conception and action common to all members of the same group (page 86, Outline of a theory of practice). Notice it is not a model. It is a theory, to be applied. A sense of value is conferred by living together. These pieces depict a relational environment, relationships are core to everything. We share by listening, we listen by doing. Meaningful doing is an expression of recognition of another person's presence.

Mill Grove follows no fashions. It has continuously refashioned its routines and patterns to meet present needs. The patterns might be characterised as a non-directive practice by words we do not now use prominently in, but are the roots of, professional discourse, like benign, healing, recuperation, sanctuary, unconditional.

Today's concerns push people to relieve immediate anxiety. Interventions predominate over environmental thinking forgetting Winnicott observing that the most effective therapeutic intervention is the "everyday", and Trieschman writing on "the other 23 hours", meaning those outside of the therapy room.

In writing this foreword two words keep coming through: dwell, and dwelling. Mill Grove offers space and time for both, for someone to be amongst, an acceptance.

Life at Mill Grove as I appreciate it offers opportunity for accompaniment, an idea used by Archbishop Romero in Latin America. Two people sharing a relationship through activity and conversation. The ordinary is extraordinary. Each had opportunity to make of it what they needed and to contribute what they could, sometimes less, sometimes more.

If Mill Grove offers an appropriate protection from the world, it provides the foundation to reconsider it and to re-emerge at your own pace and time, when you have found what you came looking for. Mill Grove supports a relationship with the world in manageable doses. What you might find is not specified beyond an environment that is being created consciously and unconsciously, to enable a connection. Once made, often unexpectedly, it propels. So it is with this book.

These are days where governments want to know "what works" and a model that can be replicated. Could Mill Grove be replicated? Probably not. Could it be scaled? Probably not. Why? It has a unique history. Perhaps this book could help you make one of your own? If so then it has served a good purpose, and that, again perhaps, is where we start and start again.

Jonathan Stanley
Principal Partner, National Centre
for Excellence in Residential Child Care

NCERCC is concerned with supporting best practice in research, theory, policy and practice for English Residential Child Care

Foreword

It is a pleasure and privilege to be writing this foreword to Volume Three of *Reflections on Living with Children*. My thanks go to Keith White who is the author of these articles which he has collated for this third collection. All the papers in this edition are based on observations and reflections from his daily 'lived experience' of life with emotionally troubled children and families at Mill Grove. My thanks also go to Jonathan Stanley with all his experience from the residential sector, who has kindly offered to edit Volume three.

I am writing this just a month before I retire from my role as CEO of The Mulberry Bush Charity, where now our School, Outreach, Research and MB3 services continue to grow and meet the needs of all those affected by early years trauma.

In doing so, I am conscious of the role that 'reflective practice' has played in the evolution of The Mulberry Bush, and the papers published in this edition are illustrations of the reflective capacity of Keith White who has used reflection 'in action' bringing together the use of his 'clinical sensibility' and observational skills, and filtered through the lens of psycho-dynamic theory, to deepen his understanding of communications, in service to the construction of positive therapeutic relationships with the children and families at Mill Grove.

So much has happened since my last foreword for Volume 2 of *Reflections on Living with Children* which was published in 2016. The papers in this collection have been previously published in our bi-monthly *Therapeutic Care Journal* (*TTCJ*) which we rebranded from the original *Children Webmag* and started publishing in 2015.

Another major change since that last edition has been the establishment of The 'International Centre for Therapeutic Care', which at the time of the last edition was still 'The National Centre', so this also reflects the growth of the reach and influence of the *TTCJ* across the world since 2016, and this reach and the positive shared connections with practitioners and researchers from around the world continues to grow and strengthen.

Issued bi-monthly, *TTCJ* is essentially the voice of the International Centre for Therapeutic Care, and we continue to invite practitioners and writers from across the globe to share best practice, research and training ideas to meet the needs of emotionally troubled and traumatised children and those who work with them.

The following is information about the International Centre for Therapeutic Care and *TTCJ*.

Our mission
To share models of therapeutic care, and to extend the influence and insights gained from our member networks, in order to improve services and outcomes for traumatised children, young people, their families and communities.

We aim to achieve this by
Sharing models of therapeutic care, and extending the influence and insights gained from our member networks, in order to improve services

and outcomes for traumatised children, young people, their families and communities

Our core values

We support and promote:

- Models of care that are relationship (attachment) based.
- Models of care that promote 'living together as a group or family', where adults, children and families use the lived experience to create 'a way of living and learning together'.
- Models of care that make use of the culture and ethos of the psycho-social and physical environment.
- Models of care where the culture is influenced by a 'conscious use of self' and shared responsibility.
- Models of care that aim to develop a sense of belonging and promote resilience in children and young people.
- Models of care that support high expectations for children and young people, and authentic stability of placement.

If you would like to join the International Centre or write for *TTCJ* please contact: **ic@mulberrybush.org.uk**

We hope you enjoy reading these articles which offer an introduction to the world of therapeutic child care, and especially the importance of being able to stay with 'not knowing' in order that deeper understanding emerges in support of emotionally troubled and traumatised children and families, through the discipline and skills of thinking and reflective practice.

John Diamond
June 2022

Author's Preface

Despite the prediction of David Lane on page 14 of the previous collection of papers, it has come as something of a surprise to discover that his calculations were spot on: there have indeed been over 80 more pieces written for *TTCJ* since Volume Two of *Reflections on Living with Children* was published in 2016. This means that there are roughly 260 articles in total.

In introducing Volume Three it occurs to me that some readers might wonder why I have been so committed to writing this kind of material since March 2000, first in what was called the *ChildrenWebmag*, and subsequently in *TTCJ*. There is the obvious reason that I continue to be a passionate advocate of magazines and journals written for the benefit of those who are seeking to understand and help children and young people. And from an early age I have been drawn to writing as a primary means of communication. But there is something deeper, more personal, and possibly more significant. At some stage I realised that I simply had to write regular pieces as a way of processing the many experiences, thoughts, feelings, questions, anxieties, that I had because of my life at Mill Grove alongside children and young people.

Before describing the reflective process in more depth, here is a summary of the nature and history of Mill Grove, the place that forms the context of my life alongside children, and is present in every piece directly or indirectly.

Mill Grove

Mill Grove is the name of some houses in the East London suburb of South Woodford. They are very close to a roundabout named after a legendary cockney publican, Charlie Brown, which is now where the A406 and the M11 meet. Since 1901 generations of my family have lived in these houses together with over 1,000 children, young people and families who have turned to us for help, support and care. It began life as an informal foster care arrangement and developed into a voluntary children's home until, in 1974, it had outgrown this label, and we chose the name "Mill Grove".

The story began with an act of compassion which embodied a step of faith. My grandfather, Herbert, offered to care for a little girl named Rosie who had just lost her mother. A fellow Sunday-School teacher known affectionately as 'Ma' Hutchin welcomed Rosie into her flat, and within a short time there were so many other requests for help that a children's home housing up to 60 children had come into being. It became known locally as "Whites Homes", although this was never its official title.

From the very first encounter between Herbert and Rosie in November 1899, the founders were determined to keep in touch with all the children who came to live at Mill Grove throughout their lives. In the first decades this was often by letter and visits, but in more recent times as the family has spread around the world, electronic media have helped immensely as we seek to stay connected. There are also records stretching back to 1899 which serve as an indispensable resource for former residents and their families as they explore and try to recreate their life-stories.

My grandparents, Herbert and Edith White, were the first family members to live in this place. My father, Victor, who was also born into the Mill Grove family, continued to make this his home together with his wife Margaret. Ruth and I are the third generation of Whites to live here. There was just one period when the family of Mill Grove had to leave South Woodford: 1939–1945. Remarkably, a farm in Tiptree was offered as a holiday home, and this became a haven in time of war, during which the property in South Woodford was seriously damaged by bombs.

The name Mill Grove was chosen to incorporate these two locations: the houses in South Woodford are the site of an old mill that used to stand beside near the River Roding; and the farmhouse in which the children lived during the Second World War in Tiptree, Essex, was called 'The Grove'. Thanks to this timely resource, the family was kept intact during the war years, when many other children in the East End of London were evacuated to families and schools in rural areas. Over the decades it developed into an extended family or residential community with its roots in South Woodford. If interested, you can find out more from the website: www.millgrove.org.uk

One other part of the United Kingdom that figures prominently in the articles, is North Wales: Eryri (Snowdonia). Beginning in the summer of 1976 we have holidayed there, and since 1984 we have had accommodation in Borth-y-Gest, a harbour village near Porthmadog. This has been an adventure playground for generations of the Mill Grove family, a context for much shared exploration, fun, reflection and conversation. It doesn't take much to see what a great blessing it has been, whether to individuals or to the family.

The reflections are set in this context: sometimes they describe daily events in the place and in the lives of current members of the Mill Grove family; there are mealtimes shared with members of the family living locally; annual celebrations, notably Christmas; holidays in North Wales; descriptions of the dynamics of the Pre-School and Rose Walton Centre based in our premises. But the extended family is so large, and so widespread, that often I find myself alongside those who come back after many years, trying to make sense of their own childhoods, families and feelings.

This is where I was born and grew up, and where Ruth, my wife, and I made our home after we had met in Edinburgh in 1969 and married in 1971. Hopefully it has already become apparent that the place and its life are not easily labelled or pigeon-holed. It has developed organically and represents a kind of safe space not envisaged in its entirety by existing categories, definitions or guidelines. A simple way of trying to understand it is to identify what it is not: an orphanage, a foster home, a children's home, a residential school, a therapeutic community, and children's centre, and so on.

As it happens it has always been rather liminal and difficult to define. An early inspection report by R.J.N. Todd of the Home Office noted that "it was not like any other home". As far as I have been able to discover there is no other residential community in the world that has been in the same family, house and neighbourhood for over 120 years, in which the family and over 1,200 others have lived. I have continued to search across the continents since 1979 to no avail. But if anyone can point me to something similar, we would be delighted to hear from them!

Having taken a radical approach to naming the place, one of the knock-on effects is that anyone reading about it probably needs to come and visit to get any sort of idea of the buildings, the grounds, the locality, and the flavour of the community and its life together. So, for those reading this volume who have not come to see us, there is preliminary challenge, before hopefully some of the dynamics and values become clearer.

Whatever the best description of what Mill Grove is, and whatever happens day by day and year by year, life alongside children and young people who have experienced trauma and loss in their early years makes some specific and very challenging demands. And because we are seeking to create a therapeutic milieu, integrating rhythms and seasons of life and nature, informed by individual and group therapy, where our lives, our personhood, are key factors in the process, some way of reflecting on what is going on around and within us is essential. The raw stuff of everyday life is so mixed, unpredictable and often painful, that this reflection has to be disciplined, informed and rigorous.

We are often asked whether Mill Grove is a 'therapeutic community'. It has much in common with other residential communities that have cared for children during the twentieth and first part of the twenty-first centuries. As you read some of the articles you will quickly see the point. An introductory leaflet put it like this: "We believe that shared living based on God-given rhythms and patterns can provide a therapeutic context in which the deepest personal and social wounds can be healed, and creative growth and expression encouraged." Life that has developed here has been informed and shaped by the work and models of many of the pioneers of therapeutic milieux and psychotherapy. Yet we have eschewed formal therapy of whatever sort on the premises as something integral to our way of life.

Through training, reading and experience we are familiar with various types of approach, but we always seek to live our lives here in as normal a way as possible, while drawing on professional knowledge and experience from those people and institutions around us. I hope that this collection of articles helps to unpack how this approach works. It values above all else the 'use of the person and relationship' in daily living, while always aware of the significance of the physical context and practical demands of life.

Another question is how far it might appropriately be described as a religious or faith-based community. From the beginning to the present day, those responsible for running and supporting Mill Grove have been committed followers of Jesus. And yet the place is inclusive of those from different faiths, as well as those who find the word faith problematical. It is not like a residential community comprising solely committed believers.

How the Christian faith and tradition informs, and is informed by, psycho-social theory and practice is the subject of the book, *The Growth of Love*, which is summarised below. I write as a follower or disciple of Jesus, but it has been heartening to find that there are those who are not followers who identify so much common ground. My colleague John Diamond used the framework of *The Growth of Love* in a paper to describe what he found in his experience of living with hurting children and young people in Mulberry Bush School, a residential therapeutic setting, for example ("The Mulberry Bush School as a Therapeutic Community", *ChildrenWebmag*, June 2008).

One of the ways in which I have been exploring the relation between pyscho-therapeutic practice and the Christian faith is through engagement with the work of Professor James E. Loder, and particularly his book, *The Logic of the Spirit: Human Development in Theological Perspective* (San Francisco: Jossey-Bass, 1998.) This led to a conference at Princeton and a symposium, *The Logic of the Spirit in Human Thought and Experience* (Eugene: Pickwick, 2014). The important thing to stress is that it a dialectic, a conversation, not a one-way process, and I hope that becomes clear in what follows.

The work of Loder is little-known outside the circle of his students and post-graduates, but I hope that its time will come. For forty years he beavered away at the intersection between psychotherapy, his own personal experience of life and traumas, and the Christian faith. His knowledge of the work of Freud, Piaget and Erikson, to name but three, is second to none. The frameworks and concepts he developed are not dogmatic or prescriptive, but rather create space for further thinking and research. He is particularly alert to the nature of the human spirit with its built-in commitment to overcome setbacks and work with paradoxes and contradictions.

If you want a label for this process of

reflection it might be 'work in progress'. As you will see, it is anything but finished, and very far from being polished. Underlying what is written is the growing sense that human and child development theory need to be re-thought in some pretty fundamental respects. At present they seem to sit comfortably within the overall idea of human progress and civilisation: "society" is getting better and so, given education, people will improve. I am not persuaded of the truth of either maxim. It follows that I believe that the theory and theories should reflect history and contemporary evidence more accurately.

Love, like grace, requires that we see human lives and the history of societies in many dimensions, and I follow Pascal in acknowledging that "the heart has its reasons that reason cannot understand". If this sounds rather heavy and formidable, I hope that the articles will demonstrate something of the joy, playfulness and creativity that thrive where love grows. At the same time, I have no intention of throwing the baby out with the bathwater. It is simply that all theory must be tested in the crucible of real life, cross-cultural and historical experience.

Reflective Therapeutic Care and the Role of these articles for *TTCJ*

One continuous feature that has been vital to reflecting on life alongside children at Mill Grove has been supervision by a consultant psychotherapist. There have been just three over the forty or so years in which Ruth and I have been serving the community. One moved to North America, and the second retired. In monthly sessions we are encouraged to express our questions, feelings, anxieties, ideas, frustrations, and hunches. The framework is professional, carefully agreed and discussion is noted. Without such a process it is not difficult to see that the demands of everyday life would tend to get out of perspective, and our reactions to unfolding situations and challenges be overly guided by unconscious feelings and emotions.

A discipline that has become indispensable is the attention to detail in narrating any interaction or incident. It may be possible to trace evidence for this in the pages that follow. This is not simply about quoting exactly the words spoken, but also filling in the social, physical and emotional context and dynamics.

But writing for *TTCJ* is another part of the reflective process. In case you hadn't realised it, the title of these three volumes is important. Over twenty years since penning my first piece I have come to realise that I cannot do without them. Whether or not they are published, they would still have to be written. You could see them as an extension of the supervision, but they have a life and momentum of their own. One of the resources that they draw from is the experience and wisdom of the ages around the world and throughout history. It is not that I go in search of practical insights and advice when reading novels and poetry or watching drama. Rather I am surprised by their deep insights into what might be going on in the lives of children, families and the community of Mill Grove.

In sharing my reflections in *TTCJ*, I also hope that others engaged in forms of therapeutic life and intervention will respond to some of my questions and emerging hypotheses. And I continue to encourage all practitioners, including students and those who experienced life in some form of care as children, to share their thoughts, feelings, experiences and suggestions.

Neat and tidy prescriptions and programmes seem to me unlikely to do justice to the many, varied and fast-changing situations on the ground. My thinking is constantly being interrupted, challenged and disrupted by what is happening daily at Mill Grove. This helps to explain why I continue to draw comfort from the comment of a psychotherapist, Kurt Pick. Several years ago he told me that he envied my life at Mill Grove. I was rather puzzled because he knew that life in such a place is anything but a picnic! He said that because he was retired, his own theories were now settled, whereas mine were always being challenged. In fact, he continued, "I bet that sometimes your theories are in smithereens!" And when that has been so, I am always thankful to Kurt for helping me to see the positive side of the de-construction of cherished thoughts and ideas. This is one of the serendipities of reflective practice.

The original articles have been edited lightly and occasionally presented in a different order to that in which they were written. Some repetition has been cut, but a few favourite incidents and quotations are retained to avoid more major editorial surgery. One piece has been extended, and one deleted completely.

Preparing the articles for publication has allowed yet another layer of reflection: on the changes in emphasis and discoveries along the way. One of these is the recognition that ambivalence plays in all forms of substitute care. This has thrown light right across the spectrum of my experiences alongside children, but also made sense of some of the hidden nooks and crannies: unexpected comments and behaviour. If love is to grow in and among those who have experienced childhood traumas there must be an awareness on the part of those seeking to help them of the double-edged nature and implications of any action or responses. Such ambivalence affects all areas of life and relationships, conscious and unconscious feelings.

Another discovery, made during walks during the Covid lock-down, was of the pervasive and serious effects of separation from, and loss of, parents or significant others on the sibling relationships of those affected. I am still unaware of resources for those seeking to respond therapeutically to this, so have begun to tease out what I hope are some sensitive and sensible lines of approach. These entail discussions with separated children in a care setting, and also with those who have left.

The discovery about the unique problems that mathematics, particularly subtraction, poses for those who have experienced separation and loss, shared in Volume Two (pages 113-115), means that all play and interaction is careful to avoid re-opening raw wounds. Games and discussions focus on positives (addition and multiplication).

Everything combines to reinforce for me the significance of resilience in the characters and lives of those who have experienced trauma and loss in childhood. It remains a mystery, but

I now wonder how far there is a latent, collective unconscious in households and sibling groups which can be drawn from, and which serves as some form of inspiration or model.

Having written *The Growth of Love* nearly twenty years ago, it was high time that I became acquainted with works such as *A General Theory of Love*. This has served to confirm intuitions and hunches, as well as to open new questions and avenues of explorations. It is part of a body of writing and theory that refuses to see the concept of love as unscientific, risky or imprecise.

The place of kith and kin, of nests, nestness, habitus had always featured in my life alongside children at Mill Grove. Relationships were embedded in contexts and settings that I knew, whether from what children shared about their own family homes and backgrounds, or from shared life together during my own childhood. I am now convinced that this emphasis offers imperatives and practical lines of approach whether in family support or in residential settings.

Meanwhile as life becomes more playful, and more distressing at one and the same time, the learning curve on which I find myself is ever-steepening. The questions and pleas for help in piece after piece reflect this. And a growing sense of privilege that I should be part of such an extended family and process of shared discovery.

The Growth of Love

The bulk of the articles in all three volumes of *Reflections on Living with Children* have been organised using the five main themes framing *The Growth of Love*. This means that some acquaintance with that book is an advantage in understanding them. There is an extensive description of the book in Volume One. This brief overview draws from the summary at the beginning of Volume Two.

The book seeks to draw together much of my thinking on daily life at Mill Grove and the lives of those for whom it has become home. The reflection is informed by psycho-therapeutic theory and practice, Christian faith and tradition, sociology, history, literature, and much else, all of which is distilled into five themes. They are not stages, steps or levels of growth or development, but rather ways of understanding the context or framework in which love thrives. They are also inter-connected, which means that an article might have been appropriately placed in two or more sections. I have continued to use the five words as a way of maintaining consistency between the three volumes of articles.

The first is **Security**. This represents the primal need to be safe, to be held in a healthy mind. Without this, love cannot find any purchase or base for exploration. And where it is absent in the life and experience of a child, there is no more important task than to seek to understand why, and to begin the difficult and painstaking process of establishing or re-establishing it. For love to grow there must be safe space. This can be configured in various ways, but it will always involve a secure context and at least one other person, usually an adult, who is completely reliable.

Perhaps the best pictures of this security are that of a baby being held in a mother's arms, a yacht in a harbour, a lamb with a flock in a sheepfold. In each case we are reminded by the symbol itself that this is not a static state, desirable for the rest of the life of the child, boat or sheep, but essential for the flourishing of the particular 'species-being'.

The second theme is **Boundaries**. As the baby, toddler, little child begins to grow there is inevitably movement. This is found in the environment around the child, where mother comes and goes, where others appear and disappear, where leaves and branches sway, clouds pass silently, and where many other moving parts are accompanied by all sorts of sounds. But it is also true of the little child. She begins to realise that parts of her are moving, and in time discovers that she is in control of some of them in however rudimentary a way.

In the process of moving the child encounters all sorts of boundaries. There are lots of things like walls and furniture that do not move. There are things like water, bubbles, leaves, insects, cars, that do move but seem to do so irrespective of her wishes or control.

There are movements within the child as air, liquids and solids are ingested, and substances excreted. Human beings, including adults and peers come and go, sometimes predictably, but always not quite at the beck and call of the little one.

With some of these boundaries come additional warnings in the form of physical intervention or the word "No!" Some actions are approved; others are disapproved of, often strongly. The collision between some of the feelings of the child and the expressed wishes of significant adults is sometimes very painful, and often confusing. There is a lot of navigating to be done to find a way through, physical, psychological and emotional. And what helps trust, confidence and love to grow is the discovery that there are predictable, reliable, consistent responses from significant adults. There are healthy patterns, rhythms and boundaries to the world of the growing child. The child is reassured by the familiarity of daily living and interactions with others.

The third is **Significance**. In time the growing child begins to discover her significance (though she will not use that word for many years). Others notice her, what she says and what she feels, and they take these into account (even if they do not always agree with her or grant her wishes). They are attuned to her, and there is a form of intricate social dance going on between them and her. She starts to use the word 'I' and acts with increasing intentionality. At the same time others are becoming increasingly significant to her, perhaps her mother, a sibling or another relative, friend or teacher.

As this healthy process develops there is a congruence between the 'I' of the child and the 'me', which is how others perceive and relate to her. She comes to discover that one or more others feel very deeply for her, as she does for them. And over time what has been called unconditional love for her is detected and internalised. At the heart of the growth of love is a relationship where a child and an 'Other' are uniquely special to each other. The child comes to welcome and treasure the truth that she is so special to a significant other that she means the world to them. In short, a child is loved, and is therefore able to reciprocate that love. Bonds of secure attachment have formed.

There will be eruptions, challenges, storms a-plenty both within this relationship and that affect it, but it becomes a rock, a base on which the rest of life can be confidently explored and embraced.

The fourth is **Community**. The result of the discovery of significance is not self-absorption or an obsessive exclusive relationship, but rather a way into a range of different relationships. The phrase "It takes a village to raise a child" has become commonplace, but much change in twenty-first century life, locally and globally, makes it difficult for many parents and children to identify that village. Love thrives on a variety of different social connections from friendship, to team member, elders, grandparents, fellow workers, siblings.

Part of the argument that runs through *The Growth of Love* is that we can easily become so attached to the primacy of biological parents in a child's life that we do not realise the role that all villagers have in parenting a child. When I have invited students to tell their life stories focusing on the significance of others in their lives (including, but not exclusively, family members) they have always been surprised by the sheer number of significant others (whether neighbours, teachers, friends) who have been special to them, sometime pivotal in their development.

The fifth is **Creativity**. If love is to grow it will be nurtured by and result in imagination, play and playfulness, productivity, achievement, poetry, dance, games, representation, conversation, music, exploration and discovery. Love depends on symbols, signs and metaphors from the earliest stages: a parent holding a child's hand or stroking their arm, a game of peekaboo, special words and gestures. Love cannot be bottled, labelled, reproduced. To begin to understand it requires creativity. And where it grows creativity will flourish.

Where there is love in a relationship, well-being in a group, there will always be jokes and humour. It is not about cause and effect, and it cannot be prescribed. This is to do with the nature of love. Perhaps we can see this more clearly by thinking of the opposite: where there is sterility, sameness, grey routine, oppressive demands and expectations or fear, then love is not growing.

These then, in brief, are the five themes described in *The Growth of Love*, and that form the framework for the arrangement of the articles in this volume. The words were selected after much experimentation, and the intention is that they should be inclusive of ideas and concepts drawn from psycho-therapeutic practice, theology and everyday life. Over the years I have been asked where one might find, say, 'transitional objects', grace, relationships, forgiveness, the unconscious, identity, trust, self-actualisation and many more subjects. It has usually been possible to accommodate each with integrity as we have worked at a shared understanding in conversation.

Context

The articles in this collection span the period from the summer of 2016 to the summer of 2022. As reflections on everyday life and events they inevitably refer to contexts, local, regional and international. There are four of these that merit a mention here. The first is the growing awareness and concern about Climate Change and Global Warming, not least as it affects and will affect the lives of children and young people. The second is "Brexit": a name given to the renegotiation of the relationship between the United Kingdom and the European Union with December 2020 as the official leaving date. The third is the global Covid pandemic which began to have serious effects in the UK from March 2020. The fourth is the Russian invasion of Ukraine which started in February 2022.

Reflections that take seriously nests, nestness and the stuff of life are bound to devote attention to those factors which go to make up the common contexts or settings of children's lives, whether as threats or resources. Especially so, if those who seek to care for children therapeutically are listening to the voices of the children themselves.

REFLECTIONS

Part
ONE

INTRODUCTION TO THEME ONE
Security

These pieces constitute descriptions of the foundation on which
genuine relationships involving trust, love and understanding are
built. They underline and confirm the importance of secure
attachment and a secure base as described and advocated by John
Bowlby.

One of the concepts developed is that of "nest" and "nestness"
(Articles 1–4). This stresses the totality of ingredients or parts that
go to make a homely home. It includes significant others of course
but also sees the importance of place, culture, language, objects,
pets and much more. The implication is that leaving the nest needs
to be understood and handled with great care. Also that any
substitute home needs to be seen as a nest too. It is not enough
simply to identify appropriate adults, however empathetic and
skilled they may be.

Another of the key concepts is that of being held. This can easily
be misunderstood, but here there is a detailed and imaginative
account of a Christmas meal at Mill Grove with reflections on what
it was that combined to make a warm and welcoming "holding
environment" (Article 5).

A discovery we made during the Covid period was of the
disturbing effects that separation and loss have, not only on
individual children but on the relationships between siblings who
have experienced the same loss (Articles 11–12). I have not done
any substantive research on this, but sense that it has not received
sufficient attention, possibly professionals are unaware how
common and serious it is.

The final two articles, relating to war and survival, are reminders
that the security of children is often threatened by fears about
death. And set in a global context such existential threats are far
more common than we do, or probably can, imagine.

Of Nests and "Nestness"

In this column I want to revisit the subject of attachment and loss not only in the light of my experience and reflection on what those who have lived at Mill Grove have shared with me, and the work of pioneers such as John Bowlby and D.W. Winnicott, but also using some of the insights and words of Jay Griffiths in her book, *Kith: The Riddle of the Childscape* (London: Penguin, 2013).

Those of us in the field of child care, child psychology, the residential and foster care of children are indebted to the likes of Bowlby and Winnicott (among many others) for sharpening our awareness of the primal significance of bonds and attachment, and the overwhelming catastrophe that their loss can engender or trigger. Professionals have explored aspects of this over the past sixty years or so and developed vocabularies including "transitional objects", "held in a healthy mind", "object relations", "replication of sameness", "defence mechanisms", and many more. These aid our listening and inform aspects of our responses to those who have experienced, or are experiencing, loss.

The reason Mill Grove was established by my grandfather in 1899 was because he was moved with compassion in his unexpected encounter with an eight-year-old girl called Rosie, who was distraught at the death of her mother. As one who had lost his own mother as a young teenager, he was particularly touched, troubled by her presence and feelings. Ever since then our home has been a place where we have welcomed and sought to be alongside those children and families suffering loss in one of its various forms. Because we are committed to "being there" for all who have lived with us throughout their lives, I have had the privilege of hearing the recollections and stories of countless "members of the family" who experienced loss as children. This has given me an unusually extensive reservoir to draw from as I seek to distil and learn from the essence of their combined, yet irreducibly, particular narratives.

But it was only on reading Jay Griffiths' book that I added "nest" to my vocabulary and began to make the connections between elements of these stories that hitherto had remained dissociated in my mind. Part of the argument of Griffiths is that the word "kith" does not simply refer to significant people in a child's family or community, but to the "nest" in which a child is born. The Anglo-Saxon root of the word is *"cydd/cyd"* and means "home ", "country", "region" or "place" (compare the German, *kunde*). So the phrase "kith and kin" is not just a poetic alliterative phrase referring to significant people in a child's life, but also alludes to the context, the setting, the place, the homeland, the culture, the soil, the dwelling, the community, the natural world in which a child lives. And pace the English poet, John Clare (1793–1864), Jay Griffiths uses the terms "nest" and "nestness" to describe this aspect of kith.

It follows that when a child is separated from her parents and or family, she is also separated from her *"cydd"*, her nest, and the loss that she experiences is a combination of all the people sights, sounds, smells, objects and associations that combine to make up that nest, both literal and imagined. The term nest is beautifully apt, both because it is primarily associated with the original home of the fledgling bird, but also because a nest is made up of a range of objects taken from the local environment. It is, if you like, the embodiment, re-membering, or re-creation of that context.

In pursuing this line of enquiry, there is no intention to detract from the shattering experience of the loss of a mother or father (or family), the significant others in the life of a child, but rather to expand our understanding of the nature of this loss. When Winnicott spelt out the role of transitional space and transitional objects what he wrote was consonant with this evocation of *cydd* and nest: such objects were valued precisely because they were part of the nest and so when taken into the new strange environment represent some continuity, some connectivity, some relatedness to it in the mind of the estranged child.

Once the importance of nest is appreciated,

isn't it the case that in the field of social work and social care we have tended to under-estimate the role of the non-human objects and symbols which the child loses at the point of separation and transfer to a new home or environment?

A thread in the narratives to which I have been privileged to listen to over the past forty years or so is the way in which the details of a place are embedded in the descriptions of experiences positive and negative. People describe the scents, the weather, the sounds, the light, and the texture of the context as if it were still present. A powerful experience is inextricably linked to the setting in which it "took place" (that very phrase is interesting in itself). Poets, musicians and novelists have seen this to the point of taking it as given: a novel sets human stories in specific contexts, and every detail of the context is meticulously chosen and crafted. As I write this, there is in the UK a renewed interest in the writings of Thomas Hardy. The way in which natural landscapes and culture play their part in his novels is epitomised by Egdon Heath (which has been described as one of the main characters in *Return of the Native*).

When listening actively to the life-stories of people it has become almost second nature to ask them to fill in such background details from time to time, and in the process the memories and associations seem to be stirred and heightened, and new connections made.

Now there are many implications of this insight and line of thought: we must record and understand the *cydd* of the child; transitional objects are as vital as Winnicott revealed; photos; visits back to a place with positive associations may play a part in healing; this is also true with regard to places that were the setting for trauma and even abuse (the novel *The Shack* by William Paul Young [London: Hodder, 2008] begins in exactly this way); we can perhaps seek to replicate aspects of *cydd* in the new setting, though this is fraught with ambiguities and risks; we may use place and context as a way of exploring the dynamics of human attachment and loss; and so on.

The single thread that I want to trace concerns the essence or nature of *cydd* in the new

home environment. As I have listened to a plethora of childhood stories of people who lived at Mill Grove there are aspects of the place (that includes South Woodford, Tiptree in Essex, and holiday haunts particularly in Churston Ferrers and North Wales) that return again and again like old friends, aged oak trees in a familiar landscape. Among them are: the lockers in the ground floor of the hall where toys were kept; the window in the corner of this hall where children watched on a Saturday afternoon hoping against hope that a parent would appear approaching the front door; the pear trees in the orchard inextricably linked with tales of scrumping; the damson trees where glue was collected during the summer holidays; the outside toilets; the wash-places; the scrubbed tables at which meals were had; the dormitories and the curtains on summer evenings; the clothes store with is smell of moth balls; the food store with its tea chests, and metal food bins in which rice was kept; the lake at Tiptree; Tiptree Heath; the ducks and their eggs; the horse and the plough; the open-air swimming pool at Maldon; the trig point at the summit of Moel–y-Gest. You probably realise that the only way I can halt this avalanche of memories is by an arbitrary and abrupt full stop.

Some of those who lived at Mill Grove have been able to speak of experiencing a considerable measure of healing (forgiveness is one of the words that often creeps in at some stage) since their troubled childhoods, and the primary loss that lies at the very heart of things. I cannot remember a single description of aspects of that healing that are dissociated from place. If there were songs and verses from the Bible that have been constant companions and sources of encouragement, the place where they were learnt (the "top hall" usually) are always mentioned; if there was a caring, empathetic response to inner anger, turmoil and loss, the room or the place where this was experienced comes alive in the telling; it is not long before sounds, colours, smells begin to emerge in the encounter.

And woe betide us if and when we change anything: furniture, the colour of the walls, the shape of a room, a flower-bed in the garden, a clock, a picture … It is as if things should remain as they were in order to help preserve the sense of and acceptance that began to grow as small as mustard seeds, "fresh as a leaf" (R.S. Thomas) in the unpromising psychological and emotional crater caused by separation and loss.

I have found other metaphors and symbols helpful in describing the dynamics of loss, and attempts to respond to them, including a harbour, compost heaps, being held, a rock, a village, seasons, rhythms. But when I read the words "nest" and "nestness" at the bottom of page 26 in *Kith*, I knew that I had been given an idea full of potential in the quest for understanding the anguish hinted at by the words separation and loss, and also the nature of the response to that anguish.

Unless we can help to provide "nestness" then all our efforts are as wide of the mark as the attempt to rescue a fledgling bird that has fallen out of the nest by placing her in a laboratory or on a conveyor-belt.

A Homely Nest

I have written before in this journal about the connections between the theories of attachment and loss by Bowlby and others, on the one hand, and the concept of "nestness", on the other. Put simply, it is possible to limit thinking about attachment largely or solely to the relationship between a child and a significant other, whereas the idea of nestness sets the loss of bonding and attachment within the wider context of the whole of a child's life, locality, culture, environment and relationships. Thus, to move a child away from a significant other will always involve the loss of some, if not all, that is familiar, including place, school, sights, sounds, smells and all that goes into making the metaphorical nest we call "home". I am persuaded that any understanding of the nature of the trauma of separation and loss that does not take the very stuff ("nestness") of a child's life will be inadequate. If such a limited understanding informs actions taken to remove a child from a significant other, then the trauma of separation and loss will be intensified. My hunch is that D.W. Winnicott had something like this in mind when he emphasised the importance of transitional objects.

So now comes the crunch: putting this hypothesis to the test. And this is how it happened. On a recent Saturday, a person who had lived as Mill Grove throughout his childhood returned after a gap of something like twenty years. He was accompanied by his long-term partner and their first child. Without breaking any confidence, I think it could be said that his life and relationships in infancy and before he came to Mill Grove were seriously problematic, neglectful and chronically emotionally abusive. And his troubled and uncertain relationships with his own family contributed to his behaviour of avoidance, lying and stealing while with us. All I am seeking to do at this point is to alert the reader to the fact that things were anything but settled, secure and easy either for him, or for us, during the long period that he lived with us.

Why did he come back? Well, he knew from years of experience that this is what happens routinely at Mill Grove. There is always a welcome for those returning, however lengthy the interruption of contact and however problematical the relationships with us have been. The way he put it was that when his son was born, he knew he must share the news with us, and he simply had to come back. One of his profound and haunting fears (he called it a recurring nightmare) was that if he ever had a child of his own, history would repeat itself, and that child would follow a script inherited from himself and his family. So he was coming home for many interwoven reasons, but one of them was for us to see how determined he and his partner were to help their little boy (just taking his first steps on Saturday) know security, predictable boundaries and affirmation. He was also introducing partner and son to us as his family, with a view to re-engaging with us, knowing that we would always be here for his son, and would support his family as we had been for him one generation earlier.

This is hopefully enough background for us to move on to explore nestness. As the time to come back home got nearer he had become more anxious, and it was only the encouragement of his partner that finally made it happen. He was quite open that there were times when he felt it would all be too much for him.

But he arrived, and we spent an afternoon together: the three of his family, two of whom we were meeting for the first time, and three of us: Ruth and myself, and the person who cared for him within Mill Grove from his earliest days. The visiting family came, like the Wise Men, bearing gifts, and he was tearful from the start, aware of the lies and stealing that had characterised so much of the time with us, and how such behaviour had hurt us, and come between him and us (that is the nature of lying). Throughout the time he occasionally asked for a tissue as tears were never far from his eyes. There was an exchange of photos (he estimated that they had about two thousand of their son at that point in time), and we had lots of him. Sadly he had taken many personal photos with him when he moved on from Mill Grove, but at some stage in the many moves that he had subsequently made he had lost them.

The photos were of course of him and people he knew, but they were also a link with the stuff of his life with us beyond the actual people. We soon found ourselves talking of holidays, of school, of clubs (including Boy's Brigade and the Air Training Corps), of churches, of Epping Forest, of ten-pin bowling, of football (he was a goalkeeper and supported Arsenal), of sailing, swimming, kayaking (I still use his buoyancy aid) locally and in North Wales, of cricket played on the beach at Borth y Gest, of breakfasts and mealtimes and the topics of conversation that recurred, to name just a few of the connections and experiences that simply rolled out. His partner was frankly amazed at the richness of the experiences of his childhood, and the sheer amount and quality of our shared life. The conversation was

effortless. And we all began to realise that despite the challenges in our personal relationships with him (we all knew that we loved each other, but the lying behaviour consistently got in the way) there had been a very rich and homely nest in which he had grown up.

Here are a few examples. He had been with us on at least one of our trips to Switzerland to see our friends in Appenzell. He and his partner told us that they had tried unsuccessfully to find some etchings on the internet by our friend, a Japanese artist, and remembered the Swiss lady he had married and with whom we had stayed. He spoke of how much he had loved being in the mountains with this family, and talked with warmth and appreciation of days spent skiing, swimming, filming and playing in snow. I left the room and came back with a book, still gift-wrapped, by this very artist, and said that it had been waiting for him and his family. He and his partner were so overwhelmed when they held it that they didn't even risk opening it. He said that it was unbelievably precious. He knew that there were etchings of the very house in which we had stayed, of the villages around, of the local mountains and tree-covered wintry slopes. They held the book together, unforgettably as far as I was concerned. This meant the world to them. Days in Switzerland were a treasured part of his nest.

Those who know of the Mill Grove connection with North Wales will not be surprised that there were lots of shared memories about people, events, adventures and places there, including an attempted dive into the sea off Trefor pier, a hole dug in the sand on our beach, some of the neighbouring families, and expeditions into the hills, tents, caravans and the houses in which we stayed.

We also talked about a couple at the church where he went to Boys Brigade: they had taken a personal interest in him. He called them uncle and auntie. Uncle was an architect. He spoke of his fondness for them both, and was amazed when I reached up to find the autobiography of the uncle, and who for those who remember him, was an early Christian mentor of Bob Holman: yes, that Bob Holman! The text of this life-story was punctuated by many photos, and once again they were a record or reminder of his nest.

I could go on to talk of memories of ice-skating, of conversations at mealtimes, of specific incidents and adventures, but I want to focus on just one object in the hope that this will convey most fully and accurately the nature of nestness that I am seeking to convey. It was a silver tea-leaf infuser, in a colourful, miniature tin box, and had been given to him by my mother. When he left, he had asked us to look after it for him, and now he was handling it for the first time in twenty years. He was evidently moved to see it again, and eventually asked us to continue looking after it. What was that about, I wonder? Was he wanting to leave part of himself in the nest, perhaps? A very precious part? And why, we mused, had my mother given this valuable personal possession to him, rather than to anyone else, as a birthday present?

Strange to say for some reason his little boy seemed to sense that the tea-infuser was significant, and he and I spent an hour or so playing with it on the carpet, putting it back in its tin, and taking it out again. It was wrapped in tissue paper, and so as we handled it and placed it back in the tin before shutting the lid, it had all the appearances and texture of an actual bird's nest. As I sat on the floor playing in this way, the other five adults continued their free-flowing conversation, until it was beginning to be evident that we were approaching the little boy's bedtime!

It doesn't take much imagination to realise that this little silver object could well form part of the little boy's nest in the years to come, that Winnicott was right about transitional objects, and that when building or rebuilding the bonds of attachment, it is the stuff that a person knows to be part of their nest that is important, possibly vital. And that this is integral to relationships, not just a background to them.

On reflection I have been reminded of just how homely, richly textured and varied is the nest that we call Mill Grove for some of the children who have lived with us. There have been significant others here for them, but there is something crucially important about the nature and stuff of our shared life.

. . . .

Coming Home

A short while ago, Cilla (that is what I will call her) came back to Mill Grove. She had lived with us between 1986 and 1991 and was returning after a period of 25 years during which there had been no contact or information of her or her whereabouts. It was a Saturday morning, and she brought her youngest (pre-school) daughter with her. Ruth and I were thrilled to see her again and eagerly absorbed news of her life as an adult and mother. And she was demonstrably full of joy to be back. We explored parts of the inside and outside of Mill Grove in an informal way, and she asked for copies of *Links* (the annual newsletter) covering the whole time that she was with us as a girl.

Photos and memories were supplemented when she met some of those whom she knew in childhood: one was a carer; another was one of the children who lived at Mill Grove (along with her brothers) during the same period. It was a sunny Spring Day, and so much of our conversation took place in the playground and orchard. We had lunch together and then I had to explain to her that a practical crisis had arisen in the lives of another family who were also part of the extended community of Mill Grove. They were moving into a new house and the arrangements for moving their furniture had fallen through at the very last minute. I had promised to help. Without hesitation Cilla offered me her four-by-four truck to use. I had never driven one before, but this didn't worry her. And it proved exactly what was needed as we piled it high with mattresses, bicycles, bed frames and cupboards, all tied securely by a trusty climbing rope that had been used on the rocks and crags of North Wales even before 1986, as well as during her holidays there with us!

When I arrived back with her vehicle, now emptied of its load, and completely intact, she seemed so relaxed that it began to feel as if she had never been away. She then started to put into words what she had been feeling in the years and months leading up to her decision to return. "This is where I learnt all the things that have provided me with a foundation for life and for parenthood", she said. "The values that I teach my children all have their roots here with you. I came to realise that this was the one place that was genuinely secure for me as a child." This was reflected in the way she allowed her daughter to explore the place and to move among the residents for herself: there was no hint of anxiety or concern. It was just how it is when a parent who is a confident swimmer enters the water with their child: it is a pleasant and safe environment and experience.

Well into the evening it was time to bid her farewell. She made sure we had her address and contact details and said she would come back for the gathering of the clan (we call it "Our Day") that takes place each May. As it happened, she had arrived just a few weeks before Our Day 2016.

Meanwhile, a few days later, Margaret, another of the extended family of Mill Grove, arrived from the USA. She and her sisters had lived at Mill Grove during the 1940s and 1950s, and she was coming back home. She told me that her friends at work and church in Colorado find it impossible to understand what she means when she says this. "How can an orphanage or children's home be your home?" they always ask. She has given up trying to explain, but it doesn't really matter because it is as evident to the significant others in her life, her brothers and sisters in the Mill Grove family, and her friends in the UK, that Mill Grove is indeed her home, a place she loves to come back to. I have known her and her family of three generations all through my life, and it is difficult to make much sense of our relationship without some concept of a filial connection and shared childhoods lived in the same place.

Not only does she come back as often as she can (with her one remaining sister who lives in Kent), but her children and grandchildren have come back home with her too. It so happens their father (her first husband) was a German orphan and so Mill Grove probably represents the nearest thing they have to family roots and identity.

Strangely however, Cilla did not appear on Our Day and, at first, I was surprised because she had spoken of her enthusiasm to come back to meet others with whom she grew up as a child. I think she will be back again, but the fact that she came just once caused me to reflect on "coming home" in a new and deeper way.

The archetypal homecoming as represented by, say the biblical story of the prodigal son, who is welcomed with open arms after a pretty reckless period away, is a prelude to a renewed stay at home, albeit with different roles and expectations. Many of those who lived at Mill Grove as children return regularly, not least for holidays and Christmas. But what of someone who comes home just once? What might that mean? As I reflected it began to dawn on me that a single visit may be of inestimable significance. For a start the home that provided security and foundational values was still there: solid and real, rather than just a nostalgic memory or figment of sentimental imagination. Then the people who cared for the homecomer when she was a child were also still there; they recognised her and welcomed her with open arms. We were obviously delighted that she had returned, and from her point of view that delight should not be underestimated. On top of this, she had the diaries and photos of her time with us, so she could remind herself and her family of her childhood home whenever she wanted to do so. And to cap it all, she was assured of a ready welcome whenever she wanted to pop in.

In the light of all this I realised that a single visit was potentially full of meaning of itself. It confirmed that the secure base was still secure, that memories were correct (not imagined), and that there would always be a welcome on future return visits. Put these three things together and it becomes apparent that there is no need to return regularly to substantiate the true nature of things. It has all been realised and confirmed.

This line of thinking led me to consider more deeply the whole idea of "home". As readers since March 2000 will realise, it has been explored in these columns in a variety of ways already. The title of the first book that I wrote about Mill Grove is *A Place for Us*, and was chosen because of the significance that those who have lived here attach to coming back and staying in touch with the place which functioned as home for them during their childhoods. Then there is the understanding of the importance of "kith" in the sense of "nestness" as described so creatively by Jay Griffiths in her book *Kith: The Riddle of the Childscape* (London: Penguin, 2013). The whole idea of a nest conveys a sense of home and security.

But what about the idea of "home"? Clearly builders of new accommodation find that it is a far more attractive word than "houses", "flats" or "dwellings". But is "home" confined to a building in general, and restricted to the place where one lived during one's childhood? What about the whole idea of *sehnsucht* which I first came across in the writings of C.S. Lewis? I find it interesting that the Wikipedia entry links this sense of longing for something still not experienced or attained, with home:

> "It is sometimes felt as a longing for a far-off country, but not a particular earthly land which we can identify. Furthermore there is something in the experience which suggests this far-off country is very familiar and indicative of what we might otherwise call "home"."
> (www. en.wikipedia.org/wiki/Sehnsucht. Accessed 23.05.2016)

This is a reminder that "home" is an evocative idea or symbol, perhaps something that functions as a Platonic idea beyond and behind any practical manifestations of the "thing in itself". And this led me to another German word, *heimat*, that I had come across through two different sources. The first was in the German-speaking part of Switzerland where I came to understand the rights and sense of life-long belonging to the place or community of a person's birth. Wherever they might have lived during their lives *heimat* was always there for them, awaiting them throughout their lives. I also came across it in the writings of Janusz Korczak. His parting speech or final words to children leaving his orphanage in Warsaw included the following: "I cannot give you a Homeland (*heimat*), for you must find it in your own heart ... Perhaps I can give you but one thing only, a longing (*sehnsucht*) for a better life, a life of truth and justice: even though it may not exist now, it may come tomorrow. Perhaps this longing will lead you to God, Homeland and Love." (*Voice of the Child*, page 144)

These two coordinates combine the twin elements of "home" that I had in mind: the place where one was born and/or grew up as a child; the place that one is seeking or longing for throughout life that is like a harbour one dreams of on a long ocean voyage, or the nest (or proximity to the nest) to which the returning swallows are drawn on their long migratory journeys.

I see both elements epitomised by both Cilla and Margaret. Yes, Mill Grove was indeed their childhood home, but it also represents what they are seeking for themselves and for their children throughout life.

So coming home is brimming with meaning, both conscious and, in my view, unconscious significance. It reassures a person that what they dreamt of as part of the good old days, on the one hand, and wish for their children, on the other, really exists. Not of course in a perfect Platonic form, but as something they know from direct experience to have been a secure base, a place of "good enough parenting".

No wonder that whenever I meet with those who have been responsible for residential communities, they always speak of those who come back. This happened just a week ago when I met a carer from the London Borough of Hillingdon. And no wonder I rejoice that some of these places remain, as well as the people who cared years earlier for those returning. Of course, sadly the converse is also true: one wonders what it means to so many to find no home to come back to, and no one to welcome them … just once!

Saving Grace

Let me begin by quoting the title of this article in context. It was in a letter I received at the beginning of November 2016 from the daughter of someone who had lived at Mill Grove as a child. The sentence reads: "My mother always told me that being taken into [Mill Grove] was her saving grace". Not you will have noticed a "necessary evil", or the "end of the road" or "last resort", but something beyond the other end of the spectrum. With hindsight it might also have been called "a positive choice", the title of the 1988 Wagner Report.

I have heard others who lived here (or their offspring) use this sort of language to convey a similar sentiment, so in some ways it came as no surprise. And yet … it always does. The thought of a child leaving familiar faces, context, nestness, neighbourhood, and school, and starting to live in a foreign new world comprising home and environment, and with strangers, is far removed from the thought of saving grace.

As it happened the letter arrived the day we received an unexpected visitor in the early evening: a mother of three who had lived with us for a short period as an adult before making an attempt to end her life during a period dogged by depression and alcoholism. She had come without warning to share with us her joy at being free of her addiction, to bring us up to date with her three children, and to describe how the twelve steps of the Alcoholics Anonymous programme had led to a deepening of her Christian faith. Rather than seeing her difficulties as a source of suffering and oppression, she described them as part of a process of personal insight and understanding, and of the growth of love and respect in relationships. She described how she had written down the names of about 200 or so people in her life,

noting how they had affected her adversely, and acknowledging her wrongful attitudes and asking for forgiveness.

The letter, and this extraordinary conversation, used concepts and words that I do not think I could ever ascribe to someone else unless I were actually quoting what they had written or told me. Here are people who in many respects have every right to see themselves as victims or survivors of a range of neglect and abuse, personal and societal, but who have chosen a road less travelled.

I re-read and then pondered the whole (saving grace) letter and found myself writing a second letter in reply. It was profoundly moving. And I will share a little more in a moment. Likewise I have been revisiting that searingly honest and open conversation. In both cases I find I have been taken beyond what I can fully comprehend. I can understand what they are saying, but fail to fathom how they have the courage and grace to say it. These people have encountered chronic suffering, but they have hung on, and have come through. In the process they have developed richly as people. Both the letter writer and the conversationalist focused primarily on others: the mother in the case of the writer, and her children in the case of the recovering alcoholic. And that is eloquent testimony to the quality of their mental health and well-being.

The person who had written the letter had come to stay at Mill Grove for one of our annual gatherings. She had visited us often with her mother, but this was the first time she actually lived with us for a few days. She was a great help with a number of practical tasks (which she delighted to recount) but went on to refer to times when she was "sitting quietly and listening to family members recount memories of being raised as part of the family at Mill Grove … [and] being able to talk to those who knew my mother as a child." She continued that she found herself "closing my eyes and being able to see my mother as a little girl in all of those places ..."

I wondered how many children of those who have been in residential or foster care have had this opportunity and experience. And of those, how many have seen it as a personal blessing expressed in these words: "I feel very privileged to have spent those few days with you all. Whenever I visit Mill Grove I am very mindful of the fact that had it not been for the care my dear mother initially received from [Pa] White and Ma Hutchin, I might not have been here to be able to write this to you."

I can't say how the three children of the mother who came to see us think about their mother and her childhood experiences and theirs, but what I do know is that their mum is close to and proud of each one of them. She holds them in what as far as I could see is a healthy mind, and they are clearly gifted and creative, achieving in chosen fields both formally and informally.

The human condition prevents us from ever knowing how things might have been. T.S. Eliot put this memorably in *Burnt Norton*:

"What might have been is an abstraction
Remaining a perpetual possibility
Only in a world of speculation.
What might have been and what has been
Point to one end, which is always present.
Footfalls echo in the memory
Down the passage which we did not take
Towards the door we never opened
Into the rose-garden."

We cannot possibly construct a reliably imagined, alternative route for these people, plotting convincing fictitious lives that did not involve such separation and loss. But I have an intimation that in some ways they are more fully aware, sensitive, insightful and understanding than they might have been ...

But we can infer from such life-stories that we dare not and must not settle for second best, on the assumption that those who have suffered childhood traumas are therefore necessarily debilitated or affected in ways that prevent them realising the potential and fullness of what it is to be wholly alive as a human being in relationships. It may be the very reverse.

One of the practical problems is that there seem to be so few opportunities for this sort of intergenerational interaction, conversation and reflection. Perhaps this is one of the particular gifts of Mill Grove: not that it was a place always full of human empathy and understanding, but that it remains and provides just such opportunities.

And to end on a seasonal note: Christmas is one of those times when there is this kind of reflection and conversation in abundance. For it is full of happy childhood memories and associations for three and sometimes even four generations. It is a season with real potential for saving grace. We will be performing a version of Charles Dickens' *A Christmas Carol* on Boxing Day, and that's a story of saving grace if ever there was one!

Being Held

It is axiomatic in the theory of child development that children need the security of the experience of being held safely in healthy arms and a healthy mind. For the very young child this is an absolute and essentially physical experience, although its presence or absence has a profound effect on her life. As a child grows, there will be physical holding from time to time, but it becomes increasingly a matter of internalising the truth that there is a person, or people, who continue to hold them in their minds and hearts whether or not such a person or people are actually physically present.

When there is separation and loss, one way of conceiving what happens is to compare it with the feeling that the child has been dropped into a chasm, or even a void. The person who they expected to hold them is, for whatever reason, no longer there. Security has been shattered and the centre will not hold. In such situations it is no easy matter either to replace the significant person or to begin to kindle (rekindle?) and nurture the trust that went with the now-broken relationship.

This is where the best of psychiatric and psychotherapeutic insights come into play (notably for some of us engaged in some form of residential care, the work of pioneers such as John Bowlby and D.W. Winnicott). In various manifestations of such substitute care (that is based on people and settings other than the original parent or family home) one of the primary tasks is to find appropriate and sensitive ways of providing a secure and healthy way of "holding" the child. For the avoidance of doubt, it must be stressed that this is not about restraining or pinning them down, but about creating an environment which is able to reassure them that they are accepted and safe and will not be let down or abandoned (as they may well see it) again.

Such substitute or alternative environments come in many shapes and sizes, with a diversity of philosophies, methods and practices. They range from foster care to residential therapeutic communities and psychiatric hospitals. Mill Grove is somewhere in all this, although it has never been easy to describe its essence or to locate it satisfactorily on the spectrum. Perhaps the truth is that it has represented different things to different children. Be that as it may, this is not the point or focus of this article.

Rather I want to describe an evening meal just before Christmas 2016 where I was particularly conscious that every person present was "being held" in one way or another, and then to attempt an enhanced understanding of what might have been going on. Put another way, I am seeking to identify some of the elements that might have contributed to the healthy holding process.

We had finished our evening meal which on this evening we had around a single table. There were eight of us present, and when the dishes had been cleared one of the young people collected the Advent wreath from the sideboard and placed it in the middle of the table. We each had a Bible open in front of us, and when the appropriate number of candles for that day had been lit by the youngest person present (that is the longstanding tradition), we read the next part of the story leading to the Christ-child event. Before a short prayer we shared family news and looked at one or two of the Christmas cards that had arrived that day.

This was the context and the content of the moment when I became acutely aware that each of us as individuals, and the whole group, were "being held". It may be helpful to share one or two things about those who comprised the group before continuing. There was a mother chronically troubled by childhood abuse and diagnosed among other things with OCD. There was a child of junior school age who was experiencing bullying at school. There was a young person who had never experienced predictable relationships with either of his parents throughout childhood. There was an adult who has struggled with the essence of her identity and finds fantasy and fabrication a way of maintaining some sort of purchase, though tenuous, on life and meaning. There was a young mother who had recently had her children placed in foster care and who was mourning their loss. And there was a young adult who had experienced abuse, serial separation and loss.

Until this moment I had not categorised the group in this way because they are all part of the extended family of Mill Grove, and I have known them all for most of their lives. This means that I tend to think of each other primarily as people with names, rather than by formal classifications or diagnoses. But this is the group that was evidently, in my view, being held.

What, I went on to wonder, were the elements that combined to make the holding possible? I am musing at this point and so my reflections do not come in any logical or reasoned order. There was of course the fact that each person knew precisely how the mealtime and the Advent reflection would go. It was safe because it was predictable. What is more each one valued the ritual. They had contributed to it before, and so they knew that it meant a great deal to many others who had been part of it over the years and decades. Some of those who had sent Christmas greetings and cards referred to this tradition.

Then there was the candlelight. This creates an atmosphere that is inherently soothing (as distinct from say, strobe lighting for discos and concerts, or the visual stuttering of a television screen). But it also holds the gaze. The verb "hold" is used deliberately here because sight is involved as well as other senses, and the emotions. If you are together around a table with candles in the midst and the electric lights turned off (as they were), then the gently undulating light of the flames draws each pair of eyes, and therefore of necessity, brings the whole group together in a common activity.

Another element is the Christmas story. Whatever your faith and beliefs, the Christmas story recounted as narrative is inherently inclusive (that is, good news for all people). It is about a family that is ordinary in many ways, and under extreme pressure. But the stories of Matthew and Luke are bursting with hope and expectation. This chapter of the story, or this act of the drama, is but a small part of an epic narrative story that spans history and the whole of humanity. So, properly understood (that is, on its own terms) each person around the table was being affirmed as significant. The birth of this baby named Jesus was somehow intended to bring help, even healing and reconciliation, for everyone. In Wilfred Bion's terms the story contributes to the wellbeing of the group as a provider of strong symbols that "contain" the processes and dynamics, the stresses and contradictions within each person's life, and the relationships within the group as a group.

In no way do I want to imply that this is what each person was thinking, or how they were processing things. I have little idea of what was going on in the recesses of each mind and heart. Unconscious processes were surely at work. But it would be unwise to try to understand the "holding" without at least considering the nature of the story that was being told.

Another factor was the presence of Ruth, my wife, and myself together at the table. We have been constants in each person's life. We have always been there for each and all the others present. We are married ("in a stable relationship") and there is no doubt in anyone's mind that we will be together for the rest of our lives. In other words, everyone present could rely on our presence in their lives, our acceptance of them, and our commitment to them. What is more we are practising Christians ("followers of Jesus" is my preferred term) and so even if the Christmas story is just a convenient and agreeable seasonal fiction to someone in the group, there is a vicarious holding going on during our celebration of it.

Then there is the length of the history of this tradition. The cards are reminders of this. Some senders had lived at Mill Grove 70 years earlier, and they still feel part of the family. Many of them are known to those who were sitting around the table. This is not an initiative or pilot project, a unit or a time-specific package of treatment or care. And the place in which we were sitting has been the home of this family for well over a century. Buildings matter when it comes to "being held".

I could go on, but this is probably the right place to stop for now. Perhaps others might help with this working out of what might have been going on. But there is one final thought that occurs. What if the deepest truth (if we can suspend our disbelief for a moment) was that this holding was largely in my own mind, a product of my imagination? Perhaps I was projecting my personal feelings on to the event and those present. If so, then the significance was that it was a holding experience for me, which enabled or helped me in the process of seeking to be present for members of the Mill Grove family who needed care and support. I don't think it was just in my mind because I could recount many other times when "being held" was not a shared experience, and over the years I think I have come to know the difference!

What I can't do is to ask the others about it, because as Keats the poet realised, "cold philosophy", or analysis, can dispel the very object of its gaze (*Lamia*). In my view what was going on was far too precious to risk discussing it with this group. It is even possible that what was going on lay too deep for tears. Perhaps it had to do with "reasons of the heart that reason itself cannot fathom".

A Rock That Will Not Move

You could say that all things considered, her life had been hollowed out, whittled away, taken from her: the only exception being the most basic things of life such as the clothes that she stood up in. She is in her 70s, but without a husband or partner (one died; she and the other are separated); she is estranged from her children and grandchildren; was hospitalised after having taken an overdose; and is currently living in emergency accommodation for homeless people. As one who served for part of her life in the armed forces, all routine and predictability, teamwork and camaraderie, accountability and purpose had disappeared from her life. When I first saw her after all this, I couldn't get out of my mind a picture of a tree struck by lightning silhouetted on an empty landscape, or King Lear on the blasted heath.

So it was that she came back home: that is, to Mill Grove, the only place where she says she had known security and consistent care in her childhood. She had accepted our invitation to stay for Christmas. The last time she had been here for the festive season was well over 50 years ago. She was with us for four days, right through the celebrations. A couple of weeks earlier we had met with time to talk and without risk of interruption, but Christmas at Mill Grove is a continuously social, bustling gathering that doesn't lend itself to prolonged personal conversations. We chatted over the course of the four days of course, mostly at mealtimes when she sat at the table just beside me to my left. But for the most part she needed to find her own level of engagement with the people who were there and the activities that were happening all around her.

She noticed and talked about the things that had changed since her childhood: there were less children living at Mill Grove than in her time (when there were about 50); life was less prescribed and organised including mealtimes when boys and girls were no longer segregated by gender and age; there was television (although we did not watch it much, with only the Queen's Speech on our list of planned activities); there was more choice of food; there were no daily chores or rotas for washing up and cleaning; clothes were a matter of personal choice, even for the very young; the bedrooms were designed mostly for just one person, rather than the dormitories that she recalled with anything up to eight beds in each; neighbours and friends seemed to come and go naturally without invitation, and evidently felt at home around the place and mixing naturally with those who live here. And so on. There were also changes to furniture and décor, and to the playground, the grass bank and garden. I have learnt over the years never to underestimate the significance of changes to the buildings or way of life for those who are returning to their childhood home.

She also noticed the continuities. There were several people who had lived here at the same time as her. The shape of life, including grace before meals, and mealtimes bore traces of how she recalled it. And the growing excitement about Christmas was something she sensed immediately as one who had experienced it all those decades earlier. Two traditions struck chords with her. One was the singing of carols by candlelight (real candles) in the hall, and the sense of stillness and wonder as the lights went out, leaving the pillars and beams, as well as the faces of young and old, lit by the subdued, warm, but evidently living light. In her days there had been what were called parades with candles in Chinese/Japanese-type handheld lanterns. As a little child, to be entrusted with a candle, and to be part of such a moving celebration, remains as unusual today as it was in her early years.

The other tradition is a strange one when described without reference to its context. What happens is that Father Christmas makes a personal visit with a big grey sack full of wrapped presents for everyone up to and including those 18 years old. Each child or young person is called to receive their gift in person before returning to his or her seat or lap with the whole family looking on. But not a finger stirs on the wrapping of the presents, and no one will think of beginning to open them until a designated person stands up to say: "One, Two Three, Open". As you may have guessed, on this occasion it was Myrtle (as I will call her). She stood up and delivered the prescribed words with clarity and dignity. At once the dining room was like a hive of activity, exclamations of joy, discoveries and shared excitement as footballs, paint-sets, games, jigsaws, books and racquets appeared as the wrapping paper was discarded.

Perhaps a bit twee or over the top in this day and age? Quite possibly, but she, like me and others, were there when the tradition started. It was Christmas 1951 and my grandfather, Herbert White, the founder of Mill Grove was terminally ill, confined to his bed in a house just along the road. One of the "old boys" as they were called then – his name was Will Cowling – had ingeniously devised a relay system (unique in my experience at the time) by which we could Herbert White's voice, and he could hear us. We sat down to receive our presents and then while we held them, he spoke to us as if he was in the room with us. In an age of smartphones, it is all but impossible to convey the sense of amazement and wonder at what was happening. As children we little knew that for most of us this would be the last time that we would hear his voice. He reminded us of the first Christmas and its meaning, and then prayed for us. Those who were older at the time said that his voice was surprisingly strong given the weakness of his lungs. The last words he spoke were (as you by this time have guessed), "One, Two, Three, Open!"

And with this in mind it begins to dawn how privileged Myrtle felt to be entrusted with the performance of this little annual ritual. It took her right back to her childhood, and to memories of one who had been there for her in her hour of need. After that, things happened at pace, and before I knew it, she had gone to bed while there were still games to be played into the early hours of 27th December. By the time we awoke later that morning, she had hit the road and was away to her emergency accommodation.

She was deeply appreciative of the invitation and of her time with us, but I am left to imagine what was going on in her heart and mind. Perhaps she will share it with me in due course, but in the meantime, I will hazard a guess. For some weeks, as I have indicated, it had seemed as if everything had been taken from her, perhaps even her childhood. Several people have said or written this phrase to me, and I still haven't had the opportunity of finding out what they mean. But I think it has something to do with a trauma or loss clouding over the whole of childhood and its memories so that nothing good is left. It is too painful to revisit the happy times because the process is overshadowed or contaminated by the unhappy experiences, thoughts and associations. Anyway, she was feeling virtually alone in the world, and then, when she entered her childhood home, she found that not only was she welcomed warmly, with a full stocking hanging on her door on Christmas morning, but that she was in a place and with others who had shared happy experiences with her, not least of Christmas itself. Of course, sad memories and associations were stirred, but there was no denying that the place was still there, she was loved and remembered, and it remained intact so that whatever happened to her in future it would always be there for her.

I have been persuaded by the basic thesis in John Bowlby's book, *A Secure Base*, that a child needs a haven, harbour, nest, safe place, rock to which they can always return after times and periods of exploration away from that secure base. There are, no doubt, many possible candidates for what constitutes such a base, but it seems to me that Mill Grove was just such a base for Myrtle, and that in returning to it and finding it secure, she was able to draw some nourishment, comfort, even affirmation as she set off to wrestle with the uncertainties of the year ahead. And she knows that she is held in a healthy mind there wherever she happens to be.

Mill Grove is a residential community or extended family that seeks to live in a way that makes creative and therapeutic space in which children can be, regress, develop, thrive, and from which they can move out to explore the world around them. In an uncertain and often far from friendly world, there are times when it is necessary to return to base, and my guess is that Christmas 2017 was just such an occasion for Myrtle. Whatever else Mill Grove is, or attempts to do, being there like a rock that doesn't move is surely one of its most positive and therapeutic contributions to the life of a young person throughout his or her life.

Making a Difference When Attachment is Insecure

In an article written just before this one I confided at some depth, and with more feeling than I had envisaged at the outset, observations about children who were "un-held in a healthy mind". Unsurprisingly, it was a worrying and rather distressing scenario, and it has not been reprinted in this volume. In this piece I would like to chart some of the modest progress that has been made in relation to one such child. As always, I will anonymise the young person, and call him Jim.

He is an intelligent boy of junior school age, and over time his parents and teachers have been aware that he has had difficulties relating to members of his family and to other children at school. Worryingly, he finds it hard to distinguish between reality, and his own imagined view of stories of events. This means that anyone with whom he is in conversation is unsure how to understand and interpret the truth and meaning of what he is saying.

Ruth and I have been alongside him on a regular weekly basis (at least) for several years, and this is a note of some of the positive changes we have witnessed during and since the summer holiday of 2018, when he spent a week with us in North Wales. This was his first time with us in Snowdonia, an area which everyone else knows very well, and where we feel safe.

During that period we, and the rest of the Mill Grove family, provided him with secure boundaries and structures. There was a predictable and reliable pattern of life from the time that he woke up until bedtime. This involved mealtimes, behaviour at the meal-table, expectations of him being part of a small team ("squad") that prepared breakfast on two or three occasions, daily preparation of his picnic, engagement in a planning and sharing meeting each morning. There were also clear explanations of what was expected of him and others during the day's activities on hills, trains, boats and beaches. He revelled in this and wanted to be fully involved in everything. This meant that he quickly learned new skills such as swimming, kayaking, crabbing, sailing, shrimping and scrambling. He has good hand-eye coordination and was confident whether joining in games such as cricket and football, or informal fun such as throwing and catching balls and frisbees.

Once he had got the daily pattern or rhythm of life clear in his own mind, he surprised us all one morning by laying the tables from breakfast by himself although it was not his turn on squad. Worth pausing to consider what this meant, but obviously a desire to get involved, to do something positive, and to play his part as a member of the group or team.

By common consent, and certainly according to his view of the holiday, he enjoyed every minute of it. So, the next question was whether, and if so, how, this experience might affect his life and relationships back at home and school. One of the great positives of course was that we had shared the time with him and so could reinforce the truth of what he said, and where necessary gently ensure our mutual recollections of events and happenings tallied. And that underlines the potential significance of a concentrated time away together in a new context full of varied, shared experiences. You might call it "quality time" together, but it also provides a secure base for conversation and relationships after the event.

On return home and to a new school term we noticed that some of the changes were becoming so pronounced that they were visible and/or noticed by most around him. Here are a few that stood out for me. Conversations at mealtimes were now more relaxed because when we talked of North Wales, we had something reliable to reflect upon, and to do normal things like give our different experiences of the same events. This is, of course, the stuff of ordinary relationships in families and among friends.

He was keen to take part in shared tasks such as food preparation or putting out the rubbish and recycling. And he used his initiative rather than awaiting instructions. I don't mean by this that he had ceased to be a reasonably normal boy, who would prefer playing to doing jobs. But he did get a lot out of being part of a team.

On Founders' Day, the anniversary of the beginning of Mill Grove on 20th November 1899, he was relaxed and at home with lots of those present (many of whom had been in North Wales with him), and he was given the honour of asking the key question of the event: "Could you tell me what this celebration means?" Four adults, sitting in different parts of the dining room, responded to him by name with their own heartfelt reflections on what the place meant to them as family and friends.

Then it was time for the first showing of the slides of the North Wales holiday. He featured in several of them and, watched by his family, proudly stepped forward to receive his "Milk Bottle Top Award" given for feats of bravery, adventure or creativity. This moment brought together everything and everyone in palpable solidarity. This is where he was, and this is what he had done and achieved. The fact that he was "Man of the Match" for the beach cricket contest did not pass without notice!

A month later, Christmas provided opportunities for him to be with us engaged in several very enjoyable activities.

He joined the annual evening trip to London where we explored the pre-Christmas atmosphere along with hundreds of other families. Again, he was the youngest of the group but revelled in the informal spontaneity of our walk between the Embankment, Covent Garden and Leicester Square. Once again, there were shared experiences that could be discussed on subsequent occasions.

He was the youngest in the cast of the annual Boxing Day pantomime. In 2018 it was Dick Whittington and he played the part of the captain of the boat that took Dick to North Africa: memorably trying to keep the wheel steady as a storm intensified.

Just one other moment. On Boxing Day there is a football match in the playground at Mill Grove. It is a friendly game between teams of mixed age and ability, but over the decades it has achieved something like legendary status. Stories of great goals and saves have been handed down the generations. For some time before the game Jim would bring his own ball on to the pitch and practice scoring goals. On the weekend before Boxing Day, he confided in me that the previous year no one passed the ball to him, so he wasn't expecting to enjoy the forthcoming game. I sympathised as one who had played at his age, and who knew how it felt to be seemingly invisible to bigger members of your team.

I needn't have worried. This year, he scored five of his team's goals, all from passes! He chose to locate himself near the opponents' goal and people soon cottoned on to the fact that he had a nifty left foot! A few days later, in the gloaming he and I walked to the very spot where he stood and relived his triumph.

Life carries on, and there are difficulties and challenges in abundance for him and his family, but it is becoming apparent that he is being held in some healthy minds, and more importantly that something of this is recognised and relished by him. Nothing I have described is rocket science, but therapeutic communities like Mill Grove, and places like Snowdonia, are comparatively rare. Where else and how can we replicate some of the elements that are making the difference in his life, I wonder?

"These Are the Stairs Where I Was Told I Was Going Home"

Most of the subject matter for the columns I have written in *TTCJ* is fresh, in the sense that it relates to what has been going on in the days or weeks immediately prior to writing it, but the content of this piece is so fresh that it is raw. In fact, I am using this reflection as a way of trying to digest, even off-load some of the heaviness and shock that I have been absorbing over a sustained period of four hours.

Today the person I will call Eric came back to Mill Grove for the first time since he had left on 20th March 1963 (that's 56 years ago). His daughter came with him, and it was her first visit to the place where her dad had lived with his brother and sister for five years of their respective childhoods. Only after the visit did I learn that he had driven a long distance to come to Mill Grove in 2010, but that he then sat outside and decided not to enter, before returning home again. This trip was nine years after that.

He was instantly recognisable to me because of his eyes and smile, even though his hair and frame had changed a bit over the intervening decades. He told me that the reason for the return was the need to try and understand more of his life-story, why he had been placed in a home so far from his home in Hampshire (and across the Thames, at that!), and if possible, to find out who his father was.

Before we got down to this, I told his daughter that I had been chatting about him with my wife over breakfast, and that I remembered him as a child who seemed to be to be centred, mature, neither withdrawn nor defiant. This was something of a contrast to his brother, and to many others who lived at Mill Grove. She smiled and nodded. "That's him," she said. "He is just that sort of person, always has been, and he has been a great dad." She then surprised me by telling me how grateful she was that I had saved her dad's life. This I could not recall, so I had to ask him for more details.

He told me that it was at the seaside resort of Lowestoft, where we were on holiday in the early 1960s. He was playing in the sea, and when he got on to a Lilo (an inflatable mattress designed for use on water) an offshore breeze took him out into the North Sea and beyond the groynes that are a feature of the beach south of the pier. Apparently, I swam out to catch him and then brought him safely to dry land. I have only very hazy memories of the incident, possibly because I thought he was playing, or it was part of a game. But there was no doubting the truth that for him it was a matter of life and death, and that he and his family had been thankful that I had preserved his life.

I reminded him of contemporaries of his at Mill Grove during the later 1950s and early 1960s, but apart from an unforgettably energetic and flamboyant character named Henrietta (as I will call her), and a couple of others, he couldn't remember them.

At this stage we began looking into the folder that contained forms, letters, reports and one or two photos all relating to him and his two siblings. We started with his admission form, and this provoked a simultaneous gasp of astonishment from both father and daughter: for the first time in his life, he saw the name of his father. Until that moment he knew that the surname by which he had been known was not that of his biological father, but despite much effort spent tracing his family roots, he had not been able to find out what it was. His father had emigrated to Canada before Eric came to Mill Grove, and he had never seen him or heard of him.

Then there was the question of why he had been placed so far from home (Aldershot was his family hometown, and South Woodford is a long way both physically and in terms of mental maps). He could only remember that he and his brother had spent a couple of nights in a big house before they came to us. The riddle was solved by documents and correspondence in the folder. A welfare officer had contacted a local Christian children's home, called Mr. Fegan's Homes, to ask if they would receive the two boys into their care, but they did not have the necessary staff at that point in time.

They referred the family to Mill Grove, the home founded by Herbert White and known to them on the Christian grapevine.

But why did they need to come anyway? The reason on the form was that his father was living abroad, and his mother was homeless following a recent eviction. Eric was tenacious in his view that the problem was a deeper one. His mother had four children by different fathers, and he felt that she was trying to settle down with her new partner and wanted to make a new start with Eric and his siblings out of the way. She was, in his view, and this was confirmed by his daughter, always hoping that she could make a new start in life, at the expense of any commitment to her own children.

So how come the three children (the sister came to Mill Grove a year later than her brothers, but left at the same time as them) went back home with Eric at the tender age of 10? What had changed, and what were the attachments and bonds? Sadly, the records made it clear that their mother was under pressure from her family to have the children home, despite the evidence that she was never attuned to them or their needs, and that one of the boys had been on the receiving end of physical ill-treatment.

Lots more came out of the woodwork as we nosed our way through letters and reports, and it was heavy stuff. There was deceit all through, like Brighton through rock, and letters that had been written under duress. The mother and the current stepfather put pressure on them to give the impression that things were going well at home, when this was anything but the case.

As the time drew near for their return journey (to avoid the London rush hour and keep childcare commitments) he got up and put a gift of money into my hands. It was, he said, a way of thanking me and my parents for the love he had received while living with us. He would not have it back, even when I assured him that just seeing him again was worth its weight in gold.

With that we started to head for his white Renault builder's van, when his daughter said she would like to have a brief look around the place where he had lived for five years of his childhood. He was a little reluctant, but agreed, and so we walked slowly looked around the familiar garden and orchard, and then the lounge, kitchen and dining room. Last we headed up to the room we call "the hall", which houses an indoor badminton court, and is the indoor base of the Mill Grove Pre-School. I said that the handrails and the brickwork were exactly as they were when the pair of us were boys. He stopped by the window halfway up, and suddenly recalled that this was the place where one of the staff, Miss Baker, by name, had told him at exactly this spot that he would be going home to live with his mother.

He said that at the time he had no idea what this might mean or entail, but over 50 years later he had found the spot where the news that transformed his life was broken to him. It had not been easy, but on reflection he was pleased that he had taken this fork in the road. Life had been OK for him, and he had two wonderful children, as well as grandchildren. Things hadn't turned out as well for his brother or sister.

The time had come to leave, and we hugged each other and promised to sustain the conversation and relationships. I agreed to scan and then send them all the relevant documentation from the family folder. And then a final word to his daughter from me in which I told her of my admiration for his resilience and good faith in and through a very rocky childhood, and of my joy that he had been such a good father to her. It was my parents who had provided the primary care for him (along with Miss Baker): I was effectively an older brother who enjoyed the fun of having so many de facto siblings with whom I could play all day long. But what a blessing to see her thriving, and their relationship so obviously caring and kind.

We are often asked about "outcomes" at Mill Grove, and whether we have analysed them. We haven't, for two main reasons: the first is that the story is never over (there are always more generations), and the second, that the whole ethos of the place since 1899 has been to welcome each child by name and to love and care for them. In this, statistics have little or no place. Perhaps someone will feel it incumbent upon them to do an analysis, but I will continue to focus on welcoming children, and children's children, by name, and by listening to their stories, laughing, smiling and as today, sometimes weeping with them. And being guided by them so that when the time is ripe, they can stop on the stairs and recall the moment when the next chapter of their life-story began.

The Loneliness of the Long-Distance Child in Care

It's been another of those weekends at Mill Grove, and I need to find ways of understanding not only how to describe and frame two extraordinary encounters that took place, but also how to identify and stay in touch with the personal feelings they have provoked in me. Each of the people in question had spent part of their childhoods at Mill Grove because their family situations were so chaotic, fraught and fragile. Neither of them knew their fathers, or even their fathers' names. And although they both had half-brothers and sisters, neither of them felt close to any of their siblings, or to their mothers. So, they have had to navigate their long and lonely way through childhood, teenage and adulthood trying to find ways of making what sense they could of their own stories, of education, work, relationships and life by drawing mostly on their native wit, their intuitions and hunches.

The male (who was substantially older than the female) had been abandoned twice by his mother, before later in his childhood she invited him and one of his half-brothers to live with her and her new partner. Predictably this ended in disaster for both brothers. Floyd, as I will call him, came back to live at Mill Grove for a time. He then spent many years living independently before coming back to live with us as a mature adult. He had encountered serious problems with housing and employment due to his lack of citizenship in any country. We promised to help him with this, and the good news is that he is now a British citizen with his own passport.

My conversation with him was completely unplanned, and so for most of the time he stood holding a broom and a yellow work-vest. It was only as the subject matter deepened that he sat down beside me. There were times when tears welled up in his eyes, notably when he talked of how independent he had been all his life. This was, of course, a matter of necessity. From another perspective you could say that he had never formed a satisfactory attachment as a baby or young child. Rather there was a succession of moves involving a variety of substitute carers, and his inner world had become separated from that of others. It was heavily fortified. Though we are very fond of him, none of those who know him best feel that we have developed a close relationship with him,

Next he began reflecting about the fact that he understood his mother better than one of his older brothers. His brother was under the illusion (that was Floyd's word, not mine) that their mother loved him, and that if he could live with her again everything would be happy ever after. Floyd knew that this was untrue. And I began to see that he had formed sensible and realistic views of not only his mother, but of other people in his life. There was nothing in his re-telling of his story and experiences that was at variance with the facts as I knew them. But at the same time his deepest feelings seemed suspended or frozen. He interacted with others politely, caringly, but (understandably in the circumstances) without risking a genuine engagement of his inner world and theirs. The emotional scars of serial abandonments were far too raw.

But the moment came when I felt it might be appropriate to ask him if he knew how much he meant to us and our family. He had always been dear to us, and it had been excruciating for us (as we knew it was for him) when he had been forced to move into unsatisfactory settings. I had been affected deeply by the distress he felt at being deemed a non-person (i.e. stateless and without citizenship by officials in Germany, where he was born, and the UK where he has spent nearly all his life). His siblings dropped everything and came to see him when they discovered the fact that having been abandoned by his father, mother, he was now being disowned by his nation-state. There was no response that I could detect involving his own feelings until, that is, he began to compare his life, his values and the person he was with that of others he knew (including his siblings).

Without mentioning him by name he described how he owed most of what he had become to my father. From him he learned about right and wrong, about respect for others, about truthfulness and honesty. And there were gentle tears as he spoke. That is where our conversation ended. And I am aware that it may not seem very significant. But it is the farthest and deepest we have ever got. For he had talked about another person, one whom I knew loved him dearly, and who was fully aware of the pain that Floyd's traumas, rejections and losses had caused. My father did all he could for Floyd and was always there for him. It seemed to me that there was a hint of an acknowledgement that my father meant something special to Floyd, and that, risky as it was, Floyd had admitted it, though in a rather tangential way.

Later that evening (it was a Saturday) Floyd asked me if I would pray for a friend of his who was in a hospice and dying of bone cancer. He knew that I would be leading worship in a church not far away the following day, and I assured him that I would do so, touching him gently on the arm as I did so. Of course, you could say that this request had little or nothing to do with our earlier conversation. But my intuition is that it was an eloquent, though probably unconscious continuation, of our emotional interaction. Here was someone he cared about, and that was part of his inner world, and he immediately wanted to share it with me.

In view of Floyd's long-held way of coping with the hand of cards he has been dealt in life, it is likely that there will be little chance of substantial change for the rest of his days. But experience has taught me not to rule anything out, so I would not bank on it. But in the meantime, it was such a relief he was able to receive just a hint of love, concern and care.

The other conversation was planned. Melody, as I will call her, had arranged to come over to see Ruth and I on our return from North Wales. It was the second visit since she had lived with us a young girl. She was now self-employed and with a daughter at junior school. Her mother had struggled with chronic clinical depression and had undermined any relationships that we could establish with Melody. After a desperately unhappy spell at home Melody spent the rest of her childhood and adolescence in the care system, with the relentless pressure from her mother to believe that she was bad, and that so were we.

Melody has always been intelligent, creative and outgoing and the fact was that we loved her dearly and were devastated when things turned out the way they did. So you can imagine the joy we felt on her return. As we chatted however, the loneliness that she had experienced and felt year by year became all too evident. She wanted to know if she really was "that bad", and it seemed incongruous that someone so confident, bright and mature should have had any such doubt. But she had not had anyone alongside her continuously to affirm her. As a result, it took her ages to realise that her mother had failed her, and that she would have to move on. One of the ways she does this it to call her mother by her name rather than speak of her as her mother.

In her lonely journey through the care system, she had virtually no recollection of several people who were alongside her while she lived with us, including at least one who was particularly understanding and close. And it was only when we started looking at a diary that events, like cycle rides and a gym club, a friendly Sunday School, began to be recalled. Unlike Floyd, she was able to relate to us with openness and feeling, and to express her own inner world and journey. But in both cases I was left with a deep feeling of sadness that they had had to try to work things out for themselves when the world in which each of them was living was so chaotic, confusing and sometimes even mad.

The two conversations took place on the same day, and that was just 24 hours ago. What are the elements that go into the mix of my own emotions, I wonder? A regret that I/we could not do more for each of them? A sense of guilt that they journeyed alone when I/we would dearly have loved to walk with them?

The exposure of my own inner vulnerability and loneliness? I am not sure, but there has been plenty of transference: that's for sure.

Meanwhile Floyd continues to live with us, and there will be more opportunities to share, before hopefully he is able to find his feet again. And Melody is keen to come over with her daughter as soon as possible. The stories continue, and so there is hope. There is always hope. But in the process raw nerves have been touched. I am not sure there is any other way after such lonely personal journeys.

The Long-term Effects of Separation and Loss on Sibling Relationships

The effects of traumas associated with separation and loss on individual children and young people are well-known, and those seeking to help, whether social workers, residential carers, or counsellors and therapists, usually have strategies that they employ when they come alongside. A notable example is *Building the Bonds of Attachment*, by Dan Hughes.

I wonder however whether there is either an awareness of, or resources, to help siblings who have all suffered trauma and loss, in their relationships with each other. Put simply, how might their mutual loss have affected the bonds and attachment between them not only during their childhoods, but in later life?

On reflection I realised that we are in an unusually privileged position to comment on this at Mill Grove, for two reasons. First, because we have been blessed with unusually spacious accommodation, we have been able to welcome and care for many groups of siblings over the decades. On occasions we have received up to seven children from the same family or household. Secondly, we have remained committed to, and in continuous contact with, many of these right through their lives.

My experience of living with and caring for children during their childhoods, and then listening to them in their adulthood, has left me in little doubt that their relationships as siblings have often been strained and difficult. Let me give some examples from the many available.

Three girls, who lost both their parents when they were young, have always found their relationships with each other tortuous. One is withdrawn and has resisted any contact for months, even years, at a time. Another is depressed and feels she does not get the support she expects and would like from the other two. The third occupies the middle ground while struggling with her own feelings.

Five of a group of six siblings, sharing the same biological parents, find one impossible to get on with. And the others have tended to pair off.

A brother and sister who came and left Mill Grove at the same time have drifted apart and have had no contact at all for years. One feels this keenly, finding it inexplicable.

A younger sister takes care to find out how her older siblings are, but discovers it is a one-way street: they don't want to know her.

A family of six siblings is gregarious and they regularly meet up, even though they are spread around the UK, but one of the six is out of touch with all the rest.

Another group of five siblings have scapegoated the youngest sister ....

When discussing this with Ruth, my wife, we realised that the list could be extended virtually indefinitely. Although there are exceptions, a pattern was worryingly clear:

relationships between siblings who have all suffered separation and loss are often fragile and unpredictable. Now it needs to be acknowledged that sibling rivalry, and difficulties in relationships between sisters and brothers, are not the sole preserve of those who have suffered trauma and loss. In so called "ordinary" or "normal" families there are often tensions, and broken relationships. But is there, I wonder, something going on here that deserves careful scrutiny?

My sense is that there is, and so here is a working hypothesis, representing work in progress, based on the steady supply of evidence that I receive. The siblings whom I have known over several decades have all at one time or another shared with me how deeply their separation from their parent or parents affected them, and how they have struggled to understand and make sense of what might have been going on, including the reason for the separation (rejection). In several cases, we have been able to work out together some of their survival strategies. Often there is a sense of guilt caused by a feeling, unconscious for much of the time, that they might have been one of the causes of the breakup in the first place. And when there was a return to one of the parents (as often, but not always, happened) some years later, this was associated with very mixed feelings and often went badly. This exacerbated tensions between siblings, and sometimes led to a parting of their ways.

The initial separation from kith and kin often resulted in relations with the siblings' extended family being attenuated, thus cutting them off for potential sources of understanding and empathy.

Given all this, here is a tentative suggestion as to what might have been going on. The loss caused by separation has been deep, and the siblings have usually tried to cope with this by themselves. As with those who have served in the armed forces during conflicts, there is often a reluctance, even inability to share their painful experiences with anyone else, including their closest relatives.

It is therefore no surprise to have discovered that during their childhoods the siblings rarely,

if ever, shared what they felt with each other. Unconsciously there may have been a feeling in each sibling that the other(s) had been the cause of the separation. Or that others did not feel the pain of loss and separation as much as the one struggling with his or her own feelings of anxiety and depression. A pattern therefore builds up in which each child cuts off from the others as a survival strategy, conscious or unconscious. Later in life, things are too emotionally charged and precarious to begin to build bridges and explore feelings together. When the siblings start their own families, these are often sealed off from each other as if to avoid contamination of emotions. This may sound dramatic, even overdone, but the thoughts and feelings shared with me are of this intensity and nature.

There is not space here to develop this line of analysis. But in the process, I have come to see that understanding what is going on between such closely related people involves complicated emotions such as guilt, blame and shame. My hunch is that the last of these three may be the most universal.

If this is so, and I would appreciate comments from readers on the subject, what might our strategies be? At the outset I suggest this dynamic receives proper attention. One of the ways of dealing with it might be some form of groupwork, even family therapy. It is apparent that the problems identified will not be resolved without some form of intervention. Each sibling will find this difficult, but there are individual wounds as well as wounds in the sibling relationships, so each and all may benefit if this is done sensitively and in an informed way.

If this has not been available during childhood, then the question arises: what can be done later in life? My initial experience here is not encouraging. It seems that trying to change behaviour and patterns that have become entrenched over decades is nigh on impossible. It is that serious. So, the task in later life may well need to focus on damage limitation. This may mean one can be there for each individual sibling who wishes to share, and sometimes for more than one, whether they are in contact with each other or not. In doing so there is a tacit acceptance of the unfortunate status quo.

In the process, as intimated earlier, it may be possible to discuss survival or defence strategies that have been employed unconsciously. If so, this can lead on occasions to insights into how another sibling might have been trying to cope. An example is of a person who had lived at Mill Grove while I was a teenager. Recently, he had suffered three deaths of people close to him within a matter of months. He contacted his older brother who told him that he should have got over it by now. I was able to suggest that the older brother could well still be suffering from the loss of his home and family five decades later; and that he might be unable to come to terms with the death of an in-law two years ago, where he had felt in some way guilty, though objectively there was no reason to do so.

This assumes of course that there will still be contact and relationships all these years later, and this is one of the benefits of the continuity of Mill Grove since 1899. In some ways what is happening is similar to what goes on in ordinary, good-enough extended families through the generations. Which takes us back to the beginning: the problem is that these groups of siblings lacked this sustained relationship with their blood relatives. This was the starting point of the long-term effects of the initial separation and loss.

Relationships Between Siblings Who Have All Suffered Separation and Loss

This is a follow-up to the previous article, "The Long-term Effects of Separation and Loss on Sibling Relationships", in which I shared a dawning awareness of an issue that arose during a walk in the woods with Ruth, my wife, during the first Covid 19 lock-down in the UK.

It is because of the long-term connections and relationships that there are in the extended family and network of Mill Grove (sometimes spanning as many as four generations) that we find ourselves in a rather privileged and unique position. We know not only the life-stories of hundreds of children who have experienced separation and loss in early childhood, but also the stories of their children and children's children. That such a breaking of the bonds of attachment causes serious challenges in the lives of individuals is now incontrovertible, but the focus of the first of these two pieces was on the effects that such traumas had on the relationships between siblings in the same family or household.

I ventured one or two working hypotheses, based on what the people themselves had shared with me. These included a sense of guilt (conscious or unconscious) that each individual child felt that they might have been the cause of the separation; or conversely, that one of the others was the cause; unresolved feelings and emotions that jeopardised attempts at rehabilitating or reuniting the children with their parents later in life; the disturbance or severance of relationships with the extended family (kith and kin). The nett effect of these was an isolation that each sibling felt, and a consequent attempt to find ways of coping with their feelings by what might be called defence mechanisms. Some looked for external boundaries (joining the armed forces or uniformed organisations), some blocked or froze painful experiences in their memories, so that there was literally nothing that they could share with siblings later in life; and there were often serial failures in establishing resilient marriage or family relationships which compounded the feelings of separation and loss, and reinforced divisions within the sibling group.

I suggested that there were three predominant types of emotion to be considered: guilt, blame and shame. In the UK we are reasonably familiar with the first two, but I shared my hunch that shame might hold some of the keys that might unlock what was going on. Shame is a widely understood feature of social relations in many cultures: quite apart from any personal shame, there is a dimension that an individual or her family may have been embarrassed or humiliated, because they have done or been involved in something of which wider social groups and networks disapprove. It compounds the tendency to split such things off, to try to force them underground.

The point of revisiting the subject is not that I have further insights to offer, or that others have been in contact to help us understand things more deeply, but that since writing on the subject, the extent and depth of the problem has been reinforced with worrying and uncanny intensity. I am now convinced that it is a major problem that has been rarely observed, recorded or addressed. So, if you are reading this and can point me to resources that have eluded me to date, please contact me as a matter of urgency. We find almost daily more evidence of the fractures and fissures between siblings over the whole of their lives, and then passed on to their children: something perhaps best left for another day. These are not minor irritants, but rather substantial blocks to personal understanding, a sense of identity and self-worth, and good-enough relationships with others outside the family.

Further evidence has been accompanied by one or two significant avenues of thought or possible explanation. While now convinced that there is a major, largely unnoticed and unattended issue within sibling groups, we find a counter or accompanying strand of evidence strengthening steadily. This is that some bonds between members of what we call the extended family of Mill Grove are thriving. (For the avoidance of doubt, this is between those who have lived at Mill Grove as children, but who are not related by blood.) By their very nature these relationships are largely outside of our knowledge and influence, but we receive regular concrete evidence of them. Some who are now in their 70s and 80s often meet and are in telephone contact even more frequently. The commitment and devotion that they have to each other is frankly inspiring. They genuinely empathise with and support each other. When questioned about why this is, they tend to be

surprised: "We are family" is the gist of their response. This, although they are neither biologically related, nor geographically close.

Crucially significant is the fact that these relationships are between those who struggle with their own sibling relationships. So, what is going on? The first line of thoughts assumes that the capacity to overcome some of the effects of separation and loss remains intact in some individuals. They have lived with others in the same residential community, and during this time new attachments and bonds have formed. There was no formal encouragement of this, and perhaps this is the point. What all these individuals have in common is a shared experience of separation and loss, whether spoken or not. There was no expectation that they would care for each other, but they instinctively knew how others felt.

The healing that this represents has not come about through specialist counselling or therapy, but from shared experiences in a place where there was empathy (however imperfect), and a modelling of unconditional commitment. No one was rejected or abandoned. There were none of the usual types of splitting, denial or defensiveness. It may sound trite, but one of the obvious conclusions we should draw from this is the importance of maintaining links between those who have lived in residential care and who wish to continue them. There are a host of other factors to be borne in mind, including the quality of the carers, their motivation, their values and their faith. But a core message concerns potential connectivity between those who have experienced separation.

The second and related avenue of thought relates to marriage and covenant relationships. On the 50th wedding anniversary of Ruth and myself, several of those who had lived at Mill Grove and who belonged to a Facebook group appeared. Their coming as a group was a surprise to us. We had not seen some for years, but they had kept in touch with each other. We reflected on possible meanings of this with our consultant psychotherapist because we were genuinely puzzled. Their evident concern and care for each other was consistent with the first avenue of thought. But why should they choose to return together to Mill Grove on our wedding anniversary? Was the fact that it was a personal family occasion of ours, and that they were invited and part of it, significant? Was our marriage something that provided unconscious security for them? We will be processing this for some time. But there is an inkling of a possible explanation emerging. What if our marriage symbolised something substantial and reliable that they could take for granted as a source of consolation? What if it was something they respected? What if it was integral to the household or family of which they felt a part when their own families had drifted apart?

One of those who returned for the first time since my father's funeral (that is no doubt significant too) told me that she had lost contact with her two younger brothers. She then went on to say that Mill Grove and the Facebook group constituted her family. What if traditional nuclear families fail to provide security for some of their members, and alternatives (even substitutes) are needed? By attending the rites of passage in a family such as a wedding anniversary or funeral, it may be that some individuals find what they have been seeking, whether consciously or not. If so, then where are such households and such occasions? This is not to undervalue the place of counselling and therapy, but rather to listen to the voices of those who are expressing a desire to belong: to love and be loved. Kith and kin reimagined and rediscovered.

Making Sense of War With a Child

Last night (Monday 7th March 2022) the six-year-old boy sitting beside me during our evening meal at Mill Grove paused over the plate of spaghetti he was enjoying, to inform me that there had been a Tube strike. He then described how children and families were ducking and running in underground stations because of bombs and loud explosions.

As he had gleaned from television, there had indeed been an Underground strike in London at the beginning of March, but the pictures he had seen of families reacting to the sounds of war were unrelated to that. They were from far away Ukraine. Perfectly understandably he had elided two sets of images. And that was it. As the adults at the table pondered what he was saying, he was already tucking into the food in front of him.

Sometimes as adults we discuss what we should say to children about war or distressing events shown on television, but we should not be in any doubt that many young ones will be trying to make sense of what is going on without such thoughtful input from us.

It reminded me of the time when I returned from a meeting in London on 9.11.2001. Our youngest daughter was sitting alone in front of the television screen looking strangely mesmerised. When I saw repeated clips of what looked like model planes flying into two towers, I asked her what film it was. She replied that it wasn't a film: it was real. She then interpreted what was happening in New York to me. As I began to take in what seemed frankly so bizarre as to seem incredible, I felt a pang of fatherly pain and guilt, that I had not been there for her, and with her, as she had been witnessing one of the appalling atrocities of human history.

After the meal yesterday evening, I was at a meeting of the local community association in what we call the Waverley Lounge of Mill Grove. It suddenly struck me that it was in this very room in the autumn of 1956 where I had first met Hungarian refugees from Budapest, who had come to stay with us after fleeing from the Russian invasion of Hungary. Memories of these people, where they sat, what they wore, what I felt, came flooding back as I sat, over 70 years later, wearing a Ukrainian flag on my fleece. I knew that this childhood experience had left me emotionally wounded, but now I was reminded just how deep and raw the scars still were.

I recall how adults, notably my father, tried

to explain to me why we could not respond to the cries of help from the freedom fighters in Budapest by taking up arms. He told me that we had to pick our battles, and this one, against the USSR, was doomed to failure. It sat very uneasily with all I had learned about World War II, and the speeches of Winston Churchill (who happened to be our MP at the time). In short, I was not convinced, but realised with the sort of shock associated with being plunged into a cold bath, that I was living in a world where people made compromises, were sometimes economical with the truth, and where there were many shades of grey. This was at a time when I saw things in terms of good and bad, drawing my inspiration from fairy stories, and children's literature, notably Enid Blyton.

So as adults, how do we help children to make sense of war with sensitivity and integrity? Instinctively I feel that the question has already betrayed itself. Is it possible to make any coherent or genuine sense of war? What does that sense look like, and how could it possibly be conveyed to a six-year-old? In the process, time and place are likely to become confused or conflated, and there is a risk that any attempt at explanation might make the child's immediate world, including for example, the local underground station, feel unsafe.

In the book, *The Growth of Love*, I invited readers to imagine a child's world or kingdom. Borrowing the idea of big and little people from Jonathan Swift, I described events in the life of a child using the language of nations and governments. So mum and dad were king and queen of the kingdom, there were expeditions to supermarkets, and there were summit meetings with friends at school. When things went wrong things turned very chilly. Parents quarrelling was like civil war; divorce like the break-up of the kingdom; physical or sexual abuse like invasion.

Whether we are talking about actual big things like governments and wars, or more local, personal things such as weddings or divorce, they are all part of the same world to a child, and this world looms huge in her thinking. As the poet Gibran realised, we may give children our love, but probably not our thoughts, for they dwell in their own world that we can never fully enter.

In case you are wondering what I actually did, or said, yesterday evening, let me describe the sequence without any attempt to explain or defend it. During the meal I chatted with the adults for a time as a way of indicating to them as well as to the little boy that what he had said was important. It wasn't something to be laughed out of court or ignored. Later I pointed out the Ukrainian flag I was wearing, and why I was doing so.

Then we had our usual prayer time. Accompanied by the guitar we sang a modern version of Psalm 23, The Lord is my Shepherd, culminating in the verse, "and though I walk the darkest path, I will not fear the evil one, for you are with me, and your rod and staff are the comfort I need to know." I told the story of the shepherd boy who had learnt this psalm, and how he used it as a prayer holding each of his fingers in turn: "The"; "Lord"; "is"; "my"; "Shepherd". He died protecting his sheep, but when his body was found, he was holding his fourth finger. And then we had a very brief prayer which concluded, "Lord, have mercy". At the end I explained to everyone that I had first heard it in Russian, in Moscow.

In recounting this I am not offering an answer to the question. But rather asking myself and others who seek to care sensitively for children who have experienced trauma and loss, how we can respond appropriately. By this I mean, in a way that somehow "holds" the child and all his or her conflicting and ambivalent memories, sensations, feelings and emotions. By drawing on Psalm 23 and the Russian "Jesus Prayer" I was digging very deep, because there was no way in which I was a dispassionate observer or counsellor. For me this was far too close for any other sort of comfort.

The Cost of Survival

I had planned to be with this particular person for over a month, and when I was with her ready to listen to what she wanted to share, it began to dawn on me just how costly the conversation was for her. She told me through tears that in anticipation of it, she had not been able to stop crying all night.

Judged by a word count, the conversation got off to a slow start: nothing was said for several minutes, but it was perfectly understood by both of us that the words would come in their time. And they did. She summarised how she felt by using the word "disappointment" and left me to work out to what it might relate. Any childhood hopes had been "smashed"; she felt "bound" (when saying this she used her right hand to encircle her left); "abandoned"; "ignored" … These were her exact words.

Her early childhood was indeed traumatic and distressing enough to warrant all of these harsh verbs. She was an unwanted baby in the sense that her mentally ill mother knew that she would be unable to care for her. And from that time onwards she had never felt genuinely accepted as someone having her own identity or sense of self-worth. What abilities and gifts she had were not recognised by others. This is still the case in her mind.

She had in short never formed a secure attachment.

So it came as no surprise when she confided in me that it was so difficult "to trust". This was the point in the conversation when I paused to reflect that the context in which she had grown up meant that she couldn't trust. In fact her survival was testament to the fact that she had not trusted anyone. Her trust would have been smashed or ignored (to use her words). Perhaps that was part of what she meant when she described her feelings.

The paradox or dilemma at the heart of her existence was that she was a survivor who had shown quite remarkable courage and resilience, but to survive she had been unable to trust. And so trusting was a quality absent from all her relationships including trust of herself.

It was almost unbearably painful listening to her story unfolding, accompanied by her tear-filled eyes.

But why was she telling me this? And why was she doing it now? Why in this place? As she pondered these thoughts there was a distinct hint of brightness in her eyes: a smile. She saw in a moment that the very fact of her sharing something so painful demonstrated some form or element of the very trust that she had been absent throughout her life.

The extended conversation we were having (this was the second part) was only possible because in some way, however tenuously or implicitly, she trusted me. And she was insightful enough to say why it was. "You came gently alongside me … You had time to listen … You had no agenda of your own …"

Before long (90 minutes all told) it was time for me to leave, having agreed when we would next meet.

But the paradox or riddle would not let me go: her survival testified to the truth that she had not trusted anyone. Had she trusted her mother through and through, it is perfectly possible that she would not have survived the loss. And with that lack of trust came a way of life: to survive meant that trust was not a quality that she could afford to explore.

Immediately I thought of another person whom I have known for many years of her life: since she was a girl just embarking on secondary education in fact. She is now in her thirties. Her early life had been a sad sequence of losses, moves, changes and abandonments. There was no one alongside her continuously who was able to help her maintain any consistent sense of her story, her identity in relationships, through time and connecting place. Social workers, foster carers, prospective adoptive parents came and went as regularly as new school uniforms. And slowly but surely she created her own narrative, which changed from day to day, and situation to situation. (The word narrative is not a wholly accurate way of expressing what I mean, but it is possibly the nearest available. The problem was that it was not a coherent story so much as a kaleidoscope, or collage of recollections and fabrications.)

Understandably it has now reached the point where no one believes what she is saying. It is sometimes called "lying", but it is more deep-seated than that. It is the necessity as she sees it to jettison inconvenient and contrary facts with each new day or encounter, so much so that she cannot understand that no one believes her. She has survived, but at what cost? For example she regularly pleads for help to save her from an abusive and destructive relationship, but equally regularly she is drawn into its clutches yet again. Her sense of time, continuity, identity, the world is warped to such a degree that no one can share it with her.

In both cases I have resisted using the term "defence mechanism" because it comes with so much baggage, and it can be assumed to be a conscious strategy. But in these cases (and many others) in my experience what is going on is of primal depth and significance. In order for the most basic survival two human beings have had to dispense with two of the most vital aspects of human life and relationship: trust and truth.

It is painful to witness. In the former case there is hope. For she has not jettisoned truth, even though how she sees herself and others is hugely coloured by her personal feelings and pain. As we continue the conversation it is just conceivable that a seed of trust might grow within her so that it might start to develop however falteringly in relationships. But where truth has been abandoned it is hard to see what hope there is of anything other than a replication of sameness.

Having reached this point in my article I found myself reading about child soldiers and the long-term effects of indescribable traumas, suffering and brutality on their personalities and characters. They are often decisive and resourceful, but the cost to their sense of personhood and relationships is incalculable.

All of us who are living are survivors by definition, and we have all had to make choices, compromises and sacrifices in order to survive. There is something admirable about the resourcefulness and resilience that survival betokens. It should never be under-estimated, but sometimes the cost is immeasurably great and sad.

INTRODUCTION TO THEME TWO
Boundaries

The term Boundaries was chosen in *The Growth of Love* to enable the description, analysis, critique and contextualisation of many different levels, layers and scales of pattern, rules and categories.

One of the boundaries considered is the organisational setting of therapeutic child care (Article 1). This can affect the shape and contours of a child's life indirectly, often without comment or reflection.

There are two pieces describing practical issues of setting in counselling and therapy both appreciating the benefits of informal and non-threatening contexts (Articles 2 and 3).

The fourth article explores the effects that diagnoses and labels may have on a child or young person's sense of identity and agency.

The fifth considers some of the unique challenges when in familiar holiday haunts, and the boundaries between childhood memories and the activities of those who are children experiencing places for the first time.

Article Seven explores aspects of the boundary between professionals and family if there is to be an appropriate and effective therapeutic alliance.

The last pair of articles describe in detail how Ruth and I set about creating safe space for someone new to meals at Mill Grove. This involves a range of guidelines, norms, patterns, rituals that combine to form a context in which self-expression and shared living are balanced or integrated. They probably come closest to what is on our minds each and every day, often without the need for words or conscious planning.

The Organisational Setting of Therapeutic Care

With the demise of Kid's Company in August 2015 there has been a groundswell of critical comment about charities in the UK. (For example, "It will take more than a fundraising overhaul to restore faith in charities": Ben Summerskill in *The Guardian*, 30th September 2015; "Fat cat charities rely too much on taxpayers" by Libby Purves in *The Times*, 8th February 2016.) Without getting into a debate about the issues raised, the modest intention of this article is to consider which type of organisational setting might be most appropriate for the therapeutic care of children.

The broad range of ideal types includes the following: local government; central government; private sector companies; charities delivering contracted services; charities that are entirely voluntarily funded. In reality of course there are many variations on each of the types, such as central government funded regional residential centres; educational and social work settings; social enterprises; and no doubt various other hybrids.

What's more there are many other factors that come into play including location, resources, training, personnel, knowledge, experience, support networks, faith and belief systems, and so on. This means that we are not discussing some neat or universal way of assessing what might guarantee the quality of care, but rather contexts which might best favour that care all other things being equal.

It is also theoretically possible to argue that the organisational settings are not as important as the rest of the factors that contribute to the quality of care.

That said, let's move on to reflect on some of the assumptions and thinking that may be at work.

One idea behind the provision of the care of children by local authorities is that of "corporate parenting", and in its favour is the possibility that an authority in which all departments are committed to such a vision has considerable resources (at least theoretically) to offer. This is something that other forms of provision will find hard to match. Perhaps it can be linked to the wisdom that it takes a village to raise a child.

At the other end of the spectrum is the concept of parenting that focuses on the household or nuclear family. If this is seen as a desirable norm, then something akin to adoption might be seen as one of the best options.

When considering the residential care of children in the UK, there has in general been a shift away from voluntary provision by charities towards the private sector; while support services for children and families, together with foster care, have tended to be provided by local authorities either directly or by being contracted out.

More recently (in historical terms) the regulation and inspection of services has changed significantly fuelled by concerns for safeguarding children, professional standards and the concept of evidence-based services in a risk averse society. Children and families are routinely being monitored by agencies who are working together using common assessment frameworks.

Sadly, it is not difficult to point to glaring failures and/or abuse in every type of organisational provision, so none is immune to falling short of acceptable standards.

With this brief summary of some of the context in mind, let me share one or two observations about what I have learnt from over 40 years researching and working in this whole area, before I close with a suggestion.

Large charities have the resources to provide professional support for the care of children that is hard to match in any other setting. They can offer "added value" for a time at least, and in some places. Very small charities and local authorities on their own are unlikely to be able to compete (an unfortunate word) with national organisations such as Barnardo's, The Children's Society and Action for Children. At the same time these large charities are increasingly being described as "corporations", not in a legal sense, but because that is what they feel like when you are working with (negotiating with) them. And although they are charities (and thus strictly speaking are free to do anything that is not proscribed by law, provided that it is consistent with their charitable objectives), they are mostly tied into contracts which restrict their room for manoeuvre, not least the freedom to innovate and experiment.

The private sector works well where regulatory and inspection frameworks intensify, because it will seek to meet the increasing range of demands and standards by recruiting appropriate professionals and raising the fees that it charges to provide care. It took me some time as a sociologist to realise that bureaucracy and the market worked so well hand in hand (symbiotically is perhaps the best way of describing it), and this may help incidentally to make sense of the trajectory of the European project in some of its manifestations at least.

Local authorities tend to vary immensely and where they are struggling with quality it does seem to require an immense amount of patience, tenacity and will to change the ethos. On the other hand, some of the best care that I have witnessed has been in various local government settings.

This leads me to close with a suggestion based on personal experience of the organisational context that I know best: Mill Grove. Over nearly twelve decades it has received a limited amount of local government funding, but this has never been attached to contracts or performance indicators. It has also received government funding for its pre-school in the form of parent vouchers. There are no corporate donors or sponsors, no charity shops and no fund-raising events or days. There has never been any fund-raising or publicity. It is overwhelmingly funded by voluntary contributions.

And remarkably the place is thriving well over a century since it began.

Who supports it? Individuals and households who know of it locally; members of churches; a few local schools; members of the extended family of those who lived there as children, and one or two small trusts.

And what effect might this specific charitable context and ethos have on the sort of care that is going on? It would be as inappropriate as it would be invidious to claim for Mill Grove any advantage over any other organisation in terms of the quality of care (for the reasons given above and many more). That is not the point. There are vulnerabilities and weaknesses that I would be happy to go into if there were an interest in them, but there is a combination of advantages. These include the freedom for the place to grow and develop organically (without prescription and labelling); the ability to stay with children throughout their lives, and to support their children and grandchildren in a personal way; the opportunity to allow children to find their own ways of navigating relationships (without the pressure of time on one hand, or expectations of particular norms on the other); vibrant and creative relationships with the surrounding community; the support of a faith base and community; rich contact with the natural world; long-term commitment by carers who are able to learn, train and develop insights and expertise …

So, the suggestion is this: would it be possible for local authorities and charities to identify some people, households, small organisations embedded in local communities that could be supported by high quality personnel and resources? That's it.

Face to Face or Side by Side?

"Lovers are always talking to one another about their love; Friends hardly ever about their Friendship. Lovers are normally face to face, absorbed in each other; Friends, side by side, absorbed in some common interest."
C.S. Lewis, *The Four Loves*

This distinction between lovers and friends is a memorable one in a book rich with potential quotations. It came back to me one evening recently when I was in conversation with a child therapist. We were chatting about the best settings for therapy when, using this image from C.S. Lewis, a very creative distinction began to emerge.

Both of us were engaged in therapy. In his case it was mostly formal one-to-one sessions with children, and in mine it was in the context of Mill Grove where there is no formal therapy on the premises, but where daily life is organised in such a way that the place is a therapeutic milieu. In fact there is a lot of overlap because he often uses play as part of his way of working, and recreation is at the heart of our family life. He listens actively to life stories and so do we. He is aware of conscious and unconscious mechanisms and so are we.

But what struck us both at roughly the same time was that formal therapy had much in common with the idea of lovers talking "face to face", while life in a therapeutic milieu was more like friends living "side by side". The purpose of setting aside a time and a place for a therapy session is often to allow two people to engage with each other (using a range of means and resources) in an appropriate setting without unwanted distractions. The purpose of life together in a residential setting is to engage in a range of activities and tasks together in such a way that healing and growth are facilitated.

You could argue that the therapy session (of say, 55 minutes) is a microcosm of the therapeutic community. But there is still a distinction to be made which I will try to identify with some examples and reflections.

I have often found that it is when walking or driving together with our eyes focused on the way ahead, (or sometimes on the environment through which we are passing) that some of the most significant conversations take place. I recall a boy in the back seat of my car leaning forward so that his head appeared between mine and that of his mother as she and I sat on the front seats talking about her life story. I think it was the movement of the car, the changing of the scenery that made such a memorable exchange possible. If we had been in a room with a limited time, I am not sure it would have been possible.

Then there are those times when a pet or wild animal dies and we bury it. Absorbed in this common interest or activity, again and again I have found that deep reflections on personal loss and grief have been shared. The purpose of the interment was not to have such a conversation: it emerged within that process.

The same sort of conversation between two or more people often occurs at the meal-table: possibly over meals more than in any other setting. Shared meals may be at the very heart of the therapeutic milieu. They are by their very nature repeated with predictable regularity, and over the years the whole of human life is likely to be discussed in one way or another, with hilarity, frustration, irony or deep feeling.

Holidays epitomise this dynamic: a new setting and distinctive activities related to that setting provide a context for being alongside one another absorbed in a common interest. In our case it is likely to be hill-walking, swimming, kayaking or sailing.

The movement (often physical and literal, but sometimes to do with a change in mood or narrative) models the "journey of life" itself. We are fellow companions on that journey who may be together for a short or more prolonged period of time. We did not come together to talk or engage in therapy: the conversation or therapy emerged in a particular place and context. It was not intentional in the sense that it was planned this way.

By way of contrast much therapy deliberately takes place outside of ordinary life: time and place are set aside for a particular purpose. It is quite possible that the therapist and the child see the time, the place and the dynamics quite differently, but without some agreement or alliance between the two of them no therapy can be said to have occurred.

I do not want to make too much of a distinction for two reasons. First, because some of the commonalities are so important; second, because like love and friendship, they are in many ways complementary. That said, it is still in my view worth exploring. Among other things it leads us to ask about the preferred settings for formal therapy, which is where our conversation headed on the evening in question.

The therapist had begun some personal

educational tutoring of children who had experienced separation and loss. The primary purpose of these tutorials was to help the children with particular subjects and skills such as English and Maths, but the therapist had been chosen for this because of his understanding of their intra-personal experiences and feelings.

Might it not be, we wondered, that in such tutorials, side by side, much therapy could take place spontaneously? What if the common subject or focus meant that it felt safer for the child to talk about feelings when it was clear that this was not the reason for the time spent together? After all, it has been remarked that people often talk about medical issues with anyone but their doctor: it is understandably safer to employ this strategy if you are anxious about your condition. Perhaps the same is true of those in debt who might just wish to avoid seeing their bank manager.

For the therapist in such an informal setting, there is the safety of knowing that there is no intended therapeutic outcome to be described in a document or on a form justifying the validity of the session; for the child there is no pressure or expectation that anything personal will be shared.

Be this as it may, I am so thankful that daily life at Mill Grove provides a myriad settings, times, seasons and contexts for being side by side with no pressure to share anything personal or difficult, but with the constant knowledge that it can be done if and when the time and the occasion are right.

There are times when we are face to face engaged in a focused conversation, but the norm is the journey of life side by side. And it is C.S. Lewis who has helped me to see this when it may have been the very last thing he actually had in mind! Be this as it may, I am very grateful to him.

A Fireside Chat

One of the people who I now realise has influenced me greatly from my younger days is the Swiss psychiatrist, Paul Tournier (1898–1986). He was the author of several books, eight of which I have on the shelves beside my desk. These comprise reflections on, and the retelling of, the stories of those who came to him seeking help. The most famous is probably *The Meaning of Persons*. On the front cover of three of them is a picture of Dr. Tournier sitting in an armchair beside a fire, and it becomes apparent as his writing proceeds that this is his preferred position when listening to those who come to him. They engage in conversation while sitting either side of the fire.

He sums up what is going on, in this way: "Day after day men and women of all ages and conditions, the healthy as well as the sick, come to see me in order to learn to know themselves better. They tell me the story of their lives. They take great trouble to get the details absolutely right. They are seeking to know the person that they themselves really are, and they feel that everything we are setting out to do together may well be compromised if they are not scrupulously sincere in all they say." (*The Meaning of Persons*, SCM: 1957, page 12)

Without modelling what I have done on Tournier in a conscious way, and despite not being a psychiatrist, it began to dawn on me recently that an increasing amount of my time is taken up sitting beside a fire listening to the stories and the detailed descriptions of those who come to me. The pieces I have written in *ChildrenWebmag* and more recently in the *Therapeutic Care Journal* often have their roots in exactly such conversations, usually in the same room and beside the same open fire. I had been drawn both to his homeliness and his humility: he readily acknowledged that he was a "wounded healer" who had experienced deep traumas in his early life. And he had no difficulty in confessing when he felt out of his depth with a particular patient.

As in Tournier's description above, those who have come to see me have done so for a variety of reasons, and in quite different states of mental health. What they have in common is a desire to know themselves better. In the past couple of weeks I recall the woman who feels unable to escape from the effects of an abusive and traumatic childhood; the man who finds it hard to forgive himself for some of the things he has done, and at least one thing he hasn't done; the young man with Asperger syndrome who wanted to share with me his meticulous drawings and proposals for making the world a better place; the woman who couldn't understand why most of her early years were a complete blank; the founder and director of a project, who is beginning to find himself in the process; a mother who finds it painful to share about the way she has been excluded from her family home ....

Almost always I find myself sitting in the same chair with the other person in the conversation on a settee the other side of the fire. There is a low table accessible to both of us on which sits tea, coffee or water. And, once we have got to know each other after a session or two, the pattern of conversation is remarkably similar. There is usually an uninterrupted period of up to an hour when the person shares with me what has been going on in their life, what concerns them, and descriptions of feelings. Whenever possible I seek the agreement of that person to take notes with my fountain pen on sheets of A4 paper. I file the notes and always re-read them before the next session. I usually make no reference to the notes during a session, but they serve as a record of what has been said, so that I can be aware of what is regularly repeated, what might be new, or something seen in a different light, and what might be developing insight.

I have come to realise that by now, like Tournier, though lacking much of his insight and most of his training, I have a pretty extensive store of peoples' life stories which help me to understand what is shared in human experience, and what is unique to a particular person. Always, without exception, the stories are fascinating. There is no such thing as a "boring" person. I have realised like Samuel Johnson that were there enough biographers to go around, every person's life merits a biography. True some people are anxious or depressed;

some stories are so repetitive and predictable that listening can sometimes be a challenge, but the person and their story are always engaging.

Just one more point of background information before I share about a recent encounter and conversation. I have always avoided categories and terms for our sessions together. Candidates include counselling, therapy, spiritual direction, mentoring and the like. There are some things completely off-limits such as project management and supervision, but the main thing is that it is a confidential conversation at the request of the person coming to see me ... and beside the fire in my house. And each individual conversation is part of a larger conversation, which is in turn an aspect of a developing relationship. There is no specified cut-off point, but to date there always seems to come an awareness that it is time to move on, and one or more of the final sessions proceeds with this in mind.

The man who came to see me and whose conversation I wish to share (in complete confidence and without attribution of course) had been off work for two or three weeks and was on medication prescribed by his GP for stress. He had gone back to work where he was informed by his employer that given the medication he was on, he could not continue at his job and place of work. It was not clear whether this was for the time being or for good, and this had reinforced his anxiety. He desperately needed to discuss with me what to do.

We had already had two conversations in recent months, and so although there was a specific context to the recent chat, it was part of a wider relationship and discussion. Having spent his childhood at Mill Grove, we had chatted together on numerous occasions. All through his life we have been in contact, and there have been some periods of his life when he has asked to spend a lot of time sharing his problems and feelings with me.

Before the session in question, he had told me the exact medicine that he had been prescribed and the daily dosage. This allowed me to confer with a GP friend who specialises in mental health and related medication. I relayed to my fireside friend her view that his employers were at fault in insisting that he could not continue at work while on this medication. I was also able to give him the relevant government advice and its source.

We discussed how he might go about contacting his employers and what he might say. Before long we had come up with a step-by-step plan, and he was clearly up for it. But then the conversation took a turn: "I always mess things up at work", he said, before going on to describe how he sometimes lost his temper and said things that he later regretted. Even when he had decided to remain silent in a team meeting, he often found himself speaking against his better judgement.

But there was more to come. This reminded him, or brought to the surface, what lay deep within his person and story, of his behaviour and attitudes that led to the break-up of his first marriage, and the distancing from his children. Although it was a quite complex dynamic and narrative, his predominant feeling is always one of regret and remorse. He holds himself responsible for what happened, and he hates himself for it.

There was still more to come. Now there were tears welling up in his eyes as he spoke, reflecting the flames from the fire. "I miss grandpa (that is his way of describing my father) so much. He was always there for me. He could understand me. If he had been around perhaps it would never have happened." We reflected on this for a bit before he continued, "And what makes me so sad is that he gave so much for me; he was always interested in me; he was always ready to help me; to listen, and I never once asked him how he was. I didn't stop to think about what was going on in his life. It couldn't always have been easy for him. But not once did it occur to me in all our chats to ask him how he was." The tears were unstoppable now.

From many similar conversations I have come to realise that my father was very dear to a lot of people, and that he had a Tournier-like gift of empathy and understanding. What's more as I have shared in the columns of this journal before, it has been made very clear to

me again and again that when you have lost your own mum and/or dad in early years and someone comes along whom you can really trust, their death is almost unbearable. Several people I see simply cannot get over it. There is not a glimmer of what Americans tend to call "closure" (a word and concept that I find hard to understand).

And then it dawned on me that in all the conversations that I have had by the fireside we have never once discussed my own situation or feelings. As far as I can recall no one has asked, but had they done so I would have sought a way of deflecting the enquiry. The reason for this is that the encounters are not about me seeking to know myself better (although that may well be a by-product) but because it is the life and feelings of the other person that form the subject of the discussion.

So it was that I realised that my father would not have minded in the least that a person had not asked about his own well-being. There were other times and places where that would be appropriate. But in these sessions such enquiries would be an intrusion, even an obstruction.

I tried to relay something of this to my friend, assuring him that my father would never have wanted to discuss his own state of mind or problems, but his sense of failure was so deep that it was obvious nothing was going to shift it in such a short space of time.

When we said goodbye, there was a buoyancy in the air, not least because he had a game-plan for the situation at work. But whatever happens there, the conversations are set to continue for some time, and his lack of self-esteem and self-worth, coupled with his admiration of my father, and his grief at my father's death, will continue to be somewhere near the heart of things.

It is significant that the conversation continues, just as the fire has never failed to light. And I have been blessed by his sharing, his honesty, his determination not to give up, his insights into others and their motivations.

One more thing that takes me back with gratitude to Paul Tournier. He is thankful for the realisation that his professional (scientific) work and his spiritual adventure have come together in his "personal dialogue with ... patients" (*The Meaning of Persons*, page 227). And for that I am profoundly grateful too.

The Double-Edged Nature of a Diagnosis

Recently two families with whom we have been actively engaged for many years contacted me to tell me how happy and relieved they were that one of their respective children had received the diagnosis "autistic". Although that was exactly how they put it, I made a mental note that most probably they had been informed by the professionals involved that the two children were deemed to be showing signs that they were on the autistic spectrum. Be that as it may, I began to ponder seriously the nature and likely long-term effects of such a diagnosis, and why it was so attractive to the families. After all, it is not as if they had been informed that their children were MENSA candidates, or that they had been selected for trials with leading football teams.

This reflection reminded me of one other medical diagnosis, and a more general category. The specific diagnosis in question relates to a middle-aged woman, mother of two grown-up children. She was diagnosed and has since received treatment for an "Obsessive Compulsive Disorder" (OCD). Over several years now she has been undergoing sessions with a psychologist aimed at helping her to deal with aspects of this condition. Although she had made some modest gains, she remains in a vulnerable and difficult place.

She also fits the more general category known as "victim". Of course, this is not necessarily the result of a medical diagnosis and can encompass a range of experiences and conditions. In her case she had been abused sexually over a lengthy period within her extended family, and her compulsive and obsessive behaviour (which involves excessive washing and cleaning) seems to be related to her traumatic childhood experiences.

Now it can seem like the milk of human kindness to empathise with someone as a victim. The willingness to listen to their story and to connect emotionally can be deeply affirming and supportive.

What I want to explore in this article is not labelling in general (it is a well-documented sociological construct or process), but to consider the unintended side effects of such diagnoses. Let us assume that the diagnoses are correct and have been given for the best of professional and personal motives. (In so doing we leave aside the diagnosis of political critics of the Soviet Communist regime as psychiatrically disturbed or ill, and those many other sad and cynical examples of false diagnosis in the interests of social and political control.) And I will accept that one of the reasons that individuals and families are pleased when there is a diagnosis is the way in which it can open the door to additional resources and help.

Given all this, what possible concern could there be with such diagnosis? To deal with the more general point first: the recognition that someone is a victim has many potential benefits, especially when their abusive, guilt and shame-provoking childhood experiences have been secret and hidden. To have others accepting and acknowledging that abuse happened can be remarkably reassuring and liberating. But on the other hand, for a person to develop and flourish in their lives, there comes a point where they cannot remain wholly or solely defined as a victim. It is true that they have been victims. But the growth of their personhood, identity, self-esteem in relationship requires that there comes a time when they need to modify or lay aside the label or diagnosis.

Time and again this is what I have heard when listening to the stories of those who were childhood victims, but who have now moved on. These reveal that there can come a willingness to listen to and share the stories of others, and to realise that however harrowing one's own experiences, there are usually those who are worse off. Often there is the counter-intuitive discovery that their abusers have themselves been victims of abuse. In this process it is not that the abuse is ever denied or played down, but rather more that the label "victim" does not become the defining category within which a person sees herself, and wishes to be seen by others, throughout life.

This is a very challenging and difficult process to navigate, and never to be under-estimated. It involves a letting go of the hold of the past, sometimes a forgiving of others: even those bound up in the abuse, and an embrace of one's own unique personality, gifts and blessings. Please understand that I do not and will not underestimate the sheer pain and uphill struggle that is involved in such a rugged personal journey. But this is not so much my assessment of things as the culmination of decades of listening to people who have made just such a move out of victimhood. (And I recognise that it is not possible for everyone to do this. Sometimes the damage is too intense and destructive of the self of a person.)

What I am seeking to identify is the way in which a simple and pervasive label of "victim" can stay with a person throughout their life and become the defining and limiting category of their identity, as well as become the way that they prefer to be seen and treated by others.

This leads me to the diagnoses of OCD and autism. I have no doubt that the former is correct in so far as it goes. I have more problems with the category "autism" (even when set within a spectrum). But there is also a problem with the diagnosis OCD. In the case of the mother I have mentioned, she had been holding down a regular job before the diagnosis, and I have witnessed the way in which this was lost as the category became virtually all-defining. She attends courses from time to time and goes to a day centre intended for those with mental health problems. She is obsessed with trying to deal with her obsession. And her housing and benefits depend on the continuing relevance and accuracy of the diagnosis.

The problem is, of course, that the very nature of the diagnosis, together with the extensive help offered, mean that she has become dependent on the services, advice and treatment that go with the category. And it does seem like a straitjacket from which it is hard to see her escaping or emerging. Her whole way of life (including her own patterns of behaviour and the demands of the treatment prescribed) is defined by her diagnosis. Everything is filtered through this lens. Although she has many personal gifts and abilities, they are often submerged as this diagnosis has taken centre stage and become seemingly all powerful.

We turn finally to the two children who have been diagnosed "autistic". They too will likewise receive additional support and services. This marks considerable progress from the time when such a type of condition went largely unrecognised. But not only would I like a recognition that the whole human race sits somewhere on this spectrum (males in particular?), but also that there are some inherent disadvantages and problems with it. Knowing the families in both cases, and having been close to them over many years, I know that the parents have themselves experienced chronic abuse, and that their lives, including their ability to parent, have been adversely affected by their traumatic childhoods.

The diagnosis of "autism" could well mean that attention shifts from the family as a system to the child. It is a label that can affect understandings of the dynamics within the family, and it can result in increased risk of scapegoating. It is likely that this will be so for the childhood, if not the lifetime of the child. And it is not clear if there is any way of modifying the diagnosis. Even if professionals make adjustments to their reading of the condition, the families are unlikely to do so.

In the light of this, my sense is that those engaged with the children and families should handle all such categories and diagnoses with care, and as provisional. The defining category should always be that all involved are related to as unique human beings and by name. Their lives and stories should be respected as full of potential. True professionalism, as well as humanity, will always be characterised by an appropriate degree of humility that is wary of fixed labels and dogmatism.

Whose Childhood?

Those who are familiar with Mill Grove through the columns I have written for the *Webmag/TCJ* over the years will know that late summer is the time when our extended family always heads for North Wales. To such it will therefore come as no surprise that this piece has been prompted by a recent visit to Snowdonia.

Ruth and I were with a family of five: mother, father and three pre-school-age children. Unusually both the father and mother had lived at Mill Grove during their respective childhoods. (This is unusual because we live as a family and so exclusive liaisons within the family are actively discouraged.) Both the parents had been with us to North Wales when they were children, but this was the first time that the mother had been back for something like 15 years, and the father for the best part of ten.

Now they were returning to the place that held so many treasured memories for each for them, but, and this is the crucial point, this time they came with their children. The children were in North Wales for the very first time. As we explored the local area together (the Welsh Highland Railway; Portmeirion; the Rabbit Farm in Llanystumdwy; Black Rock Sands; Criccieth; the beaches of Borth-y-Gest; and the Glaslyn estuary that leads into Cardigan Bay) I had the privilege of witnessing these two adults and three children engaging individually and as a group with this remarkable natural "adventure playground".

The children reacted much as I have come to expect from years of experience with others of a similar age in the same environment. They were attracted to that which was near and immediate. The youngest one was happy to sit on the sand, to hold it in her hands and to eat it; she found sitting at the water's edge mesmerising. This left me wondering yet again about that great mystery of what it might all mean to her and what would lodge in her memory far beyond the recall of images and words in the years to come.

The other two soon came to realise that there was a little village park virtually in our back garden and so repaired there as often as possible. On one occasion they spotted a rabbit, and so the park and rabbit seemed to be integral to the whole experience of the swings, slide and see-saw. On the beach they made and flattened sandcastles, quickly learning that dry sand was not as appropriate for the process as they had at first thought. They saw or imagined jellyfish and crabs everywhere and feared that they would be mortally wounded should they be touched by either of them.

Walking to the sea across the beach they noticed the distinctive shapes in the sand caused by lugworms. But they did not seem interested in digging deep enough to find one. They were attracted to making footprints and enjoyed identifying our shadows as we walked hand in hand. They quickly adapted to walking on footpaths and were soon identifying wild flowers, first by colour, and then some (including cranesbill), by name.

On the rocks they showed expected natural ability to scramble without fear, using raw energy and innate techniques to scale some modest climbs. At the top of hills, the views seemed to mean little or nothing to them (as I had come to expect from the reactions of other young children).

Shrimping was popular and they were fascinated by the bucketfull of fish, shrimps and little crabs.

When we barbecued, they happily gathered driftwood, and were respectful of the fire as it quickly became too hot for close encounters.

They threw sand, stones and rocks, but before long began to realise that sand is never thrown, and that stones and rocks need to be thrown with care in appropriate and approved directions and contexts.

On the Mirror dinghy the oldest of the three (a boy) took his responsibilities as a crew member very seriously, and he was relaxed in both calm and fresh conditions. On the second sail he responded enthusiastically with "Aye, aye, skipper!" whenever he heard the call "Ready about". He positively enjoyed riding over waves. And he took responsibility for holding the dinghy by a line when I needed to deposit the trailer in the boat-park.

I think that is probably enough to give you the picture. (Bear in mind that I love the area and every part of the whole experience, and that as I do not possess a mobile phone, I am able to be "present" in ways that many modern parents find difficult due to electronic social networking.)

If you noticed the title of this piece, you will be wondering about the parents. How was it for them? It was evidently very exciting for them to revisit childhood haunts, and they began by noticing the things that had changed. There was a new fence around the playground; the path to the beach now had a large wooden bridge because the dunes had eroded. Despite some changes, the beach was very much as they remembered it, and they insisted that we sat by the very rock which was the base for the family every year. But then there came the urge to enjoy the experiences that had meant so much for them.

And they wanted to share them with their children so much that there was a constant tendency to interrupt what the children were doing to introduce them to new activities which the parents were enjoying. This meant that the sand-castling of two of the children was suddenly terminated so that one of them could go for a roll down the dunes at the end of the beach with her mother. A similar thing happened with shrimping: it had to be done, and shrimps had to be found irrespective of what the children were doing or thinking at the time.

This pattern obtained each day, and in different places. At a rabbit farm the adults eagerly handled and passed on creatures from rabbits to puppies and guinea pigs, so that often the children did not have the time or opportunity to choose for themselves. The culmination of this came with the pony rides. Each of the older children were led in turn around a little field equipped with a riding hat.

The parents (particularly the mother) didn't want the children to miss out on anything that had been special for them. This meant a constant interruption of the activities and focus of the children's attention.

This is what led me to wonder whose childhood is dominant on family holidays: that of the parents or that of the children. The parents usually choose the venues and the activities for very young children. And these are obviously determinative of much that the children experience. But how much do parents mediate what goes on through the prism or lens of their own childhoods? And who is the child at any given time when rolling down sand dunes, making sandcastles and shrimping?

It is not easy to get an appropriate balance between these two childhoods: the remembered childhoods of the parents and the current childhoods of their offspring. It is therefore not easy to create the most appropriate boundaries for the actual children. I recalled the time when I had introduced my own children to a special holiday venue in my early life for which I retain much affection. It was the beach at Lowestoft where I had enjoyed some of the very best childhood holidays. My offspring were completely underwhelmed as they stood on the promenade overlooking the beach and groynes. Compared to the variety of landscapes in North Wales I can now see why Lowestoft seemed rather limited to them.

Our childhood experiences obviously affect the whole of our lives and our parenting, but in familiar holiday haunts there may be a lot more going on than usual. We want the very best for our children, and what we believe to be the very best in these locations is going to be determined largely by what we experienced. If much of the rest of a person's childhood at home and school was traumatic, disturbed and anxiety-provoking, then the comparative safety and joys of holidays will be correspondingly attractive and valued.

I wonder if you have guessed a possible way of helping address this conundrum. Grandparents, uncles and aunties may well be able to mediate between parents and their children. Of course, they are not neutral observers in all this. We have our own preferences and memories, but there is no longer the urgency or pressure to channel the young children's activities and experiences into those that we preferred … with the possible exception in my case of sailing, climbing, swimming, barbecues and beach games!

Professional Love

Recently I was asked to facilitate a seminar on the theme of "professional love". It was part of a conference organised for those involved in pre-school/early years' education. There were about 15 in the group, and I began by inviting the participants to introduce themselves and to summarise why they had chosen to attend this particular seminar and subject. It turned out that this was my last substantive contribution to the seminar.

The subject was so important to each member of the seminar group that in explaining why they had come, they spoke with such animation and vigour that there was no time for any further discussion!

And here are the issues they raised as I recall them. One who attended had just started helping in a pre-school as a volunteer, and she described how she was reading a story to her children when one of them walked towards her and sat on her lap. She was not sure how to react or what to do because she could not remember if there was a policy about this. Did it make any difference, she wondered, that the mother of the little girl was present throughout?

Another participant was responsible for several newly-established pre-schools, and he was attracted to the seminar because the two words, professional love, summed up exactly what he was aiming for (his educational philosophy) and he wanted to draw from the wisdom of those who were present.

A third person wanted to know if there was a toolkit available that included a "cuddling policy". (We were able to pause at this point and reassure her that this is exactly what Dr. Jools Page, the originator of the phrase "professional love" had been seeking with the help of professionals and parents to develop.)

Another participant told of a male member of staff whom she had just employed, although he had been dismissed from his previous job in early years' education because he had written in some notes that he "loved the children" he was working with. After scrutiny of the relevant records and having secured references, she found that there was no other criticism of his attitude or practice: the word that had been objectionable was "love". As his new manager, she realised that she was taking a risk (or making a statement) in employing him, but she felt that she could do no other. She believed that loving the children in an early years' setting was appropriate.

At this point in the introductions several commented that there was a crying need for more male teachers in pre-schools, and that safeguarding issues were particularly challenging for them because of the pervading fear of paedophiles in the sector.

Another person said that she did not find she was able to be close enough to children in the church where she had been employed as a children's worker and that as a consequence she had chosen to move into formal education provision. But she was doing so believing that love was vital in the relationship between teacher and children.

A mother (and a seasoned professional with two daughters, both of whom had PhDs) told of how difficult she had found it trying to engage as a teacher in early years' because it seemed as if much of what she had learnt as a mother, and what had become instinctive to her, seemed to be questioned. Once again several intervened to agree with this general point. How could it be right that a professional carer or teacher could not comfort a distressed child by picking them up and reassuring them by appropriate touch? What about children who had hurt themselves in pre-schools which had a policy that such accidents should not be attended to by the staff?

And this led to a reflection on the particular needs of children with disability (say, for example, cerebral palsy) where physical touch and holding were vital for their safety and learning of new motor skills.

I am sure that much more was said that I have not recounted here, but I hope that you have got the gist of the dynamics and concerns of the group.

There was complete agreement that early years' provision needed to operate within agreed professional boundaries set out in clear policy statements understood and affirmed by both the parents and the providers. Such policies should be in line with the best national wisdom, practice and standards.

But at the same time there was universal concern in the group (with no dissenting voices that I could detect) that something strange and worrying was going on in our contemporary society. How come a teacher was anxious when a child quite naturally came to sit on her lap in the presence of the child's mother? How come a male teacher lost his job because he wrote of loving the children he was caring for? Was there not a risk that the children's desires and needs were being overlooked or marginalised because of societal concerns?

Many nurseries and pre-schools have the responsibility for children as young as two years old for the whole of a day, five days a week. Surely such children are wired for the most part to seek for caring and loving responses to their feelings (whether because they are anxious, or because they want to express affection)?

All this points to the considerable value of what Dr. Jools Page and her colleagues at Sheffield University are doing. (http://professionallove.group.shef.ac.uk. The **Professional Love in Early Years Settings (PLEYS)** research project was set up to examine how those who work in early years settings can safely express the **affectionate and caring behaviours** which their role demands of them. The outcome was a set of Professional Development Materials which comprise the **Attachment Toolkit**.)

As it happens I had not come across the work of Dr. Page, nor heard of the term "professional love" until I was asked to lead this seminar, so I am most grateful for this rather belated introduction to it. When I presented my presidential address to the Social Care Association Annual Conference at Southport in 1984, I offered the example of Dr. Janusc Korczak (1878–1942) who gave his life so that he could stay with the children in the Warsaw Ghetto for whom he was responsible as they were put on a train to the gas chambers. I proffered the question, "What would I do if there was another such horrific situation affecting the children in my care?" It was not a rhetorical device. As one who has been involved in the care of children and young people most of my life there is always the underlying question about the extent and depth of my commitment to them. Am I effectively a hireling, or a good shepherd prepared to lay down my life for my sheep?

Perhaps understandably, some who were present told me that this was unduly dramatic and even inappropriate for a conference of professionals. I responded that I understood this, but that they needed to know that the president they had elected was one for whom professionalism did not exclude love. What's more the sort of love I had in mind was costly, serious, considered, faithful love that welcomed professional scrutiny and rigour.

In time I came to gather my experience and philosophy of care together in the book *The Growth of Love* (Abingdon: BRF, 2008). I didn't use the term "professional love", but on re-reading the text it is pretty clear that this is what I had in mind right through.

I hope that one of the serendipities of this remarkably lively seminar will be the development of links between Dr. Page and others of us (including those committed to social pedagogy) who have been living and working with the same basic questions and concerns.

The Place of Ritual in Therapeutic Child Care

It was an exceptionally bright, clear morning on Sunday 12th November 2017, but due to the warmth of the autumnal weather there had been no frost overnight, and the deciduous trees were still ochre and yellow. The grass sparkled and glistened in the sunshine, flecked by fallen leaves. The place was St. Mary's church, Lambourne, in the county of Essex, an historic place of worship due to celebrate its 900th anniversary in 2020. Here individuals and families gathered, as was their wont, for the Remembrance Sunday service, a local equivalent perhaps to the journey of the pilgrims immortalised in Chaucer's *Canterbury Tales*.

The order of service in the ancient building, and the subsequent laying of wreaths at the memorial in the churchyard, dominated by a huge and elegant yew tree, were wholly predictable for regular attendees. There was the reading of the names of those who had lost their lives in the two World Wars, the clarion tones of the bugle playing the *Last Post* and *Reveille* which framed the two minutes' silence, well-known traditional hymns, the National Anthem, and the presence of the British Legion standard throughout.

From my vantage point during the service, I had a perfect view of the children in the front pew and the gallery, and I was intrigued to see how they participated in and reacted to the ritual. There was plenty for them to observe and take in as the clergy processed, the names were read, and the wreaths laid in place. But I was particularly struck by their engagement with the standard and the two minutes' silence. They watched the lowering of the flag with intense concentration as if mesmerised, and stood motionless throughout the two minutes silence.

In an age of digital images and the pressures of marketing, branding and social networking, two minutes standing in silence with nothing pressing for your attention is a long time. One of the families was attending the service not long after the death of their spouse and father. I wondered what the widow and children were thinking as the flag was angled until its head rested on the stone floor, held by the immaculate white gloves of the standard bearer.

I didn't ask and so will never know, but it was evident that this ritual engaged children. I have watched children including those of pre-school age in similar settings, and there is something like a magic or spell that seems to be cast on such occasions. Perhaps it is one of the only times when they gather on equal terms with adults and stand in silence. Shared silence is unique in that every person contributes equally to the process: giving and receiving are symbiotic. I couldn't help noticing that afterwards they ran around the church playing informally. You could say that they were letting off steam, or you could read this as their recognition that the formal event was now over. Their play was spontaneous and happy, and they still wore their poppies and Remembrance Day clothes as if the preceding ritual was both satisfying and deserving of celebration. While they did this the adults chatted contentedly, thus creating the social space for the children to play in this way, in this venerable place, and on such a special day.

There can be little doubt that children need ritual: that is, given patterns or rhythms in their lives. This is as true of annual events, such as Remembrance, but also birthdays and Christmas, as it is of daily rituals that accompany getting up, washing and brushing their teeth, and having meals.

Recently I heard Jewish children and young people reflecting on the Shabbat dinner on a Friday evening. Interestingly they didn't speak of the elements of the meal itself, or the contents of anything said or prayed, but talked of the importance of being together. It was a gathering, a ritual in which they felt valued and respected as individuals because they were part of a family, household or community. If it were not for the ritual they reckoned that they would rarely be together as a family because of the pressures of 24/7, contemporary life.

It so happened that Monday is one of the

evenings when we have an evening meal together at Mill Grove, and there are several elements that go to make up the ritual (using the word to mean everyday patterns of group life and expected behaviour, most of which go without thinking or saying). So 24 hours after being at the Remembrance service, the meal was being cooked, and the two youngest children were in the kitchen making things. This time it happened to be paper houses.

We sat at our usual places when the meal was served; we had grace; we waited for everyone to be served before getting stuck into the lasagne and vegetables; we helped clear the tables, polish them, and get out the Bibles for today's story. Given the joy that the children displayed when showing their paper houses to everyone, we had the story that Jesus told about the two housebuilders (one was wise and built on a rock, the other was foolish and built on the sand); we sang a song about the story (with actions), and as we left the table we went to do our allotted jobs: some at the sink and others putting the dustbins and recycling bins beside the back gate.

As I am writing this piece it happens that I am hearing the voices of the two younger children again, but this time in a setting where there is not the same accepted and predictable ritual. It is hard going for them and their parents: gone is the relaxed, contented atmosphere of the night before.

With this contrast in mind, I reflected on the place of ritual in therapeutic child care. Any setting that seeks to provide "the village that it needs to raise a child", especially those residential communities that are guided by a therapeutic philosophy of shared living, knows that there must be rituals accepted over time (at least some of the time) by everyone: adults, children and young people. All philosophies of education (for example that of Maria Montessori) stress the importance of shared corporate behaviours, for example getting out and putting away books and resources. The critical thing is that the rituals are accepted by all who participate in them, and do not need to be spelt out or prescribed each time.

As the frosts come and the leaves finally part company with the trees, the season of Christmas arrives in Europe. It may be the annual celebration in the UK which comes closest to a regular shared national ritual. It comprises the patterns of myriad sub-groups of different backgrounds and faiths, but it is a time when we all know that this is what others have in their minds. In saying this, I call to mind Chinese New Year, Thanksgiving in the USA, the Alp Wand with the cows into the higher pastures in Western Switzerland, Eid, Passover, Diwali, Red Nose Day, and many other rituals around the world.

The practical challenge in therapeutic settings is to identify potentially beneficial rituals both within and outside the community, to discover ways of nurturing them, and where they have broken down (whether in households or nations) to work at reconstructing them. I know from long experience that they are to be treasured, and the ones that seem intuitively to me to be the most therapeutic in nature or essence are those where all ages are present, and in some way involved, and where there is a focus on a shared feature or task, rather than where one person or group performs for, or teaches, another.

It won't often be shared silence, but the Quakers surely have important insights for us all. Significantly they talk of Meeting Houses. Perhaps that's a useful term to have in mind as we seek to construct the rituals that underpin and sustain our communities.

Seeing the Bigger Picture

It's always revealing when roles are suddenly reversed. For example, when a doctor becomes a patient; when a judge is in the dock; when the strong becomes weak; when the giver needs help, or when the proverbial poacher turns gamekeeper. In writing this piece I am reflecting in situ on just such a reversal. As readers of this column know Ruth and I spend our lives based at Mill Grove seeking to help, care for and support vulnerable children, young people, adults and families. We don't have formal roles or titles, so are perhaps best described as "resourceful friends" (a term first coined, as far as I know, by one of our dear friends and colleagues, the late Bob Holman). Day in, day out we are there for others, listening to their stories and trying to read their situations and understand the dynamics of their relationships and inner worlds. Often what is shared and observed is familiar to us, with lots of replication of sameness, but sometimes radically new dimensions or challenges emerge.

So you can imagine the surprise when, a considerable distance from Mill Grove, the two of us sat waiting for the visit of a Community Psychiatric Nurse and an Occupational Therapist as we sat beside a relative for whom we were caring, and who needed help and support. Now we were the ones on the receiving end. The familiar roles were completely reversed. Because these columns are always anonymised, I won't say any more about the situation or location, except to note that the two of us had been living alongside this relative for ten days. The two professionals arrived on time and were bright, alert and empathetic. Each knew her stuff, and both were obviously skilled in assessment, as part of a team. Ruth and I were impressed by the effectiveness of the mental health services in the part of the UK where we found ourselves.

It was not long however before we realised that, despite their attentiveness and skills, the visitors were not reading vital aspects of the situation. They were with us for the best part of an hour. But in that time how did they know if what was going on, the behaviour they observed and responses to questions, were in any way typical of the person and his or her behaviour as a whole? There were rhythms spread over 24 hours that we had come to experience, and to deduce an understanding of the whole dynamics and situation from an interaction or conversation during a slice of one of them was simply not possible. Then there was the question of what impact the anticipation (we knew it included fear) of their coming had already had before they arrived. And how were our visitors to know what the impact or effect of their visit would have for the rest of the day, and subsequent days?

And how were they seen by our relative? They introduced themselves appropriately as far as Ruth and I were concerned, and their questions and responses made sense within this shared framework, but our relative referred to them subsequently as "staff" or "nurses", and after they left it was not clear whether the relative now believed they were still at home, or whether they had been transferred to a hospital. In any communication it is vital to know who the hearer or listener is, and messages are tailored to this assumption. Was our relative using her usual language, or was it completely at variance during this conversation? If assumptions are at variance with reality, then wires can become seriously crossed.

Perhaps most important of all is the question of how their intentions and motives were seen by the relative. The fact was that they had been invited by us to provide support as a way of avoiding hospitalisation. But given the above, their very presence belied this. It was as if their coming had somehow merged home and hospital. The relative later spoke often of the visit and the visitors, always with anxiety, and one of the terms used was that it was an "invasion" of their privacy and personal space. If you want a technical term, their home was being "contaminated" by hospital in the process of the visit.

With these issues in mind, let me reiterate our view that each of the two visitors epitomised the very best of professionalism. The OT saw that there was a risk of dizziness whenever the relative moved from a sedentary position to a standing one. She recommended that they always take a breath at that point and before trying to move. She also inspected the bathroom and recommended how the WC could be made safer.

And the CPN nurse helpfully identified the fact that visits to the bathroom were associated with an anxiety about the relative's safety. It was the one risky place in the current episode and very restricted world of the relative. A refusal to attend to any bodily functions might have less to do with any Freudian-type associations or taboos, and more to do with fear of falling.

So it was that Ruth and I gleaned important information and insights from the visit, for which we are truly thankful. But in case the reader is under any illusions, what we realised par excellence was that when the visitors left, we were now once again alone and entrusted with the daily care of our relative, and that without information from us the professionals would be largely at sea, apart from the most basic of observations or conclusions. The awareness and memory of our relative were so impaired during this episode that the possibility of them remembering to take a breath on rising was remote, and the conversation was so a-typical that any generalisations were shots in the dark. Two days later at the very same time our relative was engulfed by psychotic behaviour and there was no meaningful communication for five hours: just restless, compulsive, repetitive wandering. Had the visitors been there then, would hospitalisation have become seen as necessary?

It is not difficult to anticipate the conclusion of this reflection, so let me do so briefly. For there to be any remotely accurate assessment by professionals in therapy or mental health, the knowledge, experience, and feelings of those who know the story and context of the "patient" is essential. In many ways it is the only source of reliable information. And relatives need the insights and knowledge of professionals. The only way it can work is by trust and teamwork. So before closing I switch back into my more normal role, that of the resourceful friend (professional), and wonder how often my observations and notes could have been sufficiently enriched by the experiences and wisdom of family members. Unless and until I can genuinely enter into their world, I am liable to give undue weight to my own assessment and knowledge.

Yes, family members have their biases, their quirks, their loyalties, their limitations, their blind spots, but they have insights and knowledge that I will never acquire: sometimes a lifetime of knowledge of this person's kith and kin, of their likes and dislikes, their culture, their story, their friends, their gifts and abilities, their beliefs, culture and personal language. And in humility I need to acknowledge, respect and draw from that, while retaining a proper professional stance and relationship. A therapeutic relationship requires an alliance between family and professionals. We need each other. There is no other way of gaining an understanding of the bigger picture, and of seeing the wood as well as the trees.

The Creation of Safe Space Through Appropriate Boundaries

Recently Ruth and I revisited a scenario that has been part of our lives at Mill Grove for the past 40 years. A little boy was with us for a meal for the very first time, and so we had to plan how to welcome him so that he, along with everybody else, felt secure and could experience our home as a safe space. Much of what we did was unplanned in the sense of being talked about beforehand, but we were relying on years of experience. This meant, on reflection, that there was a lot to it. And I thought a brief outline might be of use to colleagues. It is, in essence, all about the creation of appropriate boundaries.

The meal and evening were carefully structured in our minds, including the time of his arrival, the arrangements for me to drive him back to his family home afterwards, and the sequence of activities and arrangement of space in between. His two older siblings were with us as usual, and they knew the ropes. His presence would change the dynamics of the evening for them both, as well as for us.

Both Ruth and I were present for the whole time (without a single break) and we knew that each of us would need to give it everything to make the visit work. To start with, his sister was inside with Ruth (who was preparing the meal). She played by herself with familiar toys and resources, as she usually did, before having a ten-minute board game with Ruth in the kitchen. Meanwhile I was outside in the playground with the young boy and his older brother. I began our time together by asking the senior brother if he would be willing to share some of the activities that we usually did together with his younger sibling, making it clear to him that I would respect his decision either way. We went through a list of possible activities, and he confirmed that he was willing to give it a try.

We began with football, drawing from a long history of such kickabouts in our playground, and with plenty of the sort of banter that arises when one of the players supports Arsenal, and the other, Spurs! The younger brother supports West Ham, so his presence was a mediating influence without any words spoken. We needed very, very clear boundaries to make this informal game work. It was "three goals and in", in strict rotation, no use of hands except by the person in goal, and with the two players in the outfield taking it in turns to shoot. There were no exceptions. And we had a happy and relaxed time. At one point their sister came out, announcing that she was joining us, but I gently channelled her focus elsewhere, knowing that were she to join in, the security of the boundaries that we had been establishing would be lost immediately.

We completed the game (no mean feat for the little boy, who is bound to be labelled ADHD when he attends school regularly), and

then I asked them to help me identify some small shrubs along the side of the pitch that Ruth had planted a few weeks earlier. Some had thrived, but others were dying, and still others covered by creepers and weeds. This was, of course, a passing reminder that my life comprised of more than playing with them (however much I enjoyed it). Then we moved to a round table outside the kitchen where I had placed three chairs. I asked the older brother to bring us the diary/scrapbook of the holiday that we had enjoyed together in North Wales a week earlier. And we soon established a way of exploring the drawings and photos together. Twice the little boy said that he was going inside, but both times I found something in the holiday mementoes which we needed his help to understand. This was meticulously planned (not the actual issues, but the process). We looked at the whole of the material together (no mean feat once again).

Then we went to look for a set of dominoes. In doing so we went past where the sister was once again playing inside, and she immediately said that she would play with us. All being well she will do so in the future, but on this significant first occasion, the risks of the game failing were too high in my mind. So Ruth and I confirmed her in her current activity (with a toy horse), and I explained that her little brother didn't understand the rules of the game, so we were going to learn it together. Once he had reached her level of understanding it would be great to have her playing with us.

She accepted this, and the three of us (that is the two brothers and me) had two games of dominoes. I was a partner of the little boy, and would you believe it? Beginner's luck kicked in. He won both games without needing to replenish his dominos at all. He and I beat his older brother out of town! At least twice during the game he informed us that he was going to play another game inside, but on both occasions I and his brother informed him that we always finished a game before doing something else. He helped us put the dominoes back in their container, with the sort of care that he has when engaged in productive activity.

It was then time for the meal. Ruth had

thought through where each of us would each sit, and so we did. This meant a change for the older brother, and he understood why. We said our usual grace with actions, teaching the little boy in a quick practice session. He loved it and learned it quickly. In saying grace his two older siblings unconsciously helped to reinforce the boundaries. The meal was chosen knowing exactly what each child liked, and we had two courses. In between we each helped to clear the table: something that required meticulous instructions to avoid the sister's customary help at this stage being spurned, and her becoming upset.

Rice pudding and peaches followed, with similar detailed boundaries about clearing away, dusting the table, and then prayer time. This was when we were all at our most relaxed because we simply returned to the stories we had shared together in North Wales, with the same illustrations, and some colouring that the two younger ones had done.

At no point was there any wriggle room, although the little boy did not know this. We always asked him to help in ways which we knew he liked. Then came washing up (we don't have a dishwasher, so it is a shared activity providing opportunities with time for social interaction). We speedily realised it would not work if he were to be added to the team. So the sister was allowed to play instead of helping; the little boy put all the dishes and cutlery into the sink where Ruth washed and rinsed it, while the older brother and I dried up and put things away. The visiting brother was given a special apron which he donned as a mark of his important role and tasks. He appreciated this very much, and neither sibling resented his accessory.

And would you believe it, it was nearly time to go home! (As noted already, that too was carefully planned). The two little ones had some informal play in an assigned space inside, while I and the older brother went outside to make sure the dustbins had all been put out for collection the following morning (one still needed to be moved, and he was keen to show me how much stronger he was than when he last helped before Covid 19 kicked in). And he

and I played a game together involving a tennis ball and a coin. There were three brief sets and he won the decider. I was so pleased that we managed to make space for just a little time together, reminding us of all the games we used to play before his younger brother arrived on the scene.

We tidied up all the toys inside (which the three of us did together). Ruth arranged the appropriate car seats in our Tourneo (big enough for social distancing), and having bade her farewell, four of us set off together. Just one hiccup on the journey: unsurprisingly, the little girl felt the need to make her presence felt by making a loud and continuous sound (somewhere between a laugh and a whine) that prevented communication between the rest of us. When we arrived at their flat, I explained to her that we would need to do better next time, and she appreciated my full attention as I did this (something I couldn't give her while at Mill Grove or when driving). They led me up a flight of stairs and along a couple of passages to their flat, where their parents were waiting for them.

I will never know how much experience and how many times Ruth and I had gone through a similar process of welcome. On this occasion it involved a little boy recognised as a "handful", and so we required all our individual and shared understanding and skills to set and maintain the boundaries described above.

The normal life of his family lacks security and boundaries. Both parents experience chronic anxiety and some depression. Life is a struggle, and the family dynamics are often strained and unsatisfactory. Hence why this evening was so important. It was vital that each child, and the parents, knew each child was safe. When I arrived at the family flat the parents immediately asked how the little boy had been, fearful no doubt that he had behaved as usual (which was largely outside their control), and were genuinely relieved to know that he had been pretty much a model child.

We know that it is possible that the whole evening was blessed with beginners' luck and that next week is likely to present a range of new challenges. But if so, we have made a good start. And unless and until boundaries are understood and internalised, the pattern and rhythms will be equally clear, non-negotiable, and firm. There is no short cut to shared understanding and relationships and the secure base that results from them. Creating appropriate boundaries for them is a lifelong art.

As it happens, I must put down my pen now because Ruth has just let me know that the three children have arrived again. It's Monday again. Where did that week go, I wonder? Perhaps I'll let you know sometime how things have been going since.

. . . .

Seconds Out: Round Three! (An Update on Creating Safe Space)

I was surprised and touched by the reaction of a reader to the previous article, describing the first evening on which a young boy came to Mill Grove, and how Ruth and I set about creating safe space for him and his siblings in what was intended to be the beginning of regular weekly visits. I completed that article just as he was arriving for the second week. Tomorrow he will be with us again. So, while his time with us is fresh in my mind, here's a log of week three. By the way, my memory of such things, with their constant interplay between physical context and activities on the one hand, and emotional feelings and dynamics on the other, has been considerably aided by the example and insistence of our consultant psychotherapist. Whenever we brief her on a child or situation, she expects an accurate description of what the child has said word for word, or done action by action, together with our responses and feelings, all set in context. At first this tall order seemed unattainable, but over the years she has helped us to hone our observations, to become more spatially alert and informed, and to grow in awareness of our own feelings and reactions.

The routine established on the first occasion was, of course, followed as far as possible, this predictable and solid structure being critical to the whole process of creating security. So, there was a drink and snack outside on the arrival of the three children from school. (It is important to bear in mind that all this is taking place within the period of Covid 19 social distancing guidelines.) The boy chose to play inside for a time while I chatted with his parents, before the three of us were joined by someone who was bringing a church harvest to add to our growing store for yet another year.

This may seem unimportant, even irrelevant, but I have come to see that one of the most significant ways in which adults can contribute to safe space for their children is to be at ease with each other, engaged in conversation, while open and alive to what the children are doing. Our task is not simply that of being with children, playing with them, doing things with them or for them, or conversely the children doing things for the notice and praise of adults. More often it is about being in the same space, close enough for them to know we are there, and available as and when they wish to make their presence felt. In my reading and experience, this group dynamic is underestimated in intentional therapeutic communities, as well as in modern families and schools.

The contentment and centredness of the little boy were, of course, encouraging, but it also gave me a little time and opportunity to play football with his older brother (something we always used to do until Harry, as I will call him, arrived for the first time). I knew that this would change the group dynamics, and it did. Harry, obviously aware of what I was doing, came out to join us immediately. And to complete the ripple effect their sister, who until this moment was happily riding a tricycle in the playground, attempted to join in too. She did this not by asking, but by riding into the very space near the goal where we were kicking the ball around. I encouraged her, successfully, to use the rest of the playground for her own safety, while we continued to play "three goals and in", taking it in turns, religiously, to shoot at goal and then with a rota for being goalie. It wasn't a long session, but it was relaxed, with lots of enthusiasm and fun. (As a ready-reckoner humour is what I am looking for to indicate a sense of well-being in a group.)

Because time was moving on (given the unexpected arrival of the harvest and the subsequent chat), I knew I needed to put the dustbins and recycling containers out ready for collection by the council the next morning. At the very moment we concluded our game, the sister arrived, on foot, to inform us that the evening meal prepared by Ruth would be in ten minutes' time. So I suggested that the brothers and I finished putting the bins out, with the older one given responsibility for lifting each one up the front steps and on to the pavement, while Harry and I used a wheelbarrow to get the bins to the bottom of the steps. This worked a treat, because there is nothing Harry enjoys more than working at a routine outdoor task with me. When we got to the steps, he carried each dustbin lid to the pavement, while his brother and I did the heavy lifting. Each time we were on the way back to the lean-to where the bins are stored, he jumped into the wheelbarrow and we pretended to be a runaway train, narrowly missing trees and a goalpost by swerving dramatically.

With two containers remaining and time running out, I thought we should pause, but Harry insisted that we finish the task. This is one of his most endearing characteristics. And so, we did, but this meant that there were only a few minutes left until the meal. And we still hadn't played dominoes. The boys rushed off to find the set and we managed to have one game together. I don't think Harry has grasped the numbers represented by the dots yet (he does know a blank from a five or six, but threes and fours are pretty hit and miss in his mind), but we completed the game, and I think he and I won (just). For the record, on the second week when we played, his beginner's luck ran out, and he discovered that it is possible to lose at dominoes!

We packed up methodically together, and Harry insisted on putting the lid on the box and returning the dominoes to their allotted place among the games on the shelves in the room with easy chairs and a piano. Then we (brothers and sister) washed our hands and sat at the table. Three weeks on, we each know our own places. We sang grace together with actions once Ruth had placed the food on the table. Grace was both predictable and fun (see above, for humour!). The meal went smoothly, one of the main snags being that Harry's diet is severely limited (so carrots, baked beans, cauliflower, fish fingers and a lot more items are out of his comfort zone, which seems limited to pasta or chips). We will work on this, of course, but there are more important elements to building a safe space than this.

We arranged how to clear the table and clean and polish the table mats, with each child having specific tasks. Then it was time for prayers. We revisited the story of Noah's Ark and the rainbow promise before singing an action song about two housebuilders, one who was wise, and the other foolish. There was a very short prayer of thanks for our meal and time together, and then it was time for washing up. The dynamics have changed completely since Harry first came, though he is unaware of this of course. Once again, he donned his green waterproof apron and put cutlery and crockery into the sink, where Ruth washed and rinsed it, before I dried up. His sister, who used to do this, feels that she has been promoted so that she can play. She and Ruth had spent some time painting and she wanted to continue with her creations. Meanwhile the older brother went outside by himself to play with a tennis ball on a string. He was near the kitchen door so that he knew I could see him. He is good at this, appreciated that I was watching with a tea towel in my hand, and I was delighted to be able to complement him on some of his smooth left-handed drives.

Having finished all the dishes (of course), Harry came outside and started playing a similar game, but on this occasion time had beaten us. We needed to get coats and find the car so that I could take the three children home. We said goodbye to Ruth and found our allotted seats. On the journey the sister had taken onboard my comments from week one (about us finding a level of noise which enabled all four to be in communication in the confines of a vehicle). And then we used stairs and fob to reach the family's council flat. Mum and dad were there waiting, and we were on time … just. After three weeks they were no longer anxious about Harry's behaviour at Mill Grove. They had begun to realise that whatever the problems he might have in other settings, he was a pleasure to have with us.

And so quietly and steadily, safe space is being created. And this means that not only do we all look forward to being together, but that it won't be long before we can have creative conversations, engage in other activities, and even begin to share about our feelings, fears and dreams. Who knows we might find a way of Harry consuming a pea before Christmas 2021! In the meantime, we will continue to have safe space as our overwhelming priority, and for now, the signs are looking promising. The boundaries are clear, and it seems as if some of them are already being internalised. But now is not the time to relax. If we did, it would not be long before the fun and humour began to wane.

It would not be appropriate to ask Harry what he likes best about being at Mill Grove just yet: far more important for him to enjoy what he does without introspection. But for what it is worth, I think he might like doing the dustbins and the washing up most of all. If you think that it is strange that a little lad might prefer work to play, just bear in mind that he is fortunate in being young enough to see all life as play, and what we think of as tasks can be very satisfying, while some play, like losing at dominoes for example, can be frustrating. Significantly the best times were when he was close to an adult (myself with the bins, and Ruth with the washing up) and engaged in a shared project. If you are thinking of possible definitions of safe space, then that is probably up there among the best of them.

Addendum

I wrote the above note in October 2020 when the Covid 19 lock-down in the UK had eased, but now it is November 5th, and a new set of restrictions has kicked in. As Harry's fifth birthday is on Bonfire Night, we brought it forward by a day and celebrated with fire, fireworks, barbecue, toasted marshmallows and birthday cake. It's going to be a while before our weekly pattern is resumed, and it will be interesting to see how the gap has affected the creation of safe space …. Oh, yes, since you asked, I think Harry most enjoyed helping to build the bonfire and keep it burning till the moment he had to leave!

INTRODUCTION TO THEME THREE
Significance

It is in this section that some of the most personal comments and stories of children who have lived at Mill Grove are shared. Their sense of identity and life-stories are therefore at the heart of the collection, as in the process described at the growth of love.

It begins with a restatement of why love matters and ends with the testimony of the father of a child who had just died of a cerebral palsy-related condition when still very young.

Along the way there is the fundamental question: How do we know we are human? This raises the spectre that as the result of loss, and without a secure attachment. a young child may have difficulty understanding how she relates to the rest of the human race.

The revelations are both moving and sometimes disturbing, but the very fact that such conversations are taking place shows resilience at work.

Meanwhile what can we offer? To be there, and to share something of ourselves: what used to be termed "person-centred casework".

Why Love Matters

It's strange, and when I come to think of it exceedingly strange, that it never occurred to me in England or Scotland, and that it was only when I was teaching in Penang, Malaysia that the penny dropped.

Just a bit of background: since 2002 I have been coming to Penang each June to teach a course called Holistic Child Development. Which is why this article is being written in Penang.

It was the first day of the five-day course and in the afternoon I had decided to show the students some of the videos recorded by Sir Richard Bowlby on the work of his father, Dr. John Bowlby. I have watched these several times before, and so it is doubly strange that the thought had not occurred to me until that Monday afternoon.

This is a transcript of what Richard Bowlby said:

> "The science of family bonds, which researchers call attachment theory, was started in the 1950s by my father John Bowlby who died in 1990. He was a child psychiatrist who was also a scientist and in 1952 he wrote a book called *Child Care and the Growth of Love*. But love had too many different meanings for a scientist and later he called the kind of love that children feel for their parents, attachment: children's attachment to their parents."

That's it. For some unaccountable reason it had never dawned on me until Monday 8th June 2015 that if Bowlby had not changed the word love into the word attachment the whole language and possibly history of child development, child psychology and child psychiatry might have been different.

Now clearly John Bowlby had to find specific terms to describe aspects of what he was studying and finding: so *attachment of children* to a significant other can be distinguished from the *bonds that adults* form with children, attachments can be *secure and insecure*, and so on.

But by putting aside the word love there may have been any number of unintended consequences: understanding how children feel and develop is dominated by scientific studies and discourses; education and learning is seen as mainly about cognitive development; parenting is about care; social work is about empathy and so on. In short, it becomes possible for every aspect of a child's emotional state and development (or lack of it) to be described without any reference to love.

It also risks cutting off this range of academic studies and discourses from poetry, literature, religion, music, imagination, nature and the many aspects of a child's life where ordinary people routinely use the word love, not only of the child or parent for each other, but of a child's relationship to many aspects and components of her cultural and geographical world.

As some readers of the journal know I have been working on this matter for a number of years and one of the fruits of this has been the book, *The Growth of Love*, which seeks to recast child development within the process of the giving and receiving of love. I chose the title deliberately to echo the original work of John Bowlby, and Richard was kind enough to write a foreword. Since then I have been realising that many philosophers of education (Pestalozzi, Froebel, Montessori, Cavalletti, Illich, Parker Palmer to name but a few) saw love as the basis, the very heart of education and learning.

I gave a paper on this theme at an educational conference in Budapest a couple of years ago. And it was very hard for the head-teachers present to connect what they were doing (their curricula, their learning objectives and outcomes, the exams, and the expectations of parents and society), with what I was saying. The message they seemed to give me was that it was a rather attractive and possibly, even, a noble ideal, but what on earth had love got to do with the realities on the ground?

And now I am finding the same thing among colleagues teaching "holistic child development": the range of subjects and courses taught includes research methodology, children at risk, childhood spirituality, child protection, participation, agency, ministry with families throughout the life-cycle, pastoral care of children, youth and families, and so on. But, as Oliver asked in the musical, "Where is love?"

An industry has grown up around children that cannot see that the emperor is naked, or to use another metaphor, that there is an elephant in the room. In the USA, millions of boys are reported to be on Ritalin; millions of girls are depressed, and this is just the tip of the iceberg. Is it not possible that they are crying out, sometimes loudly by word and action, sometimes silently by withdrawal, for someone to love, and for someone who loves them?

Just before leaving for Malaysia, I happened to find the book by Sue Gerhardt, *Why Love Matters*, and my heart began to beat a little bit faster. What she was arguing was that science was finding consistent and cogent evidence that affection (that was the word she used inside the book much of the time when referring to the word, "love", that was on the cover) could alter both the biochemistry and the structure of the brains of young children.

Now I do not believe that aspects and dimensions of our lives such as love, empathy, compassion, the sublime, loyalty, devotion, need to wait for science to give them its imprimatur, but in the case of child development we do need some movement from scientific study and techniques towards human affection, feelings, longings and desires: between psychotherapy and behavioural therapy.

I doubt if the books, *Why Love Matters* and *The Growth of Love* will have such an impact as Bowlby's *Child Care and the Growth of Love*, but like the butterfly landing on the imaginary wave they might be part of a tipping point. Until love is reclaimed in this whole field the word may well be held hostage by those who associate it with paedophiles, or sloppy, sentimental substitute versions of the real thing peddled in popular culture and the media.

Just for the record, during the past four days I have been completing a coursebook for a Masters Module called *The Growth of Love: Child Development in Cultural Contexts*. During this week I consulted a number of standard textbooks on the subject, and I realised that without the concept of love, some of these books simply listed a set of different, and largely unconnected, "stages" or "theories" of child development. It felt rather like reading a scientific analysis of a subject that did little justice to the subject, because the whole approach and methods were fundamentally inappropriate and flawed.

What students will make of the course is another matter, but it is above all an attempt to listen to the voices and life-stories of children with care and respect, and to respond appropriately.

- -

"But He Was My Father ..."

From the moment I heard these words I knew that I must write down the context and sequence of events that led up to them. It was 72 hours ago, and this is the first window of opportunity: a Sunday evening in mid-summer accompanied by the birdsong of thrushes and a pleasing breeze.

This is how it happened: I was at Mill Grove and had been talking with the daughter of someone who had lived here as a girl between 1927 and 1933. We were going through the folder that contained correspondence, photos, school reports, and a few forms of various sorts. She had brought along a photo of her mother on her wedding day, and we were trying to work out from that whether we could recognise her in some of the group photos of that period.

Her mother had left in 1933 to join her own mother and stepfather in York, where she started work at Rowntree's. She was a very hard worker all her life, and this attitude had been instilled in her children. It wasn't long before the family story of three generations was unfolding, and I was taking notes as fast as I could. While this was happening, we photocopied everything in the folder. (Subsequently the daughter sent me an email full of excitement at what she had discovered, tempered with the news that the health of her mother had deteriorated in a nursing home in North Wales.)

At this point the doorbell rang, and in walked one of those who had lived at Mill Grove as a child while I was at university: she had come over from North America and I will call her Martha. She was accompanied by an older sister (who did not live at Mill Grove because she was too old to do so) and who was making her first visit to our home. We had a great time catching up on respective family news, and her sister was trying to come to terms with the size of our house, when just as we were getting up to join everyone for Thursday lunch, Martha asked if there was a folder with her personal material in it. She had never thought to ask before, but the presence of the other folder on the table in front of us had prompted the question. I confirmed that there was indeed such a folder, and we agreed to go through it together at the end of the meal. Her sister was engaged in lively conversation with several others as the two of us slipped away. We sat on a settee in the lounge and opened the folder.

She was overwhelmed, spell-bound, moved to tears, amazement and wonder in turns as she began to read through and explored what she found. There were lots of letters that she had written to my parents as well as to my wife and me. And then school reports; references; her wedding invitation; photos; together with all sorts of correspondence … including, to her total surprise, letters from her father. Wiping the tears from her eyes she asked me to read one of these letters for her. It was all news to me because I had never seen the contents of the folder before, knowing only what she had previously told me about her past and her family.

The bare bones of the story were that she and her two younger siblings had been removed from the care of their father because they were not being looked after appropriately. To keep the three of them together they came to live at Mill Grove. Martha was the one who made the decision at a court hearing. The father, who was often under the influence of drink, was abusive to Martha (I did not enquire after the nature of the abuse), but she recounted the time when he tried to strangle her with a metal coat-hanger. She only survived because someone came to knock on the door as she was praying in desperation. When her father opened the door, she darted through it, and although he ran after her, she found that the sheer adrenaline provided her with the energy to keep ahead of him and hide.

Now she was reading letters written by that very same person: letters that she had never seen, and that she did not know existed. All except one were addressed to my parents, but there was one that had her name on the front. It had been neatly opened, and we assumed that it had not been passed to her because those responsible for her welfare still feared for her safety. In it, as well as in some of the other letters, her father told of his love and concern for her.

She told me that she had hated her father, and that all through her teens and early twenties she had resolved never to see him again … and certainly not to forgive him under any circumstances.

At some stage the conversation shifted to my own mother, with whom Martha had several run-ins while she was living at Mill Grove. Martha reminded me that she had hated my mother too. I didn't need reminding of this because Martha had come across the Atlantic to speak at my mother's funeral, when she had regaled us with several stories that demonstrated just how difficult they found it to get on with each other.

Then she reminded me that when she returned to the UK for the first time, as a wife and mother of two children, she had discovered my mother to be a frail, diminutive old lady. She described how it had begun to dawn on her that my mother had been trying to do her best, and that her motivation for everything she did was that she loved Martha. Sitting beside her, holding the folder and letters from her father, our attention moved speedily back to him. Without prompting on my part, she told me that she had forgiven her father. It was when he had died. She saw his body at a Chapel of Rest and had kissed him on the forehead.

"I knew that he could never do me any more harm" she told me, "And I forgave him." She continued, "He abused me more than anyone will ever know. I will never forget what he did. I can never forget. But he was my father … And now I can see that he cared about me. In fact, though he was so often abusive and under the influence of drink, I realise that he loved me in his own way."

I am not sure either Martha or I will ever get the actual sequence of events exactly right, but I was witnessing a remarkable journey of self-discovery. "Witness" is probably not the best word because I was part of the process. After all, it was my mother and my home she was talking about, and we were reading the letters of her father together. At one stage she commented how good it was that it was me there beside her, and that we were experiencing all this together, having known each other for well over 40 years.

As far as I can ascertain or remember she had made the discovery that my mother was a human being who had been trying her best, before she forgave her father. But I am not sure, and it may not be significant. What matters is that she was secure enough in her own identity and sense of self-worth to be able to re-think the characters and motivations of two of the significant adults in her life in the light of the fact that they too were human beings (like her), and that they had their own stories and reasons for how they had lived, how they had treated her, and why.

Some regular readers of these columns know the degree of importance I attach to the findings of the research study, *Out of the Woods: Tales of Resilient Teens (Adolescent Lives)* by Stuart T. Hauser (Author), Joseph P. Allen (Author), Eve Golden (Author), Harvard University Press, 2006. They stumbled upon some remarkable records at an institution, and through them traced several people who had lived in residential institutions as teenagers. While some had never recovered emotionally or psychologically, some had survived and felt OK. As psychologists they set out to find any common elements in the stories of this latter cohort.

What I was participating in was how resilience works in practice. Martha was a survivor, someone who was not just OK, but thriving. She was not, and never will be, without hurts and scars, but she has found a way of living that takes seriously the abuse that she experienced, those painful years away from her birth family and kith, and also the fact that the man who abused her was also her father.

The elements of her life that have helped this process include a long and happy marriage to an understanding and caring husband; friends who have been alongside her all through and with whom she could share what she felt able to at her own pace; a sense of her own life-story and the ability to re-interpret it in the light of what she had learned about herself, life and the lives of others; and help in getting at some of the key facts in that life-story.

The time came for us to get up: her sister was wondering what on earth we were talking about! Martha shared immediately with Ruth, my wife, what we had been discovering together. (Ruth is a very important person in Martha's whole life-story and journey, so that was both natural and special.) I promised to photocopy everything in the folder and to give it to her when we met again in ten days' time.

We hugged each other, took photos of the two sisters by the front door of Mill Grove, and they headed off for the holiday home that belongs to Mill Grove in North Wales.

I hope that further reflection and elaboration is unnecessary. It was my privilege to be present during this quite amazing time of discovery, honesty and sharing. I have spoken before of being inspired by the resilience, determination, faith and forgiveness of members of the Mill Grove family. Here it was again: but fresh and green as a leaf.

"It Made Me What I Am"

It was the end of lunchtime on Boxing Day at Mill Grove and there were just a few minutes before the traditional afternoon football match was due to begin outside. I sat down beside a young man who had been enjoying his lunch on a table with 15 others of all ages. Although he and his family had never lived at Mill Grove as children, they used to spend an evening a week with us and join us for our summer holiday in North Wales. Unlike other members of his nuclear family, he had rarely been able to come back to see us, so this was a special window of opportunity.

For a time as we sat together there were others around, and I told them that he (let me call him Ishmael) was one of my heroes. He had memorably volunteered to sacrifice one of the days of his holiday in North Wales to join me in a 500-mile round trip to London and back with young children on both legs of the journey. He kept me awake faithfully on the final leg over the Bala Hills until we arrived late at night but safely in Borth-y-Gest. That was just one of the reasons why I was so pleased that he had joined nearly a hundred others for our Boxing Day celebrations.

And that was the trigger. "It made me what I am," he said as if it was almost too obvious to state. And then without any prompting he unpacked what he meant. "It was Wales. The mountains. Swimming and sailing. Helping carry the boats and trailers. And the 'Mystery Trips'. I wouldn't be the person I am without them. I try to explain to my friends (in East London) but they don't know what I am talking about."

(Just a word about Mystery Trips: they used to take place each evening and would involve short journeys to unknown destinations where scrambling, diving, swimming, climbing and exploring would take place, usually followed by a visit to a fish and chip shop.)

Since his boyhood he had been faced with many challenges (to put it mildly) but those times spent in North Wales were an unfailing source of comfort, sense of identity and achievement. "You enjoyed them a lot." I said, "and so did I." "I know you did," he replied with a broad smile. The days on the hills, beaches and seas were shared experiences that bound us together.

Other children and young people have lived at Mill Grove for years, sometimes decades, but in his case, it was regular Thursday evenings and then annual holidays that had been the basis of our bonding and attachment.

Since then, as it happens, I have been in North Wales over the New Year period, and I talked about him with other members of the extended family. Of course they remembered him, and one reminded me that we used to celebrate his birthday often during the summer holiday. I had forgotten that.

On reflection there are two elements of this story that deserve examination for those of us who live alongside children and young people who have to navigate difficult personal and family situations. The first is that of time. The general assumption is that secure attachment takes place early in life (especially during the first two years) and that it takes considerable time for it to take root.

But here we are dealing with something like secure attachment that developed largely in a place where we spent no more than two weeks together each year. Is it really possible? If it is, then we do well to consider seriously the nature of "quality time together".

The second concerns the significance of holidays. I wonder if those out-of-the-ordinary times of shared life and experience have unrecognised potential for bonding and attachment. What if we organise our lives and "intervention" in the lives of children and young people without reference to holidays, or to put it more starkly, if we deliberately organise things so that we do not spend any holidays with the children whom we seek to understand and help?

In my research into residential child care in Edinburgh and Hull during the early 1970s I found that it was not unusual for a Director of Children's Services to spend some of his or her summer holidays with the children for whom they were responsible. With the advent of Social Work/Social Services Departments that practice ceased immediately and has never been re-established. Now it would seem unthinkable.

But meanwhile the likes of my dear friend and colleague Bob Holman has continued to spend holidays with young people from Roger-field and Easterhouse at camps in Skegness. And it is clear from the stories that are told many years later that these have been times of unique self-discovery and relationship-building.

And some alert readers will not have over-looked the fact that this conversation with Ish-mael also took place on a holiday … just a few days ago. It had nothing at all to do with work, social work, casework, therapy and the like. It was a family conversation over a family meal and about a family holiday.

There is, I believe some serious re-thinking and re-planning needed, but if that is to be done, perhaps we should fill in the picture a bit, lest we highlight two aspects at the expense of a fuller and bigger picture. It is I think vital to realise that the holidays we spent together in North Wales were connected, supported, bound by regular weekly evenings spent together, by some shared interests of the fami-lies, and by relationships that developed with other members of Ishmael's family. It was not just a matter of two individuals meeting as it were in isolation, but much more accurately another example of "kith" or "nestness". (These concepts are explored in the very creative and imaginative book, Kith: *The Riddle of the Child-scape*, by Jay Griffiths. The first article in the section, Security, "Of Nests and Nestness" is based on her work.)

It follows that thinking about bonding and attachment may need to be assessed in this wider context with its specific transitional objects and transitional space. But all the same I wish you could have been there to hear the words, "It made me what I am". They were spoken with such deep sincerity and conviction that they deserve a serious hearing. Has anyone done work on how John Bowlby's insights relate to summer holidays, I wonder?

Beyond Victim and Survivor

Even by the standards we have reluctantly come to accept over the decades at Mill Grove, Nana Peg was dealt a particularly poor hand in her early childhood. She was the youngest of three sisters (the older pair being identical twins), and when their parents separated, they were placed in an abusive foster home. For most of her life she had little or no contact with either of her parents. When the children were on the way to Mill Grove, they were told by the foster mother that it was some type of institution where delinquents were punished, and that there would be barbed wire on top of the high walls. She was pleasantly surprised by what she found, and it became her secure base for the rest of her life. In her later years she married, but this was to last just six years before her husband died. Since then, she has lived alone with deteriorating health, which has left her with difficulty balancing, eating and with a tremor. She needs to wear a neck-brace.

Last weekend she celebrated her 80th birth-day at Mill Grove, the place that is home for her, and where she meets with her extended family comprising others who also spent their childhoods there. We had been getting ready for this day over several weeks, but nothing prepared me for what I was to experience. It was, quite frankly, flabbergasting. And this is what I want to attempt to share with readers.

For a start, her one remaining older sister came over from the USA with her husband, two of her offspring, and their spouses, as well as two grandchildren. It's not every birthday that such a large family group crosses the Atlantic! But then there were several friends of Nana Peg together with their children and grandchildren. As a result, I think the average age for this 80th birthday party must have been one of the youngest on record. There was also a childhood friend who was in the middle of the TGO Challenge 2017: a walk across the mountains of Scotland inspired by Hamish Brown. (We will come back to her in a moment.)

Let's relay some of the conversations I had with those present about Nana Peg. A great nephew told me that she was his favourite person because unfailingly she phoned him on his birthdays. It was, he had told his class at school, the best present he could imagine.

Others of his generation but living in the UK told me that they thought the world of Nana Peg. It was they who had given her this fond nickname. As you can guess, she remembered their birthdays too, but she also visited them regularly, and was like a rock in their lives. They respected her not least for her integrity marked out by an unwavering sense of right and wrong. She had been a guide and inspiration to them all. Though she was not a blood relative of theirs, you would have been hard pushed to tell this from the very warm personal comments and the way that they talked about her.

I moved on to sit beside the person who was in the middle of the TGO Challenge (which in case you are unaware of it, requires that a person carries his or her own tent all the way across the highlands of Scotland). This person had travelled from her tent by bus to Aberdeen, flown down to London, and was then returning immediately to complete the expedition. What on earth had prompted such an extraordinary journey? She said that she would have done anything to be present. Nana Peg had cared for her as a nanny during her childhood. This meant that she regularly came to stay and sleep at Mill Grove. Nana Peg was one of the most special people to her, and it was therefore only right that she should celebrate this historic event with her. Like the younger ones present, she dearly loved Nana Peg. And through Nana Peg she had come to feel at home at Mill Grove too.

The picture was becoming clear. Although she had been dealt such a poor hand, Nana Peg had survived and got way beyond self-pity and victimhood. She had worked hard in retail and insurance jobs. She had taught herself to be a first-class marksman with a rifle, regularly representing the county of Kent in competitions. She found great comfort in and through her Christian faith and the life of her church. And in Mill Grove she was secure: accepted and loved. Though childless she had been a nanny, an auntie and Nana Peg. It had been a village that had helped to raise her and her sisters, and she was part of the village that had helped to raise several others.

There was a cake to cut and candles to blow out, but those present were really not overmuch concerned with the excellent refreshments and the formalities. They were there to express their thanks and love to Nana Peg. And I was there too, pretty much overwhelmed by what I was witnessing and learning. I had grown up with Nana Peg as one of the many older sisters in the Mill Grove family. She, with them, tried to teach me manners and right from wrong. I suppose I accepted her along with other older sisters as a given in my life.

Now I was coming to see how much she meant to others younger than me. I was on a steep learning curve. And it was a huge privilege to be part of an occasion that I will never forget. My parents and grandparents had welcomed Nana Peg into our big family and cared for her. She was passing it on and, in the process, I began to see one of my older sisters in a whole new light. It has become apparent to me for some time that genuine care, like love, is reciprocal. On this occasion reciprocity took on a much deeper and richer meaning than I had anticipated.

"It's Really Very Moving"

It was a Friday morning, and we were sitting in a little blue room with the sun streaming in through the patio doors. This is the place where there is perhaps as much space and privacy as anywhere in the community of Mill Grove. And Colin (the name I will give him) was holding a fawn-coloured folder bearing the names of his father and brother. These two people, now deceased, had come to live at Mill Grove as children in 1929. Now for the very first time Colin had come with his wife to visit Mill Grove to find out more about their stories, and about the place where they had lived. This part of their lives had remained a closed book to their children and families. His father and uncle had said little, if anything, about it.

The first piece of paper that Colin saw was very old, creased, and yellow. As he held it in his hands, he noticed that it was signed by his grandmother. She had written very neatly with a pen, in black ink. It was a form in which she requested that my grandfather care for her two boys following the death of their father, her husband. That is when Colin said, "It's really very moving". In that moment of time there was a compression of many years, memories, associations and pieces of the jigsaw that made up the family story.

Why had Colin decided to come to see the records at this point in his life, for example, rather than years ago, or choosing to put it off for some more years? It turned out that there was a granddaughter who was becoming increasingly interested in her family history. She was not bound by the tradition of silence about this period of the story and so prompted her grandfather to see what, if anything, could be discovered.

One of the reasons why he hadn't come earlier was because, relying on stereotypes of residential child care, he had assumed the worst: that his father and uncle had remained silent because their experiences had been so harrowing. The building was bound to be grey, drab, intimidating, institutional and unfriendly.

Another was that he had just come to accept over several decades that this was a gap in the family history that was unlikely to be filled.

He continued his way quietly and methodically through letters, medical and school reports and some photographs until I offered to scan them all so that he could have a full set to study at his convenience. We then lunched with others at Mill Grove before looking around inside and outside, pausing at places that had remained unchanged since his father and uncle had lived here. As we did so I realised that my own father who grew up at Mill Grove was of virtually the same age and generation as them. It is certain that they knew each other well. So, as I recounted some of the features of my father's childhood, I knew that they were likely to have been common to all three.

Since Colin and his wife returned home at the end of the day we have corresponded, and I have also exchanged emails with Colin's cousin. Colin was kind enough to give me a copy of his draft of the family story (without of course the new information that he now possessed). The cousin plans to come to Mill Grove as soon as he can. Meanwhile we have passed on a copy of *Links*, the annual newsletter that connects members of the extended family worldwide. The first 70 years are archived online, and so in this way there is a living link between 1929 and the present day.

I have found myself reflecting on this historic encounter between Colin and his father's childhood home, and the link between the shared childhoods of our respective fathers. One of my more immediate reactions was to share with Colin that I too found it moving to be present as he gained his first sight of his grandmother's writing and held in his hands the records of his father's early years. This reminded me of the occasion when my father was welcoming three new children to Mill Grove. As he showed them their new home, he was visibly distressed, so I spoke with him sometime later, puzzled that after all these years he had still not got become accustomed to handling the trauma of being with children who were experiencing separation and loss.

His reply had never left me: "Son", he said, "if ever I am not moved at such times, then I should no longer be here caring for children." To become de-sensitised to a child's inner grief and anxiety was to put at risk his relationship with them. If he could not empathise, their loss would be compounded. Over the years I have found that I, too, never find myself unmoved by the psychological suffering and stress of children deprived, if only temporarily, of kith and kin.

I am not thinking here about inappropriate expressions of emotion, but rather of the awareness that in residential child care the main resource that is available is that of nature, the character, the experience of the person or persons who care for a child. They must be vulnerable enough to feel the pain of others, while responsible, knowledgeable and supportive enough to express their empathy appropriately.

A further line of thought over recent weeks concerns the records of those in care. Whatever the original or primary reason for them being assembled and kept, it is now clear to me that the keepers of these records (that is, part of the life-story of an individual) are stewards of them for future generations. When a child comes into care there is inevitably a disruption of her life and story, and so these are critically important for the child and their offspring later in life, as they try to understand their own family history.

Until Colin saw the records he had feared for the worst. Now new light had been thrown on not only his father's story, but his relationship with his father, and his own relationship with his children and grandchildren. A life-story is not merely something that becomes history at a certain point (so that records can then be discarded); rather, it is a vital part of living history. Without this, the future generations of someone in care are deprived of information essential to their understanding of who they are and where they come from, even why.

While this story was unfolding with Colin and his family, I found myself engaged with someone else who has been trying to unearth his own early life and ancestry (before he came to live at Mill Grove). The absence of reliable records meant that his recent years have been something of a rollercoaster, with some profound discoveries and shocks. The concept of record-keeping as a form of stewardship or guardianship of information for children (including those yet unborn) is one that I cannot recall being given as a reason for what and how record-keeping should be done. I now commend it wholeheartedly.

But there is also the matter of place. It was not just the records that brought such light and even comfort to Colin: it was the experience of spending time in the very same home, garden, orchard that his father had inhabited, that was significant. Some of the trees are the very same, most of the bricks, some of the windows, and even some of the furniture! The fact that I could assure him of where his father slept, where meals were served, the games that were played, and something of the daily and weekly patterns of life were obviously things that he was eager to absorb. A picture was emerging of how the father he knew in part grew up, and how aspects of his character and way of life were formed.

Alongside the aspect of place went the continuity of relationships: my father knew his, and vice-versa. They grew up together. He knew his father and I knew mine, and we were able to work out that not only did they go to the same school (as did I years later), but that they almost certainly then travelled to work in the city of London together on the same train. Possibly more important was the axiom that my grandfather wanted to get firmly into the heads of all who lived at Mill Grove: "Remember my boy/girl that in the final analysis, it's character that counts," were the exact words. Not status, qualifications, connections, wealth, beliefs or the like, but the quality of your character as demonstrated by the way you live and work, and also by the way you respond to, treat and respect others. That made complete sense to Colin. If his father had not used the very same words, he clearly lived by a very similar compass bearing. It affects every aspect of your life, whether at work, at home or friendships and associations. And it gets communicated to the next generation: your own children.

Perhaps this short reflection will give a little insight into why the comment "It's really very moving" made such an impact on me. To be a small part of a process where the truth about a family story is being reliably passed on through the generations is a considerable privilege. And it gives us all cause for thought about the long-term implications of, not only the quality of the care of a child, but also the quality of the care of the information and records that relate to that child.

A period spent in care is not just an episode in the life of a child, but also an episode in the history of a family.

How Do We Know
We Are Human Beings?

The article focusing on "kith" or "nestness" sought to enrich our understanding of the nature of attachment and bonding, in order to know better some of the lesser acknowledged elements involved when there is separation and loss. The argument put simply was that we have tended (since the work of John Bowlby) to focus primarily on the human relationships between a child and her significant other at the expense of other aspects of what constitutes attachment, and what is lost when there is separation. Nestness is an image that reminds us that human relationships are set in a context, and that if there is a disruption in a child's life, there is likely to be a loss of any number of artefacts, places, associations that have to do with what we mean by "home". The first and only time I had come across the concept was in the work of Jay Griffiths, *Kith: The Riddle of the Childscape* (London: Penguin, 2013).

Before proceeding with a response to the question at the head of this article, I want to share my sense of surprise and pleasure when discovering that the concept is now being used in the field of sociology. In the Vol. 51 No. 5 October 2017 issue of *Sociology*, there is a study of intra neighbourhood trust in Great Britain and London, and key to this. According to the paper it is an American sociologist R.J. Sampson who has developed the idea in the book, *Great American City: Chicago and the Enduring Neighbourhood* (2012). Here "nestedness" is studied with a small neighbourhood as the subject, exploring how this community is set (nested) in wider or larger whole. Further investigation has revealed that we probably owe the concept to the French sociologist, Pierre Bourdieu, who gave the world that richly textured and related concept of habitus. This is heartening because it means that the idea is alive, and so there is hope that we will not lose sight of the significance of the many ways in which an individual or neighbourhood relate to their environment both personal and environmental. Since writing the piece I have listened with renewed intensity to how people describe their childhoods, always with a sense of place, context, artefacts, objects, colours and textures.

Here I want to explore another aspect or dimension of what might be involved in separation and loss in early childhood. And this issue is crystallised by the question at the head of this article. If a child experiences separation and loss from both a significant other and the nest in which they have shared their lives, is it possible that a deeper and far more primal separation is at stake? What if our sense of being a human being and part of the "human race", derives in substantial measure from our relationship with a significant other? Before reflecting on these questions, perhaps it would be helpful if I shared with you the context in which they emerged.

It happened when I was reflecting with my wife, Ruth, on the life and development of one of the children we have cared for at Mill Grove for the best part of twenty years. I will call her Maddie. She had experienced traumatic separations in quick succession in her early life that set her apart in turn from her birth parents, her siblings, two different religions and her adoptive family. It was after all this that she came to live with us. Among the many challenges that she faced was her belief or fear that she did not live in the same world as everyone else.

Another way of putting this is that she felt different from everyone else. One of the symptoms of this was that she would or could not accept the rules of any games (she simply changed or interpreted them to further her own progress). Another was her deep-seated fear of water that was not the least assuaged by the fact that on a calm day, in a sheltered shallow lake, all the others in the boat were completely relaxed and untroubled. There were many more, but in essence she seemed to inhabit a very narrow personal world, a universe parallel to that in which everyone else lived.

Now such characteristics are not uncommon among human beings. But in her case, they added up to a profound (I believe, primal) sense that she really didn't belong. And by this I mean not just to a group, but to human beings in general. Which led to the almost unthinkable and unbearable question of whether she felt or perceived herself to be a member of the human race at all. I am aware that this retreat into one's own world is a primary characteristic of the defence mechanism often termed "flight", but her story and behaviour forced me to look more deeply than this.

Developing this line of thought I began to recall other children and young people with whom I have lived at Mill Grove, and quickly I saw that this same question was just as relevant in their cases. Yes, they had different personalities and life stories, and there was a range of labels to describe them (including "withdrawn", "autistic", "personality disorder", "difficulty in making relationships" etc.) but was there at heart a common denominator, I wondered? They had all experienced separation and loss. Was one of the results or consequences of this a sense that they were on their own, not just because they were lonely or isolated, but because they experienced a fundamental gulf that divided them from the rest of the human race?

Over the many years that I have written columns for this journal (and others) I have no doubt referred to some of these children, but until now I had not considered the possibility of such a huge and seemingly unbridgeable gap between them and everyone else. There was the boy who was repeatedly excluded from every school to which he was sent, and who regularly called out in a room full of people (whether at home or school) "It's me. I'm here." Pondering this with others the only way we could make sense of its meaning was that he feared he did not exist unless we constantly affirmed and reaffirmed his presence among us as a fellow human being.

Then there was the teenage girl who never seemed to laugh spontaneously. One day I found her laughing (by the snooker table I recall) and thought that she might have broken through in some way, so I asked her whether she had found something funny: "No," she replied, "All the others laughed, and I just joined them, so I wasn't the odd one out". It dawned on me in a flash that she lacked one of the most basic competencies of what it is to be human: a sense of humour that connects people as people.

Further examples were not hard to find. Despite the variations in their life stories and their very different personalities, was there at the very core of their beings the same fundamental lack of a sense of belonging to the same world as others? Perhaps the psychological term that comes closest to this might be schizoid. Schizoid personality disorder (SPD) is characterized by a lack of interest in social relationships, a tendency towards a solitary or sheltered lifestyle, secretiveness, emotional coldness, detachment and apathy. It is not the same thing, but is there the possibility that a reason for this set of behaviours or attitudes is the sense that a person does not belong to the human race? If so, you could easily see why they see others and relate to them as they do. Is there, I wonder, research on the incidence of separation and loss among those diagnosed as schizoid?

As a sociologist I have often written and taught that socialising and relationships with people in the wider world are learned within the context of the nuclear family, household, or its equivalent. But now I wonder if there is a deeper relationship at stake: what if we learn that we are humans, like others, from the primal relationship with our mother or significant other? Does the work of Konrad Lorenz and imprinting have relevance here? His studies seem to imply that an animal will tend to behave as if belonging to the species with which there is the first bonding with or attachment to a caregiver.

It is, at very least, food for thought, and I will be considering the matter carefully over the coming months and years, keen to connect with any who would like to explore the matter. Does Bowlby hint at this in his work? What about others exploring this field?

But let's end on a positive, because true, note. How might we go about helping someone like this (who believes or assumes that they do not belong to the human race) to discover their shared humanity? I don't know how it works, but I have seen it happen. Maddie now has a full-time job helping parents with premature babies in a general hospital. She is very good at the rules of games, enjoys swimming and sailing, and is increasingly able to sense the emotions and feelings of others, and at times to empathise with them. Somewhere along the way she has uneventfully identified with the rest of humanity.

How? That's a big question. But I know it has to do with the unconditional commitment of significant others. But it also had to do with nestness. Maddie continues to spend lots of her spare time at Mill Grove, often not talking with others, but being with us, being alongside, eating some meals, joining in events, and helping with the washing up! She also takes an inordinate interest in her niece. Sometimes holding her like a baby chick. Could it be that significant others, a nest (in the sense used above), and then a baby related to a person, are three key factors in connecting her to the human race? All those of us involved in therapeutic care in its many varieties would do well to ponder the question that engendered this piece, and the questions that emerge at the end. It is just possible that we have missed something very important.

One of the archetypes or icons of human relationships is that of the Madonna and child. I now begin to see that it is not just about a parent and her offspring, but two humans in relationship, perhaps representing how understanding what it is to be human is shared and learned.

The Scars of Childhood Traumas are Deep and Lasting

Some time ago my friend and colleague, David Lane saw fit to remind me that 118 years was a long time in residential care. He is aware, of course, that I have not been in it that long, but equally aware that having been born in Mill Grove, and knowing scores of those who have lived there personally, I am in a rather unique position to reflect on some of the issues inherent in such care with the benefit of hindsight. Books on "leaving care" for example, are rarely if ever written with the wisdom of the reflections of a person's lifetime, let alone the thoughts and experiences of that person's children, grandchildren (yes, and even great grandchildren). And yet properly speaking is that not where we should be looking when considering "outcomes"?

As I write this piece I am on a train travelling back from the south coast of England where I have spent the day with one of those who lived at Mill Grove as a boy from 1951 to 1955. I knew him then because throughout this time we grew up together, and today we discussed his story, due to be published later this week (Val and Bev Savage: Somebody's Son, 2017.) He is one of those who lived at Mill Grove who has written and published their memories and reflections.

It so happens that I had already chosen the title of this piece before travelling to see him today. In point of fact I had sketched the outline of the content exactly six days earlier. But now I want to share with you, freshly-minted, my thoughts and feelings about, together with my reflections on, this encounter. He greeted me at the station and took me to lunch beside the sea. Then he immediately began by asking about Mill Grove and who would be leading it in the future. This put me on my guard lest it would deflect time and attention from discussing his own book and story. But he gently and patiently helped me to see that what happened to Mill Grove was of considerable importance to him. The future of the place that had been there for him when it really counted mattered to him deeply, and so did my family and those who are responsible for holding the future of the place in their hands. He knew my grandparents and parents, who between them had cared for him. It followed that my wife and I and our children and grandchildren meant a lot to him. So from the start the conversation was more reciprocal than I had imagined. And it was he who had taken the initiative

We finished our lunch before having any discussion of his book at all, and then drove to his flat which was a short distance from the beach. Then and only then was he ready to get down to what I had thought would be the main focus and substance of the day. He had a notebook in hand, which took me off guard, because I was thinking of a much more informal and free-flowing conversation. But I suppose it was a natural reaction to the fact that I was holding a full page of handwritten comments I had made on the first 100 pages of his autobiography!

I asked whether he would like me to share with him some reflections, or if he had something else in mind. He nodded to me that I should carry on. This being so, I ventured that there were two things that I felt might well help us get near the heart of things. The first was that he was in a residential nursery for the first 9/10 months of his life. The episode was recorded in his book but virtually without comment. This was understandable in part because neither he nor anyone else was able to help fill in the simplest details or facts about the place or those who had held him in their hands, fed and clothed him. But when I read later in his story that he following this period he "rocked himself" a lot, I realised that he was describing the experiences and patterns of life of those described by Bowlby, Spitz and Goldfarb as they observed and filmed children in institutional care as a result of having been separated from their significant others (usually parents or family). I think this connection between separation and the comfort that comes from physical rocking came as something new to him. And it was painful for us both as we tried to imagine what he might have been going through.

This led us to explore some of the likely effects of this separation and loss during the pivotal period of his life. Nothing else could be properly understood without taking account of this primal trauma. He wanted me to say more about what I knew of the effects on other children. I explained that as I understood it something called the "ego project" tended to start in all young children around the age of two. I referred to, but did not quote, the work of Professor James E. Loder (The Logic of the Spirit, San Francisco: Jossey-Bass, 1998) which had been important in my own reading of child development as described in The Growth of Love. I suggested that the "ego project" was a defence against the discovery that the significant other was not always there for the growing child, not at their beck and call, and demonstrably not controlled by the child.

To deal with this harrowing discovery, over time and unconsciously, the child was creating or constructing a fantasy world that was safe from the vagaries of actual life in which the significant other has more important people to deal with, and other matters of concern. It was reinforced by the western consensus that human history was also a project of progress in which an individual child, young person and eventually an adult is encouraged to develop this project, and receive rewards in the process. His story, not surprisingly therefore, not only showed some of the hallmarks of the "ego project" conceived in this sense, but also of a person who needed to find ways of defending desperately his fragile sense of self against all comers, and all events.

He is a very intelligent, personable, able and gifted person. So all his energy, talents and abilities went into laudable roles and activities (such as marriage, parenting, ministry and management), but his re-telling of his story was testimony to the fact that his social development was at the expense of his inner self.

This led us to a second reflection. In the introduction to his book he wrote of his wife's preliminary writing about the search for his origins as being "frozen" for ten years. I told him that this was a word and concept that had often been used by those trying to understand how children cope with traumas, and that it helped me begin to grasp something of what was going on throughout his story. He effectively coped with not only the early separation and loss, but also the many difficult and painful setbacks, losses and separations and confused and confusing relationships that would follow, by "freezing them". His wife had noticed that he was on the surface sociable and very good with people, but that he rarely risked sharing his deepest thoughts and feelings with anyone else.

Dwelling on this metaphor we compared notes on old heating systems in schools: they relied on big pipes running through classrooms. After a snowball fight in winter when hands were frozen it was tempting to put the little fingers on the pipes to warm them up. But a child only did this once because whatever the imagined benefits, the pain was actually excruciating! So after a lifetime of freezing, with occasional periods when emotional feeling just began to return for a moment, we tried to imagine what it might be like if the emotional pain of feelings, fears and traumas of several decades were suddenly unfrozen. Freezing was an understandable learned unconscious reflex in the light of this.

Referring to a term his first wife used in her part of his story (the book is a joint effort), I wondered whether on reflection perhaps the two of us had been "half-connected". And even today, I noticed that when we embraced and I called him "brother", he called me "friend".

At this point in our conversation he asked where, having written the book, did he go now, and what of the future? It seemed to me that it was his children and grandchildren with whom the first developments would be apparent. But I knew that already his book was being read by others who had lived at Mill Grove. Who knew who else would obtain the book and what the resulting connections and reactions would be?

He noticed that the time had come for me to leave to catch the train home. And so our conversation drew to a close. As I began to write this piece it became clear to me that the title I had chosen should remain as it was before our meeting. His resilience all through his harrowing but uplifting story could not disguise the depth and lasting nature of the scars of childhood trauma.

But the practical and pressing reason why I intended to write the piece was to ask, in the light of this truth, what were the purposes, parameters and priorities of therapeutic children's schools and communities. Perhaps a discussion of this will need to wait for a future column. But I close this one by reflecting that among the lessons that seemed to come from our very open discussion today, therapeutic milieux should:

- provide a place (physical and emotional) where a child or young person knows security and predictability;
- create the safe space in which a child or young person can explore inner thoughts and relationships at his or her own pace;
- offer resourceful people who will empathise with and understand something of the depth of the traumas resulting from separation and loss;
- and identify a person or persons who will be there for the child or young person throughout their life.

I guess that most of this is pretty much understood, but the last objective sounds almost fantastic. And yet, that was what made today possible. And possibly even the book: the life-story.

I have referred before to that remarkable and seminal book, *Out of the Woods: Tales of Resilient Teens* by S. Hauser et al. (London: Harvard University Press, 2006). It is a work that reflects with hindsight on how some of the resilient young people in residential settings came to terms with their lives and traumas. The researchers concluded that what mattered was that the therapeutic intervention expanded the personal narrative of the young person. There is little doubt that over a period of 60 years this is what has happened in the case of the person with whom I spent today. If a therapeutic community is not able to identify a professional who will be alongside the hurting young person for that length of time, then perhaps it should be helping to hone the skills of the young person to identify such a person themselves.

"I Don't Know What to Say"

We were sitting together either side of the fire and chatting together. It was a few months after the last time we had met. Reuben, as I will call him, had driven down from East Anglia to Mill Grove, and we began to catch up on news over a cup of tea. He and his siblings had lived at Mill Grove as children during the time I was at university, and we had spent many years playing together, sharing holidays, and growing up.

He was always fond of my father, and I'm not sure he has ever got over the loss he experienced when my dad died. But slowly over the years he has come to share more deeply with me in what I suppose is like a relationship between a younger and older brother. There were many things we enjoyed together, and lots of shared experiences and places, but the memories that we always hold dearest are those of summer holidays spent on a farm in Essex. The summers seemed endless while we were there, and it still sounds like a boyhood dream: Land Rovers, combine harvesters, tractors, rabbit hunts, barbecues, den-building, the fresh smell of litters of newly-born piglets among the straw, tennis and putting on the lawn, and games of hide-and seek that took us into nooks and crannies redolent of some of the stories of Enid Blyton.

From time to time as we sipped our tea we returned to these nostalgic memories, and those with whom we shared them. But a shadow hung over the conversation. His brother-in-law had died suddenly since we had last met, and that loss had upset him and, to some extent, destabilised him. A host of emotions, feelings and associations jostled and tumbled around untidily in his mind and heart. Sleep had become difficult. He felt deeply for his newly-widowed sister and her son, and he missed a brother-in law whom he respected and admired and whom she had loved dearly.

After the funeral he would phone her regularly to assure her that he was thinking of her. But then he gradually began to stop phoning her. This is when he said to me, "The reason I don't phone her is that I don't know what to say". He felt deeply for her, and was sometimes reduced to tears, so it was not that he lacked feeling. The problem was deeper. It was as if he stood at the rim of a crater where a bomb had gone off and there was a huge gap where formerly there had been life, laughter and shared activity. He knew his sister was still grieving deeply. Put all this together and he simply did not know what to say. In fact, he was not sure there was anything to say.

At this point he reminded me that his sister had been with him (and crucially, at his urging) on the day her husband died. After a happy day with her brother, she returned home, only to find her husband dead upstairs. My younger brother simply could not get over an enveloping sense of guilt that was associated with a sense that he had in some way caused his brother-in-law's death. Had his sister not been with him, perhaps she could have done some emergency first aid. It mattered not that nothing and no one could have done anything to bring him back to life. He was left with this death on his conscience.

It doesn't take much imagination to realise that our own conversation slowed down at this point. I was not at all sure what if anything to say, and he was visibly shaking. And so it was that we spent some time in silence. But it was not uneasy or uncomfortable. We knew each other well enough to be relaxed in each other's company without the need for words. We had spent time on the mountains in Scotland and North Wales together and he knew that sometimes togetherness is best experienced and expressed in a silent sharing of the scents, breezes, textures of rocks and flora, and the outlines of ridges and valleys.

But then it dawned on me that we were recreating something that he wanted to do with his sister, but couldn't do, because their communication was by telephone. Had he been physically with his sister he could have shared silence and tears with her, possibly smiles through the tears too. But on the phone silence is difficult, if not sinister. Hence his observation that he didn't know what to say made complete sense. Sometimes words failed. And that is when being alongside someone, in their presence, perhaps holding their hand or giving them a hug, is the only way of communicating what you mean.

This gave me cause to reflect on what we might call counselling or therapy. So often there is the implicit assumption that it comprises mostly words. That may or may not be so, but it is evident that there will be times when words will be inadequate and inappropriate. And it is the wise and sensitive counsellor or therapist who knows that not only is there nothing to fear at such times, but that they are to be welcomed and treasured. It is perhaps akin to the seminal discovery that music is not simply about notes and sounds, but in some way rooted and set within the context of silence. A rest, or a pause between phrases or movements, may be the still point of the turning world.

I wondered how Samaritans are trained to handle this in their telephone counselling, and whether we have as a society acknowledged the significance of presence, as distinct from advice and comforting words. Just to be clear, I think the term body language is wholly inadequate and out of place here. It gives itself away, by implying that there is still something to say (language), but that it is said as it were by miming or expressing it with your body. What he was getting at and I was seeing was that there are times when there is nothing to say,

and the only appropriate and commensurate response is simply and solely to be in the presence of the other.

This led me to recall two times when I had grasped this with immediacy and clarity. The first was when Cicely Saunders, the founder of the Hospice Movement, shared with me what she saw as the heart of the process of what might be called good dying. Often the dying neither seek, nor appreciate, words. What they are looking for is someone to be with them. And this presence is not just a physical body which might be drowsy, pre-occupied or asleep, but someone who will be with them and "watch with them". She knew that I knew that this was exactly what Jesus asked of his disciples when he was in Gethsemane nearing the hour of his death. He knew that they could bring no comfort, for there was none to be offered. Sadly, in his case, they failed miserably, and three times at that.

The other occasion was when I had finally arrived on the summit ridge of An Teallach: the Scottish mountain that I had longed to climb more than any other. Some Munro baggers have gone on record as saying that they would happily swap all the others for the experience of climbing this series of peaks. They somehow seem to encompass and represent all the rest in their scale, variety and grandeur. I was with my oldest daughter, who had been born in Edinburgh, and who was in a papoose on my shoulders when I first tried to climb the mountain nearly 20 years earlier. She and my son, who was also with us, enjoyed and relished every step of the way. On the main summit she finally broke her silence: for we usually climb in silence, and said, "Now I understand, dad". That was all. And after that seeming infinity of time that accompanies the pause on a long-anticipated summit, we began the descent by completing the horseshoe.

Nothing more. Silence surrounding the perfect encapsulation of all that we were experiencing. It might have been a hug, I suppose, but that would not have been right there and then. And what her words meant were simply that she realised that there was nothing to say. We were together, and she knew exactly how we felt, and what to say and when. But just in case it is unclear, none of this would have been possible by smartphone or selfies: there are times when you need to be in the same place, together, and in silence. Who can possibly understand, let alone measure the therapeutic value of such moments and times? Who would dare, or even want to? I wonder whether we can resist any pressure to reduce counselling and therapy to mere words, and recognise that in residential living there are daily opportunities to be in each other's presence without any need for them?

Less than 24 hours after writing that question I was re-reading *An Unquiet Mind* by Dr.

Kay Jamison. It is an autobiographical account of manic depression. On page 118 I found these words: "The debt I owe my psychiatrist is beyond description. I remember sitting in his office … thinking 'What on earth can he say to make me feel better or keep me alive?' Well there never was anything he could say, that's the funny thing. It was all the desperately optimistic, condescending and things he didn't say that kept me alive: all the warmth and compassion I felt from him that could not have been said."

She has put the whole thing neatly in a nutshell.

"I Can Still Hear That Scream As If it Were in This Room Now"

During the summer months of 2018 Ruth, my wife, and I travelled widely in the UK and Europe to visit and stay with members of the extended family of Mill Grove who were unable because of distance or circumstances to come and see us at home. Not counting ferries and flights we covered 4,500 miles and saw over 100 people.

Given that Mill Grove has been around for 120 years, there are a myriad connections, layers and levels to what we mean by its "extended family". These include those who lived here as children; those who came to help as adults; trustees; our own relatives; friends; and those who have supported and encouraged what has been going on. The logistics of the exercise worked smoothly, but emotionally it was a veritable rollercoaster.

We heard many stories of childhood told with a freshness that made them feel as if the events had happened yesterday. Some were well-known to us, but others came as a surprise. There is no one story or history of Mill Grove, but rather a web of interconnected experiences and recollections. This means that

we also discovered new connections between people and events. For example, we wondered why one of those who lived at Mill Grove as a girl had moved to Devon, married and made that her home. It is not what many children in the East End of London do. (What's more she had celebrated her golden wedding anniversary a year or two ago, and her husband was with us as we chatted over a meal in her brother's house.) We found out why when we visited a very elderly and frail person who had come to help at Mill Grove in the 1950s. She told us that she had recommended the farm in Devon: her home county. As we sat beside her bed and told her how well things had turned out, she wanted to be filled in on the whole story.

We also discovered that we were playing a unique role in the lives of some of those we visited. Put another way, we were in some specific ways irreplaceable. For example, a mother told us how her own parents, now retired, spent much of their year holidaying in a camper van, so they were not available to support her with her young children. Her husband's parents meanwhile had told her to her face that she would never be accepted as one of their family, and so they too would not support her in any way. It was while playing on the floor with her children that we noticed the tears in her eyes. We came to see that we were effectively their grandparents and fulfilling some of the psychological roles of parents in the mother's life.

Another person was completely overwhelmed that we had travelled roughly 100 miles just to see her. She couldn't get over it and asked us more than once who we were going to see next. We reiterated the fact that we had come just to see her. (The word "just" is an unfortunate one in English because it carries some unwanted baggage.) Our visit and our presence spoke volumes and prompted us to ask on the way home why we had not found it possible to see her years before. As you can imagine all this and much, much more took quite a time to digest, and so we were thankful for the many miles in between visits between Glasgow and St. Gallen when we could reflect together on our feelings and thoughts.

Coming to the words at the head of this article, I will anonymise the speaker the person in question by calling him Andrew. We met him and his wife in their neat and historic home in a thriving university city. I had known him as a boy because he and his siblings had lived at Mill Grove through most of my childhood. Although he was older than me, we had played and holidayed together with shared games of cricket, football outside, and table tennis, draughts, billiards and Monopoly inside. He and his wife had come back to Mill Grove from time to time and we had met when I had taken the funerals of more than one of his siblings and their spouses. (This is something that I find myself being asked to do with increasing frequency.)

Ruth and I were welcomed warmly and shown around the house at our request, and then we chatted at a table over a cup of tea. We had brought a book of photos relating to Mill Grove from the earliest days to the present. And, of course, in it there were lots of people, not to mention rooms and places that stirred memories. For years I had respected and looked up to Andrew, and I knew that he was rather like a father figure to other members of his family. But it was not long before it became clear that he was rather anxious. He was not in good health, but at his age this was not a great surprise. Then he, supported by his wife, shared with us that he was not sleeping well, and that he had suffered for some years "with his nerves". (I am not sure how widely this phrase is used, but it is common in my experience and covers a plethora of psychological and emotional conditions.)

As we continued to chat, his own story began to emerge. It was six decades ago, on the day that his mother had left the family and their family home, that suddenly and without warning the bailiffs came. When they knocked on the front door, one of his sisters screamed with a combination of fear, loss and anger. She was voicing how all the siblings felt at being abandoned and losing their home. As you can imagine, it was this incident and the whole saga and family dynamics leading up to it that led to the children coming to live at Mill Grove. And my presence in his home without the need for any words triggered the associations that prompted him to share this harrowing memory.

One of the questions that continues to reverberate in my mind is whether it might not be better to stay away, and so to avoid sparking such painful emotions deep within a childhood experience of separation and loss. But, in his case, he dearly wanted to see us, and so that wasn't a realistic or sensible option. Then there is the question of to how to respond. Over the years I have learned that it is often better not to say anything, (certainly by way of words of supposed comfort) but rather to stay alongside and to share in however small a measure the grief.

On further reflection I realised that the sister who screamed was always seen by the rest of the family as the odd one out. And she felt this too. I recalled that on one occasion when I spoke to her of my memories of how my father treated a wound of hers every day, she was amazed that I should remember this. It was as if her serious and painful condition at the time was of little or no interest to me or anyone else.

I have seen such "othering" of family members often and see it as part of family patterning. Quite often it seems to be allied to a process something like scapegoating. And perhaps it is a defensive reaction to the one who articulated the deeply felt and terrible truth that everyone else experienced, but to which no one else gave voice.

I have often been reminded that there are things that must be voiced or expressed, but that can only be said once and by one of a family, where all have suffered loss or abuse. But the cost of the speaking for the truth-teller seems to be their ostracism by the rest of the family. By keeping them, as it were, like the scapegoat in the desert, there is the unconscious hope that the pain might also go away. I guess that this is familiar territory for those engaged in family therapy, but perhaps it is under-recognised in other forms of therapeutic intervention.

This was, as I have intimated, just one short episode in a period of three months but it is, like many others, unforgettable and disturbing. How can I help, how comfort? I am not sure that I can. But at least a painful truth has been shared and, in some way, understood. This may seem a very modest, almost insignificant response, but perhaps it is all that can be done. And perhaps it helps. Because I am not sure, does not make it invalid. And perhaps this is one of the most important things that Mill Grove can do: to be alongside and to be there so that personal hurts can be articulated in the knowledge that those who listen and feel are also affected deeply. If so, we have to be prepared and alert to such possibilities and opportunities, and to be forewarned that it hurts.

Resilience Revisited

There are fashions in academic and professional disciplines, just as there are in clothing, music and holiday destinations, and there comes a time in life when you find them coming round again: endorsed and advocated enthusiastically by those who are encountering them for the first time. I well remember when I first heard the term "resilience" in the field of child care. I am not sure, but think it was in the 1970s, and had been imported on that occasion from Poland. It came as a bit of a surprise at a time when social work in the UK was focused on casework, drawing on psychotherapeutic models. The idea that some children were more resilient than others (that is that they could withstand trauma and loss and bounce back, whether the characteristic was innate or learned) was a bit of a shock to those who assumed that it was resourceful professional adults and associated services that were the key to helping children who had suffered trauma and deprivation.

Over time it became apparent to any who were involved professionally with children who had been on the receiving end of more than their fair share of separation, loss, neglect and even abuse, that these children did not all react in the same way. In short, some were more resilient than others. And now, some 40 or more years since I first head the term, I would like to explore resilience in the context of another concept: that of being "held in a healthy mind". How, I wonder, is it that some children can survive, though not being held in this way, or to put it more starkly, when some are even being held in an unhealthy mind?

As we all know, many of today's parents suffered at the hands of their own parents or their substitutes in their own childhoods, and so it is no surprise that they lack some of the most basic of insights and skills which make for "good-enough parenting". Watching at close quarters the lack of attunement of these parents to their children can be painful, even distressing. The needs of children routinely go unnoticed; they are nearly always unanticipated; and when a child resorts to crying or acting-out behaviour, the currency of their cries for help has become devalued to the point where they become used to being marginalised or invisible. The parents in question are of course trying to cope with their own needs, feelings and impulses, and it is no surprise that these tend to override the needs of their children.

When children do gain the attention of a parent by whatever means, then the response can range hugely along an axis from overindulgence at one end to outright neglect and even cruelty at the other. The one thing completely absent is consistency in the form of predictable insight and empathy. This sounds rather soul-destroying stuff, and for some children it undoubtedly is, but I have observed young children at the receiving end of all this who are so resilient that they are not only surviving emotionally, but even able to show empathy and understanding to other siblings, who are for the most part rivals for the attention of their parents and scarce resources. They are growing, developing and becoming more resourceful.

The question I have been pondering is to do with the source and the replenishing of the inner resources of these resilient children. One possible explanation is related to what might be called "being held in a healthy group mind". Please bear with me as I share with you a tentative sketch of what I mean by this. We all know that corporate memory is increasingly short (think of your bank, your GP's surgery, a supermarket, a social services department, and so on). This means that they do not, and indeed cannot, hold you as a customer or client safely and consistently in a healthy organisational mind, because such a mind does not exist.

What I now wonder, conversely, is whether in families, particularly those that are in many respects patently dysfunctional, there is a reservoir of healthy thinking between the members, somewhere in the relational dynamics, that can be drawn upon by a resourceful (resilient) child. Now clearly there are some families, sadly, where there is no such reservoir, but I come to suspect that if only we have ears to hear and eyes to see what is really going on, in many such families there is a residue, a fund of healthy thinking, care, concern, call it what you will, although it may be hard to believe, and possibly harder to identify.

What leads me to suggest this is that I have witnessed children thriving, in some respects at least, in the most unlikely of families, and I suspect explanations that posit the idea that some children are born naturally resilient. That seems too easy, even simplistic. Even saints need to draw from current resources at some stage: they cannot give out forever without appropriate emotional input. As I write this I have in mind the work of the psychiatrist, Dr. Frank Lake, and specifically his "dynamic cycle" as described in *Clinical Theology – A Theological and Psychiatric Basis for Clinical Pastoral Care* (Lexington, KY: Emeth Press, 2007), where he charts emotional and psychological well-being around "input" and "output". So whence do these children draw emotional nourishment, if their parent or parents are ill-tuned to their needs?

Through observation I began to see that beneath the obvious struggles for help, attention, approval and companionship, there was what might be called an underlying or residual vein or stratum of understanding and care. When another sibling was in a genuinely distressing situation then a child would at times lay aside his or her needs and priorities and become, however temporarily and partially, a care-giver. I mentioned this to someone who knows the children in question rather well and she was surprised, to say the least. Her view until that point was that they were the ones who needed help and were largely incapable of offering it. And I agreed with her that this was how I had framed things until I saw resilience in action.

Where there has been empathy in a family, however irregularly, does such a child draw and learn from it? Does this become reinforced by experiences with extended family, teachers and friends? Is there perhaps a collective unconscious as proposed by Carl Jung, I wonder? I honestly don't know, but the remarkably encouraging truth is that I have witnessed resilience in practice, not only in those relatively near to hand, but in children in different parts of the world, sometimes called "street children". I am not claiming that they are consistently and maturely caring, but that deep down they are able to feel the distress of another and respond with a measure of appropriateness.

As for the implications of this? I guess that it would do us all well to be alert to these positive instances and dynamics and to support and encourage them when we can. And to try to see children in the context of systems (family/ peer/school) rather than as discrete and labelled individuals. And, perhaps most important, to feed models and examples of attuned behaviour into their lives. If I am on the right lines at all, resilient children have an uncanny way of recognising and drawing from the slightest of positive emotional experiences.

I leave you with the picture that has been in my mind from the start of this piece. A little girl with untidy, dishevelled hair is sitting holding her baby sister who has been crying. She holds her tightly enough so that she is safe, seeking to comfort her in the best way she knows. She is not doing it to display virtue or to gain attention, but simply as a human response to a need that only she seems to have noticed. If you knew her background, you would be as moved as I was. All I have been trying to do is to begin to fathom how and why this act of tenderness and love might have been possible.

Who Remembers "Person-centred Casework" Nowadays?

In Section Four, called Community, there is a piece "The Wheel Comes Full Circle", which is a companion to this article.

Ruth and I were in the very same local church where the funeral of the mother of four children we had cared for at Mill Grove, that I wrote about, took place. And we were sitting beside one of the four, her partner and their three young children.

Over refreshments one of those present introduced himself to me as the secondary school teacher who was instrumental in putting the family in touch with us in the first place, over 40 years ago. He told me that the oldest of the four children had come to him during school time, pleading with him to visit the family's council house to see for himself how bad conditions were and how serious was the plight of the children.

This was in the years before safeguarding guidelines and "Working Together", so the teacher (now retired) was open with me that he was not sure how to react, and whether it was within his brief. Be that as it may he went to visit the family home that afternoon. He has never forgotten what he saw. Through his intervention I was to experience the place for myself just a few days later, and so I can vouch for his horrified reaction. He described it as something like a war zone, so bad were the living conditions. The parents seemed to have given all hope. It was obvious that something needed to be done.

He contacted a social worker and recommended that she contact us, because we were a local voluntary organisation that had a long history of caring for children and young people (that dates the intervention!), and we worked alongside the local Director of Social Services and Department (whom we knew well) to decide how best to respond. It was sadly not difficult to know that the children needed to be removed from that squalid house and the depressing social and emotional dynamics.

We cared for the four children until they moved on in their own respective careers and into their own accommodation, and have kept in touch with each one, their mother and, in due course, their children. A few years ago, one of the four children came back to live with us at Mill Grove, bringing her mother, her partner and her first child with her. We always remain committed to each child who has come to live with us, so in a way this was no surprise. But what was quite remarkable was the fact that the teacher had kept in touch with the pupil who had asked for help right up to the present day.

Over a cup of tea and sandwich he scrolled down his recent emails on his smartphone, and said he wanted me to read a paragraph of what his former pupil had just written. I was reluctant because it is not my habit to read other people's personal emails, but he said I would understand when I had read it. When I did so, I was frankly flabbergasted. Despite all the intervening years, the pupil had written to him as "Dear Sir", and the paragraph in question was one of heartfelt thanks. He thanked his teacher for taking him seriously and responding to his desperate cry for help, and then went on to describe Mill Grove. It had been the very best setting that could have been found for him and his three siblings. It was a place of welcome, of security, and where they experienced care, love, encouragement and nurture. What's more it had been there for each of them when they needed it later in life.

It was of course gratifying to read something about Mill Grove that was written to someone else: something that would hardly be appropriate to say to us, because we had become so close to the family over the decades. But something else struck me: the email was overwhelmingly reassuring and comforting for the former teacher. It is no small thing to intervene in the life of a family, and to set in train such a serious sequence of events that resulted in the removal of four children from their family house. But here, 40 years later was confirmation that he had chosen the right course.

He had no idea that any of the family would be present on this occasion at the church. But on hearing that one of the siblings (and her family) was there, he made a bee-line for her, and introduced himself as the teacher who came to her house when she was very young. And he was the reason that she and they had come to Mill Grove. She didn't know him, but had heard from her brother about him, and was able to explain that Mill Grove had been there for her many years later when she and her fledgling family needed help again.

So it was that the wheel had continued to roll, and another generation had come to experience life at Mill Grove.

This year Mill Grove reaches the 120th anniversary of its founding (in November 1899), and there have been roughly 1,200 children who have lived with us since then. Each one came to us through the intervention of one of more people, and often we do not know who or how it happened, but what a blessing all round when there is a reminder of the day it all started, how and why. And when the story is continuing exactly as the brother, who bravely blew the whistle, described to his former teacher!

There is something to consider carefully in the long-term memory and commitment of both the teacher and the place to which he pointed the children. These children, starting with the pupil, obviously meant a great deal to the teacher, so how reassuring for the now grown-up pupil to know he was still remembered by "Sir" as well as by the family of Mill Grove. I am not sure there is a lot of likelihood that children are being held in the healthy minds of their teachers and carers for decades. Is this an example of a bygone era, or is there the chance that person-centred casework and its like may be rediscovered?

The Truth of the Matter

The London Borough of Redbridge has joined a select group of local authorities in the UK that is working in partnership with UNICEF with a shared commitment to make their communities "Child-Friendly". This is something for which voluntary children's organisations in this borough have been campaigning for 15 years or more. Whatever the outcomes it is surely a good thing.

It was on a very well-run training and awareness day by a member of the UNICEF staff that one or two deep-seated queries began to surface in my mind. We were informed that the basis of the initiative was the concept of children's rights, specifically the 1989 United Nations Convention on the Rights of the Child. For some reason I have always been uncomfortable with, and wary of, the notion of "rights". And the current Covid 19 pandemic has served to confirm the substance of some of my fears.

For the period of the pandemic, work

towards becoming a more child-friendly borough was suspended, and for several weeks most children were able to go to school or play outside in parks with their friends. They were confined to households that in some cases are unhappy and, in others, downright dysfunctional. You can add to the list from your own knowledge and experience.

This, you may say, comes as no surprise. The global health crisis necessitates such restrictions. But what, I wonder, has happened in the process to the rights of children? I am not sure how many have been infringed. Has someone been monitoring the situation? Presumably they are in cold storage, ready for reinstating when the crisis is over. If so, in what sense are they still rights? What substance, status, or leverage do they have?

Now I hope you will agree that this is neither a trivial nor a fleeting matter. Worldwide there are millions of children chronically deprived of their rights as guaranteed by signatories to the UNCRC. When famine, disease, war, migration and much more come to dominate the life of their community, nation or region, their rights are denied. There is no legislation that is introduced to do this: it simply happens without notice, and usually without mention. This is the truth of the matter. And on a massive scale.

According to Eurochild's April roundup (info@eurochild.org), 60% of all children worldwide are now living in countries with either partial or full lockdowns (information provided to Eurochild by the United Nations). Many face challenges of social connection, stress, abuse, neglect, domestic violence and trauma. And all of this is exacerbated for those children living in poor households where they have disabilities or act as carers for others. Specifically, in relation to education, Eurochild has joined with the European Public Health Alliance, calling for governments to ensure that children from vulnerable groups are not left with lower educational opportunities.

Yet there are still those countries, organisations and people who speak of rights as if they are in some sense solid, real, inviolable. They were presented as such during the recent training session. And this is a characteristic of our age. It is possible that future historians could identify the period in which we are living as one framed largely by the rights discourse.

Which brings me back to children and child-friendliness. It is a comfort to think and speak as if rights were indeed non-negotiable and therefore solid. But we all know that there are times and places where they are demonstrably not. Would they not therefore be better described as aspirations or even dreams?

So what? My point is that many children and young people know that rights are not being respected in their own lives and communities. This means that they have to live with the contradictions between the world as it is portrayed in the UNCRC, on the one hand, and the ugly and often brutal reality of their daily lives and situations, on the other.

Of course, it could be that rights make adults, particularly professionals who care about them, feel better, but that they risk making things worse for children.

The Covid 19 pandemic has been a new, and in some ways perhaps a unique, period in world history because for once we are all aware of a common issue. And it is something that has come upon us, taking us unaware, and in the process has threatened treasured and hallowed aspects of personal and social life. In more wealthy countries this comes as a shock. But for the rest of the world, it is but another variation on the same old theme. And that theme is the contingency of human life and existence that threatens, and sometimes mocks our aspirations, desires and dreams.

When I was a little boy there were times when I was afraid of the dark. And I really do mean afraid. There were one or two places which terrified me. What, I wonder, was that about? It is worth pondering because my experience of listening to children suggests this is a common phenomenon. I can suggest elements that might go to make up the scale and intensity of the fear, including the terrifying possibility that a violent stranger might be lurking in the shadows. Knowing some novels by Dickens did not help particularly!

But my growing intuition is that deep down

there is a universal fear of a void, of death. This is not a particularly original idea as a passing knowledge of say, Pascal's *Pensées*, and Freudian psychoanalysis would testify. But it is worth holding on to.

The truth of the matter is that all human beings are mortal, and there comes a time in a child's life when she knows that she will die. Life is not assured: it is contingent.

And Covid 19 is an eloquent reminder of this. We are all in it. And for those children in refugee camps and war-torn cities, hungry and anxious, bereft of any comfort that can be offered with assurance or conviction, this is the simple, bedrock reality of things. Nearly all the nations on earth have vowed to respect children's rights. But none of them have it in their power to guarantee them.

So while welcoming the progress that the UNCRC represents, and the significance of rights as markers and indications of what is valued, we do well to be humble and cautious in what we say to children. Promises could resemble those that turn out to be unfulfilled on bank notes not backed-up by sufficient reserves of gold.

In another article in *TTCJ* I wrote about fairy stories. Since then I have continued to muse on the importance of stories for children. And it seems to me that good and realistic stories offer more of substance to many, if not all children, than the all too easy promise of rights.

The stories will deal with the reality of life: unfairness, loss, bereavement, mistreatment, double-crossing, poverty, hunger and death. But in the process, they offer hope that is consonant with a child's experience. That hope is not about easy maxims or solutions like the promise of a child-friendly world. But it will encourage children to dream of one.

One such story that has moved me for decades is from *West Side Story*. It provided me with the title of the book, *A Place for Us*. And the way this happened is instructive. I had written the bulk of the text but was struggling (as I usually do) with a title. I shared this problem with the children at Mill Grove. One of them responded that she didn't have a title, but she did have a tune. This didn't sound very promising, until she began to sing, "Somewhere", with its opening words, "There's a place for us". I knew that this was exactly right for the book.

But it also took me closer to her own sad life experiences. She had suffered the loss of both her parents and had not been able to come to terms with the separation and grief this was causing her. There was nothing to offer her by way of rights, but this song, a childlike dream, offered hope. She is now a grandmother, who still struggles with her memories and anxiety, but I know she has not given up on the dream. That's the truth of the matter for her, as I understand it.

A Little Child Will Lead Them

Years ago, someone made a gift to Mill Grove with the intention that we should buy some pictures for the newly refurbished building. The children and young people were keen to be involved in the selection, and because it was in the years before the internet, I obtained some catalogues from a local art shop. We then arranged a system of multiple-choice voting in which everyone could rank pictures. The process itself was interesting, and offhand I can only recall one other time when we had a form of voting. This was when the local confectionary producer, Trebor, asked us to test out a new range of toffees. While this delightful test was proceeding, I thought it would be interesting to see how far my palette and preferences matched theirs. I discovered that there was no overlap at all: I was looking for flavour, and they were attracted to texture: the nearer to bubblegum the better, irrespective of taste.

So, back to the pictures: I was prepared for surprises but had never entertained the unanimous first choice of the young people. It was a painting called *The Peaceable Kingdom*, not the famous one by Edward Hicks, but a variation on the theme based on Isaiah's prophecy that a new era and completely harmonious way of living in which the whole of creation was at peace was coming, and that a little child would be leading the process. The picture still hangs on the wall in our dining room, while others, including some that I thought might be chosen, are mounted elsewhere in the building. (In case you are interested, they include depictions of sailing, trees, and possibly Macbeth, an elephant by Peter Scott, and a Lowrie ....)

Knowing that this picture had proved so attractive to a former generation, I have returned to it as a subject for discussion from time to time since. And its theme always proves to be deeply interesting and significant to children of all ages. Now, of course, it chimes with a major shift in consciousness as Greta Thunberg, recently turned 18, has become a household name. When thinking of planet Earth, climate change and the threat of the extinction of the human race, it has been a child and children who have taken the lead. Adults and adult institutions such as governments, companies, organisations, and even educational establishments are caught up in the status quo with short term considerations such as the next election, the bottom line for the next quarter, turnover and expansion, Ofsted inspections and exam results, respectively.

But the future of the world or, more precisely, the human species on it, requires a completely different perspective and approach. It needs to be guided by long term thinking and planning: the next generation, children's children. There must be blue-sky thinking, dreaming of alternative ways of doing things, visions of a new way of living. And children are equipped with the natural capacity to do this: their neural networks are plastic, potentially able to connect with an infinite amount of data, and to process it in creative and imaginative ways. What's more, as they grow up, they become aware that, whereas teachers, parents and grandparents might just pass away before life as we know it becomes impossible, they will probably be around to experience it.

The reflections of children on the picture, and our discussions, led me to write in a book called *Through the Eyes of a Child*, in 2009 (when

Great Thunberg was about seven): "The combination of increasing global awareness and a sense of the unfolding agency of children and young people may create an environment in which we see children increasingly lead (take care of) the process of caring for planet Earth. In this way the prophecy of Isaiah 11 may find some practical expression in our own times ... if adult priorities continue to be dominated by short-term parochialism, tribalism and warfare/defence, then it may be that children will be the ones show challenge these priorities with those of their own." (*Through the eyes of a Child*, eds. Anne Richards and Peter Privett, 2009, 63)

Institutions and groups that are thinking therapeutically have been drawn to the natural world in all sorts of ways as part of the therapeutic process, and perhaps there should be more reflection on examples of this. Has someone done research in this area to date, I wonder? A brief scan of the history of Mill Grove since 1899 reveals all sorts of interactions with nature and the seasons from the Hollow Ponds, Whipps Cross Lido, and Epping Forest locally; the fruit trees in Tiptree and the River Blackwater at Maldon; the hills and lakes of Snowdonia, to the rivers in Holland and the Alps in Switzerland. It would be genuinely interesting to hear the stories of other residential communities.

But there is another point that I would like to explore before concluding this piece. It is to do with the process, or dynamics, of learning and therapeutic development. Integral to all understandings of how adults can help children cope with traumas, deal with loss, anger, anxiety and the threat of the void, is the principle that it is the children who lead, who guide and teach us. However much we need to help and guide the process, we have to go at their pace, to be attuned to their emotions and feelings, to have empathy for their situation, and to imagine how it feels to be in their shoes. This is not about authority or status; it's not guided by a romantic notion of childhood that with Wordsworth sees children "trailing clouds of glory" and therefore to be admired and placed above contradiction. It is not about children's rights and some legal-political discourse. It is about how adults relate to children who are respected as such and allowed to be children, not "adults-in-waiting".

It seems to me that the concept, A Little Child Will Lead Them, is one that deserves constant, and perhaps renewed, attention. I am not sure that the children for whom I care are aware of it, and perhaps it is appropriate that they are not, but over the years I have been increasingly guided by them: their reactions, their thoughts, their fantasies, their play. Which reminds me of a time recently when my dear friend Simon Rodway was recounting memories of Donald Winnicott. He spoke of one occasion when Winnicott did nothing but get down on the floor and play with a child. That's pretty much it. I doubt if the child realised the half of what Winnicott was picking up and learning, and how he was seeking to help, but we can be sure that this wise and sensitive psychiatrist was allowing the child to lead.

A Day to Remember

I am writing this piece primarily because I never want to forget some of the things that happened on Friday 4th June 2021 at Mill Grove.

It had already been a memorable week, because the day before one of the children who comes regularly for physiotherapy took his first steps unaided. I had been passing by the room where this momentous event was taking place in the company of someone who had lived here decades ago as a little boy. He had come back because he wanted to look around the place where he spent some of his early years. His medical prognosis was not good, and as we were sharing quite deeply, this seemingly chance encounter proved to be an unforgettable experience for him. I know this because he rang to tell me this morning!

But already I digress. Friday began with my fifth session teaching Asian graduates online. The class was made up of students from Myanmar, Japan, Vietnam, Singapore and the Philippines. I have been doing this sort of thing, though face to face, for over 20 years, and this cross-cultural perspective with all that I learn from the students is one of the unexpected blessings of my life at Mill Grove.

I then did some preparation for a sermon to be preached in Cambridge on Sunday, based on Psalm 63, before a scheduled meeting with one of the members of the extended Mill Grove family living in Colorado. He would like to make a documentary about the story of Mill Grove based on interviews with those who lived here as children. Not long before the meeting he had to call it off …

Then Ruth contacted me to let me know that another member of the Mill Grove family had arrived from Swansea with his wife and two daughters, and that another daughter of his, who is currently living with us, had welcomed them and they wanted me to join the party. This was roughly the same time as a planned birthday celebration for another member of the Mill Grove family who is paraplegic. To add to the mix, yet another member of the family who had come back to live with us after a gap of 16 years was hoping to join a meal with us. So it was that, within a short time, rather than being involved in a Zoom discussion of a film production and script, I was in the thick of things, face to face. And this is pretty much how it has been, with variations on the theme, since Ruth and I became responsible for the leadership of Mill Grove in the 1980s.

The youngest daughter of Danuj (as I will call him) greeted me with a very warm hug, and this was an unexpected start because I was still getting used to the latest relaxation in Covid guidelines. I think at that time the Prime Minister had been attributed with saying that we should hug responsibly (comedians could work through the hours of the night without coming up with a line as amusing as that). Anyway, that's what happened, and I was assured by those present that she was right. I'm not sure why, but somehow the spontaneous conversation turned towards the story of how Danuj and his two brothers – a twin, and one who was younger – came to live at Mill Grove in 1980 when they were still young, having recently been flown from Nigeria by their father and without being able to speak English.

His oldest daughter (if you are following this, the one living at Mill Grove as an adult, and who works as a teaching assistant in a local borough) said that she knew little or nothing of this part of her family history. And very soon the discussion gained momentum. Ruth found a couple of photo albums and before long we found ourselves back in time and reminiscing. We recalled the arrival of her dad and his brothers, their first meal with us, their partiality for sugar. And then, with sadness, their bewilderment about who we were, and why they had been entrusted to our care. Having been abandoned on arrival in the UK, a social services department took them into care, and then tried to find somewhere suitable for them. We had a couple living with us at the time who were on furlough from Nigeria, hence there was at least a little connection.

We told of the one time that the boys' father (her grandfather) flew over to England and came to Mill Grove to visit his sons. Danuj and I recounted some of the challenges of that encounter and the conversation in which his father wanted to draw a line under the past and plan the future, while the boys had told me how angry and bitter they were. They had wanted me to tell him exactly what they felt. Some months later we were able to find a housing association flat for the three of them near Mile End station. And as they became more independent, Danuj had a partner and in due course his first daughter (still listening intently to the unfolding story?) was born. When he was separated from his partner, her mother, she used to come on Saturdays to meet him at Mill Grove. She recounted how those were days she looked forward to eagerly, and which she always enjoyed. We said that we loved it when she arrived, and how pleased we were that she could see her dad while with us.

There was lots more of the story emerging, and you will recall that all this was happening when one of the extended family was hoping to have a birthday meal, and another was wanting to join in, as she used to all those years ago as a girl living at Mill Grove. As they listened, they both understood because they knew all the people involved, and as members of the Mill Grove family this is the sort of thing that sometimes happens.

There were two revelatory moments in the narrative. The first was for the family of Danuj when they heard of how Ruth's parents and brother had died in a car crash on their way to our house in 1985. It so happened that her late brother had included Danuj and his brothers in his will (I am of course recounting the sober truth however unlikely it might seem). Because the three family members died together at the same time by a convention that goes back, I am told, to Roman law, the three brothers were treated as members of Ruth's family and co-inheritors of her parents' estate. So it was that we had effectively adopted three Yoruba Nigerians into our family. And that was one of the reasons why we were so close.

The second concerned the death of Danuj's twin brother. It was a tragic and heartrending end to the life of someone so full of joy, of fun and swings of emotion. Danuj's oldest daughter shared how she witnessed her father weeping with grief. She had never seen him cry or even show emotion before. It had naturally affected her greatly. And this was when I shared that during their early years with us at Mill Grove, as they tried to come to terms with the loss of their kith and kin in Nigeria, Danuj's brother had sometimes wailed for hours, head in his hands, on, and sometimes under, his bed, while Danuj always remained in the same room but without showing any sign of emotion.

When I had asked him whether he did feel emotion he commented that he did, but that because his brother expressed it, there was no need for him to do so. How would it help the situation? And how appropriate would it be? I had never forgotten his words, as you can see all these years later. But now I realised the awful truth of that moment during the funeral. Now he was separated again from a brother from whom had he never been parted before, and not only had he lost his brother, but he was without the one who always expressed how he himself felt. This double loss helped to explain his desperate sadness.

It sounds bizarre, but around this point in the story we adjourned for lunch and a socially distanced birthday meal, cake and candles. There was another album of photos found by Ruth and after we had sung Happy Birthday, there was a group eagerly looking at the photos over Danuj's shoulder.

Meanwhile, in case you were wondering, the lady who had been sitting beside me during the meal, the one who had come to Mill Grove as a little girl and had then returned after 16 years to come and live with us again, spoke with me. Yes, there were one or two new things she had heard, but none of it was a surprise. It all made sense because she knew each of the people involved and this was true to what she knew of their story and their characters. She spoke as one who knew more than I would ever want to about the savage emotional effects of separation and loss. In some ways it all seemed natural to her: a birthday party at the meal when we were welcoming her back home, and alongside these two events a family discovering more of their story together in the lounge and dining room at Mill Grove.

Which made me realise that the furniture and walls in these two rooms had heard conversations of this sort again and again over the years. This line of thoughts was interrupted when the daughter of the mother whose birthday we were celebrating rang through to wish her a happy birthday and to catch up with Ruth and myself.

Before completing this piece, I looked at my diary to see how the day ended, but it was already full by this time, and so I have forgotten! I do recall that we said goodbye to Danuj and his family and wondered if they might join us in North Wales during the summer, we said goodnight to his oldest daughter and the person who had just come back to live with us. And bade farewell to the birthday mother. And I remember tidying the rooms, washing up, and seeing Ruth put the albums away.

This is the place where I was born, where I grew up as a child, and where for over 40 years Ruth and I have been at the heart of the community living at Mill Grove and the focal point of the extended family. In some ways this day was typical of many, but on the other hand every day is as unique, as each one who has lived here since 1899: that's over 1,200. What a privilege to be present when such stories are being told and retold; and when healing, psychological and emotional, is taking place at its own pace, sometimes over years, spanning decades and generations. Perhaps such a day is the best indication of what the place is all about. Whether that is so or not, I am so blessed to have been a part of, and able to witness to it.

What readers will make of this note of a day in our lives I am not sure, but it's great to have it on record!

The Father's Day
It All Came Together

For those separated from parents, annual events such as Mothering Sunday or Father's Day can be troubling, even cruel occasions. I recall the time in Cambridge when a daughter shared with me the dilemma posed by a Mother's Day card. She regularly sent birthday and Christmas cards to the mother who had abandoned her to the care system, so what was the problem, I wondered? Just this she ventured: "I cannot write 'mum' or 'mother' on it", she said wistfully, "and so I don't send one". The penny dropped immediately.

Now years later just after Father's Day 2021 I was shown a card received by someone who grew up at Mill Grove at the same time as me. He was not only happy, but radiantly so. Before explaining why, let me pass on a little of his background. I will call him Doug. His own father had separated from his mother, and as a result he, his brother and a younger sister came to live at Mill Grove. The father kept in touch regularly, but the loss of kith and kin had been painful. One of the effects he subsequently realised was that he had very little memory of his childhood.

He went into the forces after leaving Mill Grove and subsequently struggled with marriage and parenthood: he often reflected that he was short of role models for ordinary family life. A daughter died tragically while still young, and his son had a child with a very young partner, before separating and fighting a long term battle with anxiety, depression and substance dependency. The mother of Doug's grandchild moved away with her child, but Doug remained in touch. He remembered his grandson's birthdays and each Christmas without fail. I knew that he held his growing grandson in his mind through thick and thin. He used to visit regularly, every three months or so, despite the distance of between 150 and 200 miles.

The grandson was diagnosed as being on the autistic spectrum and required special schooling while supervised by the local social services. He loved it when grandpa arrived, and they did things together: predictable things. Grandpa Doug would always bring another cuddly toy to add to his collection; they would go out to the park, and sometimes to the cinema or on a local trip. That is, until Covid 19 arrived in the Spring of 2020. Then everything was done by post, and Doug wondered whether his grandson would still remember him. He kept in touch with him and his mother, also with social services, assuring them that he would always be there to support his grandchild.

Then just around Father's Day 2021 he finally had the chance to visit again. He travelled by train and was overjoyed that his grandson came running to him as he had always done before when he visited. They went to the park with the latest cuddly toy and enjoyed their time together. And then came the big surprise when the grandson handed Grandpa Doug a Father's Day card that he had made himself. It had a picture of a train on the front

with one person visible through the carriage windows, and inside there was some handwriting: "I like it when you come. Come again!" When I was shown this precious item Doug's face was aglow with pleasure. He told me how thrilled he was, how much it meant to him, and how he would keep it forever.

What was this all about, I wonder? Clearly there was the bond and attachment between grandfather and his grandson represented by this unique gift and message. But the reason for Doug's joy went way deeper than this. He had feared his grandson might be unable to express any such emotions; and that he might disappear into the care system without trace. That history would be repeating itself: a cycle of deprivation. His own relationship with parents had foundered; his marriage and family life has been disrupted. But now here was a sign that such a process was not inevitable. It was possible to break the vicious circle.

And he had done it, by his faithful, steady, love, care and contact. However difficult the grandson found it to express his feelings, it was obvious to me that Grandpa Doug meant the world to him, and always would do. And now the message had got through. Doug had done it. He was not a serial failure.

What's more after years, two decades of trying in fact, his relationship with his own son (that is his grandson's father) had begun to develop in such a way that they could both express for the first time how much they meant to each other, without fear that everything would break down again, as it had again and again since the earliest days.

My role in this had been as a mentor, encourager, surrogate brother, which is why the card had been shown to me with such pride. As it happens one of the ways in which we have worked together is by Doug preparing written communications with his son, grandson and social services that he shares with me before sending them. Over the years these have become sensitive and practical. In an age of apps and instant social media the place of letters and cards seems to have become redundant for many. But this card showed it was not over by any means. A chance to think again, to sleep on things, and to put into words and a picture important thoughts and feelings.

Often in my columns I explore psychological and emotional healing over the generations, with time, as it were, working backwards. Although it was not verbalised, I sensed that in the interaction between Grandpa Doug and his grandson, Doug was not just the older person in their relationship. He was in some respects reliving his life through his grandson. Perhaps in their play together he was able to let go (regress). And just for the record, his memory of these times together is completely intact. It is as if the deep-seated need to freeze emotions for fear of another trauma and loss has started to be lessened.

Returning to the Place Where We Started

For a combination of reasons there has been an increasing stream of requests from those who lived at Mill Grove as children, to know more about their stories and to see what records and photos there are. It would be interesting to know from colleagues whether any such trend is apparent elsewhere. The three factors that may be relevant in our case in addition to any effects of the new normal ways of living, engendered by the Covid pandemic, are the wedding anniversary last year that several members of the extended family attended and communications between former residents within a Facebook group.

Let me share a few of the issues, dilemmas and feelings that arose in three of these recent contacts and visits. The first relates to someone I will call Patton. He was one of four siblings who had the same mother but at least three different fathers. He came having been at the wedding anniversary, prompted by the wish of his daughter to know more about her family and origins. As we went through the records together it became painfully obvious to both of us that there was nothing more than a single sentence note to the effect that his father had died in a car crash before Patton was born. He had known that from childhood, but there was always the hope that there might be another scrap of information, a clue that would help his search for his father's story. He still does not even know his father's name or his date and place of birth.

He told me that when he had asked his mother about his father, she had erupted and warned him never to mention his father again. From that time on therefore, most avenues remained closed. The two of us sat in silence, looking at some school reports and photos. But these records of his life were insignificant compared to his all-consuming desire to know about his origins. I realised for the first time just how isolated and lonely he felt at heart, even among his siblings. They at least knew something about their respective fathers that they could share with their offspring as and when appropriate.

After a while we began to muse over how he might share the result of his search with his daughter. This is when I wondered whether there was any way in which Mill Grove might be one of the fixed and reliable reference points, a coordinate perhaps, in her life. If we could glean nothing more about origins, would it help in any way to see if something could be built using what he and I (and his siblings and contemporaries) knew of each other, shared times, people, experiences and places? Perhaps the houses in North Wales might be a resource when he and she were looking ahead. (Since Patton was with me that evening, I have seen the film, *The Windermere Children*, and reflected in *TTCJ* on the importance of that place and shared experience to those who lived there, and it may be of relevance.) What I do know is that as tears welled up in his eyes, silent testimonies of his seemingly absolute aloneness, I think I experienced the awful reality of the void more vividly and frighteningly than ever before. I felt close because at that moment space no longer had any relevance.

The second person, who I will call Sutton, is happily married and looking forward to his

50th wedding anniversary as I write this. He does know about his birth family, though his memories of childhood in his family household are fraught with ambivalence. In some of the letters from his mother he learned more about why he came to Mill Grove, why he left, and more of the context of his time spent living at Mill Grove. In his case, it was his school reports that were the most challenging part of the written material. He is intelligent and has been a successful accountant. So it came as a heavy blow to discover that he was invariably near the bottom of the class and poor at most subjects, including maths. I suggested that he probably had far more important matters on his mind at the time than grammar and arithmetic. He has subsequently written to me with his feelings and reflections. I was pleased that his wife was with him right through the process. He was not alone.

I will call the third person Martha. She came with her husband and was trying to understand more about her life and experiences as a child. Her identity and self-esteem had been completely undermined throughout her childhood by a mother struggling with mental health issues. She was unclear about who her father was. And after leaving us and returning home, she had gone on to live in Local Authority care. She had recently received all her files and case notes in a single bundle. This experience had traumatised her so much that she had called her psychotherapist asking for emergency help.

For this reason, as we handed over the records that we had, we tried to prepare the way for what she and her husband would find, and some of the issues that might arise. One of the reasons she came over to Mill Grove was to see her bedroom and to look around the place where there were some happy memories of her childhood. In time she hopes to bring her two children to see us. Her visit was part of a long-term strategy.

These three examples of those who have lived in care, returning to find out more through their records, reveal the complexities of the issues involved, and the sensitivity required to assist and support them, in the process. It is not easy to describe what these personal records represent in the first place. In whatever way the records may labelled or categorised by a professional or an observer, they are very close to being part, not only of the person's story, but even part of them. There are examples in history of how to know or possess the name of a person, a replica or photo of them is deemed to be somehow in a position of influence or control. The roots of this are in an understanding of how representations somehow embody the person themselves.

Putting that on one side, it was evident to me that something exceptionally personal and significant was going on. The relationship between the person and fragments of their life-story is potentially very close. They were holding a precious possession. And in each case, I had to draw deeply from experience and the knowledge gained from others to get my bearings and try to work out my part in the facilitation of what was going on. Rarely have I felt so ill-equipped and vulnerable.

Integral to the process in these three examples was the fact that we were reading about how Mill Grove had been involved in the young person's life: and that is a sobering thought. Some of the frailties and vicissitudes of the practice of my predecessors in the first two cases, and in the third case, Ruth and myself, were recorded in what was being handed over. That's a cause for anxiety, if ever there was!

But it was not this that presented the challenge so much as how to respond appropriately. It was not like a conversation with memories and thoughts being shared and exchanged. The records were more like a rugged and unpredictably shaped rock that we were confronted with and were sometimes stumbling over. How to pick ourselves up, and to navigate a way together, or possibly separately? And who else should be involved, if anyone?

At the very least, I hope that this reflection will deter organisations, including local authorities, from simply sending bundles of personal records to a person who has lived in care. But then it occurs to me that at least here at Mill Grove there is a consistency of person and continuity of memory. So who would be the best person to act in the role that I had been taking in other organisations, I wonder?

I really would value the wisdom and insights of others. Not least because each of these people were with me, I have not seen one of them yet. So I am bound to wonder what might be going on, conscious that it is distinctly possible that I could have handled things better.

(This article is an extended version of the piece that first appeared in *TTCJ*.)

Children as a Gift

Usually when I write a column for *TTCJ* based on a specific incident, conversation or occasion, I seek to get to work on it immediately to ensure that no details are forgotten. But in this case, I have waited almost a week to ponder what happened and make sense of the turning points in the dynamics. The title of the piece is the result of that period of reflection.

The occasion was the visit to Mill Grove of two families, both of whom were grieving the death of a child. We were in the sunniest room in our house which for nearly 30 years has been the place where children with cerebral palsy and associated conditions have come for regular sessions. This part of the life of Mill Grove is known as the Rose Walton Centre, and is run by a dedicated team using the Peto method of Conductive Education.

One of the features of cerebral palsy is that it commonly curtails life expectancy, and so over the years we have been alongside families mourning the loss of children and teenagers. In the case of these two families, the boys who died were both young and, astonishingly, both had died from an identical and very rare genetic condition. The first, who I will call John, died over a year ago; the second, Ethan, died just a few weeks ago. Although the parents had been in touch with each other over this period, not least when they realised the highly unusual medical condition that connected the two boys, this was their first visit to the place where they had come so often with their children.

It was a big step because there were so many happy memories associated with the Rose Walton Centre and its team. They knew that the visit would irritate raw emotional wounds, triggered by any number of associations and relationships. So although they were at different stages of their grief, the challenge of coming back was something they had in common last Saturday afternoon.

Ethan's mother came with her youngest child, and he enjoyed the opportunity to play and eat as much as he liked over a period of four hours: yes, it turned out to be a shared experience that lasted that long. John's mother and father arrived an hour later, and they brought John's older brother. He came armed with a football and spent much of his time practising on the five-a-side pitch outside.

There was intentionally no agenda or plan. Some chairs were set out in a circle around a table laid out with a finger buffet. It was a time to be together, that allowed feelings to emerge and be shared as and when appropriate. There was no shortage of clips of both boys taken during sessions at the Centre, and these were shared. Touchingly, several showed them lying side by side, smiling and with arms linked. As conversation ebbed and flowed along with tears and smiles, one of the emerging reflections was a shared acknowledgement that it was highly possible, in fact, likely, that in their togetherness John and Ethan shared much more with each other than anyone else will ever know.

The assumption that words are required to understand and respond to deep feelings had been dispelled early by years of living with and being alongside children with cerebral palsy. All the adults described how they had needed to unlearn many such assumptions, and to adjust their focus and attention to take in the many rich messages that were being passed on by other means. It probably doesn't need to be said that likewise all had discovered that the inability to speak was no reflection of a child's awareness, ability, empathy, imagination or intelligence.

Ethan's mother was often in tears and regularly used the tissues to hand. She asked how others had come to terms with their loss and grief. Several times she described in detail the stages in the death and burial of her little son. One of her realisations was that she and her husband had been processing their feelings in quite different ways. As she did so one of her refrains was that the Centre was "family". She realised this was why she knew she had to come back, although it was so hard. Having had to say a final farewell following the death of her child, she recalled the regular farewells at Mill Grove. She commented that she would never have left her boy had she been in anyway concerned that he would be anxious or unhappy. She came to have complete confidence in the team and gave them a thank you gift: a little plaque reminding them of the difference that they had made in Ethan's life.

At this point there was a moving conversation between the two mothers. Each described how the nature of their child's condition meant that holding and letting go their sons was imbued with completely different significance to that of holding their other children. From the time their sons were in their wombs, and they had held them at their breasts, to their dying days, they had held them more carefully, often and closely, than anyone else. And because of their condition, this holding was one of the primary ways in which feelings were expressed and communicated. This meant that the final letting go, the literal releasing their hold of their children for the last time, was unbearably poignant. It helped to explain why coming back to a place where they had released them into the care of others whom they trusted was so full of emotion.

There was much, much more that was shared, by words, tears, smiles, touch and hugs. But on reflection, the factor that seemed to me to have made all the difference to the parents was the realisation that their child was a gift. Both sets of parents had at least one other child, and John's mother was pregnant and expecting another baby in a matter of weeks. What they had come to see through being the parents of children with cerebral palsy, knowing that their life expectancy was short, was something usually hidden from parents. They confessed that they would never have seen it themselves except for the remarkable effects of welcoming and receiving such children into their homes, hearts and lives, and adapting everything to show them their care and love.

The father of John put it like this. Until John was born, he saw himself primarily as the provider in the family. He ensured that there was a good home, that his wife and family were secure. The arrival of John changed things fundamentally. In time, he developed a closer relationship with John as a father than he could ever have envisaged. This in turn changed him as a person, his fundamental perspectives on and values in life. He went on to say that his relationship with his wife had been enriched. She had given up her career to care for John. He was clear and unapologetic that John had been the catalyst for something resembling a revolution or conversion in his whole way of living.

What was at the heart of this? It was the dawning awareness that a child was not something to be expected by parents as of right, not a sign of future security and prosperity, not the source of pride on account of progress and achievements. Rather a child was a gift. And an infinitely precious gift, entrusted to parents who were to be stewards of that gift for as long as the child was given to them.

All three parents were in complete, joyful agreement about this. They had come to realise that they had been blessed immeasurably through the gift of John and Ethan respectively. Preconceptions and assumptions had been stripped away. There were precious achievements in their children, often hidden to others, but they did not remotely measure things by development and achievement, so much as by the joy of seeing and knowing that their children were content and enjoying life. And that their presence, not least expressed through their touch and smiles, were priceless treasures. They spoke as if they had discovered what seemed like the pearl of great price.

One of the effects for me and for the team was their help and encouragement in seeing this. Whether as parents or carers, it is all too easy to lose sight of the truth that each child is a gift. That we have no right to assume the length of a life, or the steps or levels of achievement that will be made. In the present, in the fleeting moment, life is to be lived to the full. And where that is so, though sadness and regrets linger, because there is never "closure" of loss and grief, the blessings are such that the future is enhanced. It will not be a case of nostalgia and constant looking back in grief, but of expressing the joy of the discovery that their child was a gift, that brought light and life to the future. And this discovery is transferable: all human life is a gift, so all future relationships are potentially enriched.

The presence of one of the team endorsed this. She was the grandmother of Anthony, the first child at the Centre, and having cared for him until his death aged 17, she has since devoted much of her life to sharing her discoveries and joys with others. She confirmed that she felt a lingering sadness, but that she had received so much that she wanted to give more. She is in her mid-80s, and so speaks with a quiet authority, including the experience of helping 100 or so children and families.

As for me, I have witnessed so much as a parent who has not had a child with such a condition, that I have constantly been blessed to learn from those who have. The quality of their lives and relationships is distinctive. And now I think I have the words for its source: each child is a gift.

INTRODUCTION TO THEME FOUR
Community

Love is dynamic, always seeking deeper understanding, wider horizons. As love grows, relationships develop beyond the primal dyads and triads of the nuclear family or its equivalents. Sensitive parenting and care of children welcomes and prepares the way for this. The articles in this section explore a range of aspects of this expanding social process.

Running like a leitmotif through the collection is the concept that "It takes a village to raise a child". And in some ways perhaps Mill Grove could be seen to have developed as one small version of just such a community: a single household of four generations, serving as a hub to a global extended family.

The quality of intergenerational relationships is crucial in such a village if it is to thrive.

And some form or marriage or covenant seems to be essential.

Article Fourteen contains a poem by one of those who lived at Mill Grove with her young child. Perhaps all therapeutic communities are places of mending in one form or another.

But there are also living examples, or models, of hospitality. These comprise shared living, with its welcomes and especially its mealtimes, and an acknowledgement that any categories or labels will ultimately need to be deconstructed if genuine shared living is to be possible.

Changing Dynamics of Care

The residential community called Mill Grove began in 1899, seven years before John Bowlby was born, and over 50 years before the publication of his ground-breaking work, *Maternal Care and Mental Health* (WHO, 1951). For much of its history it has sought to care for children in need/at risk by creating a substitute family or alternative household environment. Children, singly or in groups of siblings, lived away from their birth families in what was generally conceived and thought of as a children's home. However distinctive the home was, there were many in the UK throughout this period that had a number of characteristics in common.

As Bowlby's work on separation, loss and attachment began to enter academic and professional consciousness there was a gradual shift towards supporting children in their own families and communities, rather than removing them from those who had been significant others for them from birth. One effect of this over recent decades has been that less "unaccompanied" children have come to live at Mill Grove, as more parents have been living here with their children. Another consequence has been the increasing pre-school provision on the premises for local families.

In this article I want to explore just one aspect of this change: the different dynamics that it creates within a residential community. In doing this there is no presumption that one way of living is inherently better than the other. In the former (pre-Bowlby) period the adults (significantly my grandparents and my parents with others helping them) modelled and taught patterns of life and behaviour in keeping with what they believed to be best for the children. This included just about every aspect of personal and social life from dawn to dusk, weekdays and weekends, school terms and holidays, the four seasons. It included standards of dress, language, table manners, boundaries and discipline, religious beliefs and behaviour and much, much more.

Some of these patterns of life came as a surprise to children whose families had operated in different ways and with contrasting values. The home felt distinctly middle class to those coming from the working-class East end of London, for example. But over time (and often on reflection years later) they often came to appreciate the consistency in the way life was patterned and experienced. It was the caring adults who shaped the immediate social environment, not their birth families.

In recent years, when parents and children have come together to live at Mill Grove, we seek to support the bonds of attachment, and that means that a parent will continue to have a major share in the way their child is brought up. This can work smoothly when we can support it with a good conscience but it creates some chronic difficulties when we can't. Let's take eating habits. The mores and tradition of Mill Grove is that during main meals a child learns to have a little of everything that has been prepared, thus ensuring a reasonably balanced diet. Several children and their parents have a different approach, and it is possible that children will choose only the food that they like, thus having (for example) no vegetables or fruit. How is this conflict resolved?

Then there are expectations about bedtimes, both the actual time in question and what putting a child to bed entails. Baths, showers, stories and prayers may be replaced by far less predictable patterns. Electronic devices may be available to young children all through the night.

At the heart of all this is the question of what constitutes "good enough parenting". What if a parent leaves her child to cry loudly and continually during a mealtime? What if a parent leaves her young child alone? What if the way a parent responds to a child or young person is inappropriate both in words and actions? What if a parent has mental health problems and cannot relate to a child consistently because they do not hold the child in a healthy mind?

A constant thread in all this is how to balance the needs of the child on the one hand and the parent on the other. It is a chronic issue in mental health and in my experience shows little sign of being grasped, let alone addressed, in any systematic way.

The challenges in a residential community multiply when there may be more than one parent living or staying at Mill Grove at any given time. Then there is likelihood that there will be different expectations and values between some of the parents. How do we arbitrate? And how do we advocate and model consistent boundaries? Some mature readers will immediately be aware that this sort of scenario is well-known to many grandparents. Much grand-parenting revolves around such issues. Much of social work and residential care has near its core the parent-child relationship (in many varieties), so perhaps we would do well to open up the thinking and practice to the way extended families operate around the world.

Once this line of exploration is pursued it becomes apparent that there is a virtually unlimited range of possible challenges created by such a change in the dynamics of care. Imagine a classroom where the children's parents are always present, and then think of the challenges this would present to the teacher. That may clarify some of the issues that are likely to arise. The reason I ask such questions is because I do not know the answers. What's more it is dawning on me that, if anything, it is an art rather than a science.

The art requires good and open communication between the parents and the carers, but there will still be many times when a parent is unaware that he or she is acting in ways that we consider to be inappropriate. This means that some things never come up for conversation or review because they are not seen as significant. We do not have formal reviews or meetings as part of our way of life, and we are reluctant to introduce them because of the risk they pose to the normality and informality of our life together.

As I said earlier, the difficulties are not an argument for separating children and parents as used to happen decades ago. It is important to support bonds and bonding between children and parents who are "good enough". But no one should underestimate the wisdom, patience and resilience required in such a setting. And what if it is "good enough" sometimes, but not at others?

What we have discovered is that there is an ethos understood by a critical mass of people at Mill Grove that helps to provide something of an agreed way of living some of the time, but some interaction between parents and children falls outside these limits. Occasionally we must intervene to safeguard one or more children.

Perhaps most frustrating aspects of shared parenting is the knowledge that children are not being allowed or encouraged to reach their potential: the parents' view of life is understandably restricted, and it is extremely hard to enlarge their vision. If you have possibilities and options in mind that do not exist in the mind or imagination of the parent or parents, then there is little hope of passing them on. No person can understand what they do not know. This may mean that walking in the forest at autumn time is supplanted by yet another trip to a shopping mall; individual computer games replace reading stories together; playing games together inside or out is rarely considered; television is a default mode; conversation is stilted and tends towards restricted codes and sound-bites; the world is parochial.

Looking back over such a list it becomes apparent just what a gap there is between traditional working class and middle-class values. They have probably always co-existed in much social life worldwide, but it is a particular challenge when they collide in a single-family household. Given the wisdom of the nostrum that "it takes a village to raise a child" perhaps one of the keys is to conceive of Mill Grove as a village. That could make a lot of sense.

The purpose of writing this piece has not been to extol one set of values or lifestyle over another, but to muse on a dynamic that creates such profound and continuous challenges in daily life and experience that I am having to go back to the drawing board again and again. In this as in so much else I find that the learning curve is steepening. And as always, it helps to have a well-developed sense of humour.

Bonds Within an Extended Family

This article was written as Christmas approached, and I was compiling the index for Volume Two of *Reflections on Living with Children*. I was reminded of some of the factors that help to keep an extended family like Mill Grove connected. And I thought I might reflect on one or two as part of my seasonal gift to readers of the Journal!

Advent and Christmas for the family of Mill Grove this year began with a birth and a death. Readers who are familiar with the poem *The Journey of the Magi* by T.S. Eliot, know that he juxtaposes birth and death, and it is not difficult to see some of the connections, however counter-intuitive it might seem. The little baby boy has been asleep or feeding contentedly every time I have seen him so far, but the birth was rather trying for his mother, and there will be some stern challenges ahead. The death was of the oldest member of the family, Ben. He was 102 going on 103 when he died. And his funeral in Great Dunmow was on what would have been his wife's 99th birthday had she survived!

Just a week before Ben died, I happened to be passing near the nursing home where he was living and decided to drop in on the off chance. He was in good form. He finished a drink that I offered him, and we were soon talking about the old days at Mill Grove during the inter-war period, about my grandfather, and a contemporary of his, one of the boys with whom he struck up a friendship. The two of them went to Canada as part of the apprenticeship programme popular at the time. (The exhibition, *On Their Own: Britain's Child Migrants* is currently on at the nearby Bethnal Green Museum of Childhood.) And then we sang together. (I have written of this before.) It was one of the choruses that Ben had learnt as a boy at Mill Grove. This is how it happened that the last words we shared were these: "I, 'though so unworthy, still am a child of His care, for His Word teaches me that His love reaches me, everywhere."

Two days before writing this piece I was taking Ben's funeral service in Dunmow URC, followed by the committal at a crematorium in Harlow. The places were significant. Dunmow had become his home over the long last period of his life, and he was a loved citizen of this town famous for its Flitch. But Harlow was where he worked for 20 years or so as a brick-layer: yes, he helped to build Harlow New Town! (He was also a horseman as befits someone in the 19th Hussars, and a fine gardener, but that is for another time!)

Ben has one daughter, who now lives in the USA. She was unable to come to the funeral and so we were in touch regularly before and after the event. The email trail includes the following:

26TH OCTOBER FROM UK TO USA:

"Just to say that I spent a happy time with dad yesterday afternoon and learnt that you had phoned him the day before. He seemed in pretty good form, and he finished a vanilla drink while I was there. When talking about the old days, you, and horses he was in sparkling form. We sang "Wide, wide as the ocean" together as usual, and I wonder what other residents made of the duet. With love …"

1ST NOVEMBER USA TO UK:

"Dear precious Keith, Dad went to heaven around 11pm this Saturday. Will be in touch. I know he is with Mum just hurt so, God is with me, Love …"

2ND NOVEMBER USA TO UK:

"Dear Keith and Ruth, you are my family now …"

And that set me thinking. How remarkable that it was my grandparents who cared for her father; that he grew up with my father in the role of an older brother, and that I should have had the privilege of being with him at the very end. It is the essence of what Mill Grove stands for: we seek to "be there" for each child throughout their lives … and for their children and children's children.

This means that we keep in touch whenever possible by letter, phone, cards, latterly emails, supplemented by the annual newsletter of Mill Grove, called *Links*. Undergirding all of this is good record-keeping going back to 1899. In Ben's case he often used to phone, and he also wrote a summary of his eventful life.

Just before the funeral of Ben I was looking forward to seeing another member of the Mill Grove family (he is roughly the same age as me and we grew up together). He was coming over with his wife to join us for lunch, and they had agreed to take on the task of converting all the colour slides that we possess (thousands of them) into digital form. The reason for this is hopefully now clear: it is all part of the record-keeping for generations to come. But he phoned me the morning he was due to come with shattering news: his wife had just been rushed to hospital on account of multiple heart attacks. She had been operated on and was in Intensive Care.

Since then, and until today, she is still unconscious, and I have been in touch with him (and his son) by telephone and emails. This morning Ruth and I were praying as usual for the family with his latest email in front of us. There was no thought of categorising or labelling what sort of relationship we had (family, friend, colleague, etc.): we had grown up together and we felt deeply for him.

The following day (yes, it's not just London buses that come in convoys) another member of the Mill Grove family came to see me. She is a senior practitioner in social work and was coming to help one of her younger brothers who came back to live with us over a year ago, aged 41. She and her three brothers had always kept in touch with each other and with us. One of them had spoken at my father's funeral. We needed to go back over the family history generation by generation because we were belatedly trying to establish nationality and citizenship. It wasn't long before all sorts of feelings and emotions were coming out, and she was talking about her own family and her plans for the next stage of her professional life.

I was touched that she had dropped in to help a younger sibling, and she was so grateful that her younger brother had found a welcome the second time that he needed it from the family at Mill Grove. In his case it was my parents who cared for him, but Ruth and I knew him from his earliest years, and he and his family had stayed in our caravan on holiday in Devon two weeks after our wedding in August 1971!

These are some of the people I have been alongside in the past few days, as I sit with unsent Christmas cards piled neatly unattended beside me. I'm not sure what this adds up to. But the original idea behind this column was that I would write as one who lived among children and young people. Now many of them have grown up, but we are still in touch.

Which reminds me. There was something that I shared with the senior social worker. She talked of the importance of life-story work (books and personal records including photos), and I reflected that I was often asked how children who lived at Mill Grove have turned out. These days I guess people have in mind "outcomes". My response is usually along the following lines. Of the 1,200 or so children who have lived at Mill Grove since 1899 and who have died, there seems to be a spread from those who have experienced fulfilled lives, careers and families, to those who have felt separation and loss very keenly. Statistics aren't available, and I would not trust them in such an evaluation: every life is that of a unique individual and the figures would not convey the true narrative.

But then I add: "for those who are still alive, the story is not over". And in the stories that I have shared you see something of the truth of this. The baby and his family have everything still ahead of them; Ben's daughter plans to come over to see us next year, and meanwhile she will, God willing, have a recording of the funeral service courtesy of another member of the Mill Grove family. We will continue alongside the family currently holding the hand of their wife and mother. And the social worker and her youngest brother will be with us at Christmas ... along with the newest member of the Mill Grove family.

The end of 2016 is drawing near, but it's not the end of the story. And while the story continues there is always hope.

Where Art Thou Brother?

For some inexplicable reason, though summer is approaching, we have been talking about Christmas games over recent weeks. And we are all amused by the games we play at Mill Grove: traditions handed down to us by previous generations. They include Schools, O'Grady Says, Bomber Coming Over, Bigamy and Where Art Thou, Brother? This last game requires two volunteers, both of whom are blindfolded and who then lie on the floor, each holding a stick made of newspaper with which they attempt to strike the other person in turn. Like it or not, it is a very popular game and we never run out of volunteers. Often these volunteers are brothers or sisters.

Which leads me to the subject of this reflection: siblings. When planning the care of children, when conceiving of their rights, when describing their growth, we tend to assume that they are primarily to be seen and related to as individuals. And this is both understandable and appropriate. But in the process, we can unintentionally downplay or even neglect the significance of siblings in child development. One of the theorists who acknowledged this was Alfred Adler (1870–1937). While family therapy by its very nature includes siblings, in general attention focuses on each individual child. As I was writing this piece I wondered, for example, how much has been written on Attachment Theory and siblings.

Several things have combined or conspired to bring this subject to the forefront of my mind. One is my experience of China where the "one-child" policy has revealed unintended consequences, not least the absence of aunties and uncles, as extended families of cultures around the world understand them. The observation that Chinese people of all ages (including young people) made to me while I was visiting was that young people lacked personal confidence and social skills. When I probed what this was about, they told me that it was with brothers and sisters, aunties and uncles that these social skills and the accompanying confidence developed. I suppose it might help us understand their point if you could try and imagine a baby monkey or lion cub trying to develop their skills without the opportunity to play with siblings.

Then there have been many children coming back to Mill Grove as adults (often retired) who have told me that they have discovered previously unknown stepbrothers and stepsisters in different parts of the world. Social media have played their part in these discoveries. For whatever reasons these sibling groups had been split up, or kept separate, throughout the childhoods of the children concerned. And I wondered how it was that sibling relationships seemed to be a poor relation in the calculations that had been made for them.

Added to this has been the awareness at funerals I have attended of the closeness and significance of sibling bonds. These are occasions when people seem to talk about their sisters and brothers more deeply than at almost all other times. Perhaps because kin are ascribed rather than chosen, they may tend to be largely taken for granted … until that is there is separation and loss. When there has been separation from parents it is often siblings that become significant others in the life of a child, consciously or unconsciously.

I have been reminded again and again (including this very week) how often those who have lived together in a children's home, residential school or foster family become as close as brothers and sisters. Sometimes they seem to become closer friends and confidants. 30 years ago, a young lad walked into the middle of a barbecue we were having on a beach in North Wales. We invited him to join us and from that moment on he became a member of the Mill Grove family. I am not sure we thought about this consciously but when he died, aged just 48, we felt the grief and loss associated with a close and loved relative. Although this column is usually anonymised, I think it appropriate in this case to say that his name is Professor Sir David Mackay, formerly the Chief Government Adviser on Energy and Climate Change.

With these factors in mind, what are some

of the significant issues that come alive when we focus on the siblings of those who spend all or part of their childhoods in some form of substitute care? One is the shared memories that they may have of their birth parents, birth family and home. Such memories are kept alive by constant reminders, jokes, associations and events within the nuclear family home. But without that setting they can easily become hazy or wildly unreliable. Sometimes they are ideas created out of wish-fulfilment, and the projections of fears and traumas. Siblings can combine memories to create a more rounded and nuanced understanding of their parents and families. If this does not sound important then it is worth pausing to consider the problems that arise when there is no reliable history on which to draw when a child is seeking to understand her life-story.

Then there is the fact that sometimes the reason a child has been placed in a particular setting is so that he or she can be united or reunited with siblings. Despite what I said earlier in this piece, keeping a family together can sometimes take precedence over the needs or even wishes of an individual. I was reminded of this just a couple of weeks ago. A little girl had loved living with her grandmother (in Southend on Sea) when she could not remain with her mother or father, but then she was moved to Mill Grove. The reason? There were probably two. Her grandmother was getting older and saw that the time was coming when she would not be able to cope adequately. The other was that so that girl could be with her two older brothers. Although she loved being with her granny, she longed to be with her brothers, and readily confessed that she imagined the grass to be greener over the other side.

The desire to be with her brothers helps to explain why she could not remember a single detail of her life with her grandmother. She had no one to help her do this when her grandmother died because she was living with her alone. But my intuition was that she found the breaking of the attachment to her grandmother so hard that she coped unconsciously by freezing her memories of this loved and dependable significant other.

On the other hand, I have known those younger siblings who were not allowed to join older siblings at Mill Grove, and who have regretted this ever since. I recall walking around our home with one such person. She looked at the rooms and furnishings as if it were holy ground: the place where her three brothers had lived, and where she had longed to be together with them. She had felt rejected in some way throughout life because of this decision (who by we do not know).

Blood siblings can share with each other personal and very intimate thoughts and questions without it being at all surprising or unnatural. It doesn't always happen like this and sometimes, as we know all too well, things can go very badly wrong. But there is plenty of evidence that siblings have taken advantage of this. An older sister will often be very protective towards a younger sibling (a mother figure if you like). But even if there is not this closeness, there will still be conversations, often humorous, which siblings take for granted and on which they can rely, perhaps many years after the event.

Nephews and nieces play an important part in this sibling relationship in an inter-generational way. We have seen siblings struggle with their own relationships only to find themselves drawn closer together through their respective children. This is where family events like birthdays, Christmas, weddings and funerals have their place. This can be about the very identity of a person: to be called "Auntie" can be a defining moment in a person's life.

I have often been reminded that when children suffer trauma and loss they can fear that the very same things will happen in their lives (family patterning). If a birth parent has rejected them and found it difficult to remain in a committed and fulfilled relationship with a husband or wife, they are anxious that they will repeat this all over again. It is important not to underestimate the power of this fear. Once again it may be siblings that provide a ray of hope. I have often heard someone describe a brother or sister with pride: "We don't have to be like our mother or father" is the living message. So a sibling who "succeeds" in some way is not just someone to be admired, but an embodiment of the hope of a better life rather than the "replication of sameness".

Which leads me to reiterate the point about sibling-type relationships between those who are not actually related by blood or birth. And here I can speak with the insider knowledge of one who experienced, and still experiences, this in and through Mill Grove. When someone in the Mill Grove family dies there is often an unexpected outpouring of grief as we realise just how special that person has been, and

what a good brother or sister they were to other siblings in this family that brought people together from many different blood families.

It is true that we should always be careful to consider the rights and needs of an individual child paramount when decisions are made about their lives. But this should never be without due attention not only to birth siblings, but also to the potential of the group. Siblings are a vital element of the village that it takes to raise a child.

"Why Haven't You Burnt Out?"

We are blessed at Mill Grove in having those who come to stay with us as part of a formal or informal stage in their education or professional development. Reflecting on those who have done this, I now realise that they have come from many different parts of the world (including USA, Europe, Africa, Malaysia, The Philippines) and from a wide range of cultural backgrounds and learning environments (social work, children's ministry, residential care, community development, psychology, and ministerial sabbaticals and training, to name but a few off the top of my head).

When chatting (or "doing supervision" if you would prefer it) with one who has been with us for three weeks this September, she asked the question at the head of this piece. I enquired where it had come from in terms of her observations and experience at Mill Grove. The way she saw it was that there were children and families who had serious and chronic problems living here all the time, some for many years. We were involved with them pretty much continuously, without "shifts" and the like. So how come that it didn't all become overwhelming at times? What were the ways in which, the resources because of which, we were able to cope?

It was a fair question and set me thinking. This article is a response to it. First it is

important to say (as I did to her) that there were occasions during my time as a trainee social worker in Edinburgh in the 1970s when I felt that I might go under. The cases that I was allocated were all to do with rent arrears and eviction with just about every other personal problem thrown in. That experience stayed with me as I moved into Mill Grove with Ruth and our family. And it came back strongly when early on I found things beginning to get on top of me. This means that burn-out is not just a theoretical concept that affects other people in different situations. I knew from personal experience what it means.

All the same, it is true that Ruth and I have survived over a period of 40 years' engagement with the community of Mill Grove, and 30 years living as part of that residential community. So why might that be? One factor has been the presence of a consultant therapist for nearly all of that time. There have been three since the 1970s: one moved to the USA; the second retired; and we are now supported by the third. When researching children's homes in Edinburgh and Hull between 1969 and 1973 I quickly realised that the house-parents (as they were then called) were under relentless pressure that adversely affected each of them and their marriage relationships. The importance of regular support was impressed upon me. And the case for it cannot be overstated. To have a predictable and reliable opportunity and setting in which every issue and feeling can be shared is vital for sanity, let alone well-being. It is perhaps close to "being held in a healthy mind".

Another factor is the support that we have had from others, notably parents, family, trustees and friends. This has happened in numerous ways, direct and indirect. But when the screws are on it can be a make or break to have those to whom you can turn, and on whom you can rely. It is simply not possible in my experience to function independently of resourceful friends. One such friend was Bob Holman (who coined the very phrase, "resourceful friend"!). It was a comfort and joy to know that he was always interested and willing to listen to my questions and descriptions of my difficulties without ever becoming remotely anxious or seeming to be phased by anything I shared with him.

Then there is the matter of boundaries, patterns, rhythms of life. Early on I came to discover that Benedict had seen into the heart of community living, and so I took his basic rule of life as one of my guides. And this was part of a process of learning during which I came to draw insights and wisdom from a whole range of residential settings: psychiatric, religious, artistic, social and political. How did Jean Vanier avoid burnt-out, I often wondered (after that is, the time of his well-documented failure in the early days)? And what about Dietrich Bonhoeffer, Victor Frankl, Alexander Solzhenitsyn in their harsh confinements? All were acutely aware of boundaries of every sort, ideological and practical, personal and group, and they were strong in maintaining what they saw as necessary and healthy ways of living.

Another strand of the story is my engagement with other aspects of life, the wider world. When starting out at Mill Grove one of the senior trustees, a GP, advised me to make sure that I always had interests and commitments outside the residential community. This proved inestimably wise. And I have kept his advice to this very day. Without regular, lively, fresh interaction with the world outside a residential community, things, including people and feelings, readily tend to get out of proportion and become unduly negative. The result, on reflection, has been a cornucopia of different interests, partnerships, projects and initiatives that range from singing in choirs, joining professional associations, sailing, climbing, playing chess, writing books, writing and producing plays, and so much more. Such engagement helps a sense of perspective when others in the community may be losing theirs.

As this list lengthens it dawns on me that I am probably not the best person to answer such a question. No doubt others can see much more clearly than me the resources that have sustained me over the years. I think that they would start with Ruth, my wife, whose inner tranquillity and resources are second to none in my whole experience. But I guess they would also refer to my personal faith. As a committed and trusting follower of Jesus, I have often wondered how those without such a faith find sustenance, hope, grace and peace in the often harsh, real world. I have come to realise that many do, but I still fail to see how they do it. Perhaps there are other names for what sustains them and provides hope when all seems bleak, even hopeless in micro and macro worlds. Something to hold on to when, as a former colleague of mine, a psycho-therapist, said "Your child care theories are all in smithereens!"

There is no doubt a lot more to it than what I have just written, and I begin to feel that I have only begun to scratch the surface. But let me round this reflection off by connecting it with what I am doing at this very moment. For most of my life I have enjoyed writing, and it has been my joy to complete hundreds of articles and papers, to write 50 years' worth of sermons, and to author and edit several books. They are about quite different subjects (from theology and sociology to art and history), but there is a thread running through many of them. And this thread has to do with reflecting on residential care, therapeutic communities, intra-personal development, and group dynamics.

This is how I process things. I am currently reading *À la Recherche du Temps Perdu* by Marcel Proust. If you don't know it, it is so vast that I would never dare to recommend it to anyone, but if you are familiar with it, then you will know that this massive work is an extraordinary and extended reflection on his life, feelings, thoughts, relationships, and context set in the world of nature and culture. Writing pieces for *The Care Journal*, formerly *Children Webmag*, is for me a therapeutic experience which allows me to chew over issues, many of them very challenging, and some barely understood. So it is that this piece is not only an attempted answer to the question posed about burn-out, but part of the very process by which burnt-out may have been prevented. Whether it is worth reading is a completely different matter!

"The City Streets Will Be Filled with Boys and Girls Playing There"

In this column I would like to share an idea or dream with you. It has its roots in the words of the prophet Zechariah spoken to a people who had been driven out of their homes and their beloved city. He tells of a time that is coming when "once again elderly men and women will sit in the streets of Jerusalem each with a cane in hand on account of their age, and the streets will be filled with boys and girls playing there" (Zechariah 8:4-5). Recently I shared this vision at an AGM of our local community association, and one of those present, a senior officer in the council, remembered it. On reflection I think I can see why, because it is a picture that surely evokes deep longing and affection from each one of us.

In a brief paper I summarised the first 40 years of the life of the Maybank Community Association as a basis and inspiration for looking ahead. One of the suggestions I made was that we might consider our local neighbourhood to be an alternative version of "sheltered housing". Rather than building a new complex of flats and houses and then appointing a warden and resource people who would be on 24-hour call, we might encourage elderly people to continue living in their own homes. And we, their neighbours, would be the ones on 24-hour call, supported by social care professionals and networks. In an age of smart communication, it seems eminently possible that help can be as readily accessible in a closely-defined community as it would in a purpose-built complex.

The huge bonuses of the idea are not only that people can continue to live where they want to (in their own homes and familiar surroundings), but that, rather than being in a setting where everyone is elderly or in need of support, they remain within sight and sound of children. They would be able to hear them playing and, if able to do so, could sit or stand outside watching them play (given adequate traffic control).

Not long after this I heard of Nightingale House in Clapham, South-West London, where a nursery and a home for the elderly are to be located on the same site (*The Times*, 1st July 2017, page 3). The scheme seems to be bursting with creative ideas and a range of potential shared activities. But what caught my eye particularly was a comment by one of the senior staff of the charity that runs it. Speaking of an open day she said: "You could feel something different in the air with all these children running about. It just made it really happy. It lifts the mood and brings life into the home." This reminded me of the time when Cicely Saunders told me of the day that they opened a nursery in St. Christopher's Hospice in Sydenham that she had founded. It is also in South-West London. The residents/patients found that the presence, activities, comments and questions of the little children were a highlight of their day.

Despite this isolated example, it appears that the UK is coming to all this a little later than other countries: America, Canada, Australia, Japan, Singapore and parts of Europe are already engaged in what is called "co-location" of a care home and a nursery. I then discovered that in Hogeweyk, a "dementia village" in the Netherlands. It is effectively a nursing home designed as a "secure village" with houses, pub, supermarket and theatre "staffed by professionals to evoke everyday life".

Put it all together and it doesn't take long to figure out that rethinking a neighbourhood as sheltered accommodation isn't a million miles away from where others are right now. Come to think of it this is what has been happening at Mill Grove (a residential community within the Maybank neighbourhood) for decades. There is no "age apartheid", and little children, some with cerebral palsy, teenagers, young adults and elderly people take it for granted that they will be enjoying each other's company in a variety of ways. Let me give just a few. When the Pre-School has a "farm day" the parents of the children are encouraged to stay, and elderly neighbours coming to have Thursday lunch with us always look forward to joining in. It is the animals that bring everyone together. There is for example a very basic impulse in most people that makes them want to hold little chicks or ducklings in their hands (whether three years old or 102 years old!). Then at Christmas the Pre-School children and those from the Rose Walton Centre (for children with cerebral palsy) come to share with those who have gathered for lunch, singing carols, creating a Christmas crib, giving and opening presents, and lighting the Advent Wreath. These are, if you like, the formal or arranged meetings, but it is the informal times and the spaces in between where things really come alive. A little boy with cerebral palsy interrupting lunch to do a "high five" with everyone and bringing tears of joy to the faces of those dining. Or an informal football match that just came about spontaneously.

This shouldn't come as too much of a surprise when you consider that most of the human race throughout history has lived in rural or urban villages (by which I mean local communities where people can walk to each other's homes within a couple of minutes or so). We accept I think the nostrum that it takes a village to raise a child (and that this means that every villager has a role in parenting of some sort), but perhaps it still hasn't sunk in that it needs a village to bring deep joy and smiles to the elderly.

We will see how this rather radical idea of a neighbourhood re-conceived as sheltered accommodation develops, but meanwhile as we think about what makes a therapeutic community it seems to me that it is likely that the presence of young and old is a step in the right direction. The Irish and Scottish ceilidhs get it right: when a community celebrates, it can only be truly effective and real when young and old both have a part to play. It won't be the same part: the young will probably do most of the dancing, but what an added blessing it is to them that there are older people present who take joy in watching them doing so, whether or not they lean on their canes!

The Therapy of Shared Experiences and Memories

The time has come for another reflection on the holiday experiences of the family of Mill Grove in our beloved North Wales. We have been there every year since 1976 and, if anything, the wonder, excitement and discoveries have grown rather than diminished with each passing stay. Now children and grandchildren of those who were there as little ones are discovering and exploring the very same beaches, rivers, slabs, crags, pools, mountains and seas as their predecessors.

I would like to focus on just two days we had together, and then to describe the sheer joy of the spontaneous sharing about holidays past. The first day was on the local mountain, Moel-y-Gest. 15 or so walked to the summit ridge of this modest but striking hill, led by one of the youngsters on a dry but unexceptional morning. On arriving at the triangulation point we took the traditional photos and then began to look around: west along the Lleyn peninsular, south beyond the Harlech dome, and North and East towards the mountains and valleys of Snowdonia National Park. We had a picnic lunch on some rocks that provided shelter from

113

the Westerly breeze, and then there was no hurry to descend. In fact by design there was ample time for the youngsters to enjoy the local boulders and rocky outcrops that form part of the summit plateau.

And it is that period, seemingly timeless but actually over an hour, that lingers in the memory. All of the children and young people were engaged in a process which combined trying to find new routes up the rocks, with shared discoveries of ways round and down them. At times they did so as individuals, oblivious to what others were doing. At other times they compared notes, or occasionally asked for help or advice, usually from each other. The adults chatted nearby in a very relaxed mode, clearly interested in what was going on, but not in any way governed by or responsible for it. Some children chose to attempt harder routes, and to do them more quickly; others were happy scrambling in the heather and perching themselves at the top of slabs. It was a wholly contented and enjoyable experience for all. The personal dynamics were trouble-free, and the interaction with the natural world was a pleasure to witness. I felt privileged to have been present to savour such unalloyed, enthusiastic and extempore enjoyment.

A few days later we were at sea level, in the harbour of Borth-y-Gest to be precise, and it was nearing a spring high tide. It was a perfect day: a cloudless sky and the water sheltered from the westerly breeze by the headland. There was the usual hive of activity that goes with a high tide by a slipway, with various types of dinghies, boats and canoes being launched. The same group of Mill Grove family was now on the slipway putting three kayaks and one sailboard into the water. Each person had a buoyancy aid and several had wetsuits. The adults were once again relaxed and chatting with each other, as well as with people and families who were enjoying the sundrenched water directly or indirectly.

And that's about it! For the best part of two hours the youngsters played in and on the water, "messing about in boats" (to quote Water Rat from *The Wind in the Willows*). Some were competent at kayaking; others were not.

Some were used to swimming; others were new to being in the sea. It was completely unscripted and spontaneous. The adults were present and alert to the need to ensure that no one drifted inadvertently into the main channel as the tide ebbed, but that was done without words: just an occasional swim and a little encouragement. The fun and games became more boisterous and adventurous, until the sailboard was overladen and tipped everyone into the water. Two teenagers set off to see if they could walk across the harbour to the other side: they couldn't! And then as the tide emptied the harbour two of the young people started a mud slide, and soon several were caked in pretty clingy, slimy mud from head to foot.

It would be unfortunate to dispel the sheer enjoyment and fun that was had on these two occasions by analysis. Keats poem, *Lamia* is an unforgettable warning against this:

"Do not all charms fly
   At the mere touch of cold philosophy?
There was an awful rainbow once in
    heaven:
We know her woof, her texture; she is given
   In the dull catalogue of common things.
Philosophy will clip an Angel's wings,
   Conquer all mysteries by rule and line,
Empty the haunted air, and gnoméd mine –
   Unweave a rainbow ..."

But the most cursory reflection on the two sets of experiences, on the mountain and in the harbour, reveals that certain simple elements went into creating the space for such unfettered and spontaneous fun. There were carefully chosen settings and times; the children and young people were enthusiastic about the activities and had chosen to do them; there was the appropriate knowledge and equipment; there were adults at hand but not obtruding; and there was a shared understanding about the nature and limits of what was going on. It seems to me that any therapeutic context or experience will embody or replicate in some way exactly these components. Let's be clear about it: the times on the hill and in the water were not set up to be therapeutic sessions! Far from it. They were all about holiday fun chosen by the children. But the essence of life at Mill Grove is the creation of an environment where therapeutic activity and relationships, personal and group, is embedded in the warp and woof of everyday life and the seasons of the year.

This leads us conveniently to the spontaneous sharing about times past. There is a tradition in the family that means we keep a diary or scrapbook of every holiday. These will usually be a single volume per year, but can reach as many as three for one summer. They are compiled or edited by one of the adults or older children, but crucially everyone is invited to make a contribution, however rudimentary or small. The entries range from postcards and brochures to pictures, maps, diagrams, poems, drawings and paintings. For the first time that I can recall we decided to take a set of old scrapbooks with us to North Wales (about 30 volumes spanning 15 years or so). In doing so, I had little idea what might transpire. It just seemed to me a bit of a waste that they were stored carefully in London with only rare forays into the cupboard in which they were kept by someone wanting to check a particular year or holiday.

In the event nothing prepared me for what happened. It started slowly, but then gathered pace as first one, and then another person from the youngest to the oldest began to dip into the pages, and before long there was a continuous flurry of individual discoveries and shared reflections. There were people in the room who had contributed to diaries 30 years before; there were photos of adults when they were young children, and there were pictures of the very places that we knew and loved so well (yes, you've got it, including the harbour and the hill!). We realised that we were privileged to be part of an extended family with shared experiences and traditions, and that we valued the past as well as the present. We were part of a shared narrative and story.

Over several decades there has been an awareness of the importance of a child or young person having a secure grasp of her own "life story". This can be nurtured in various ways, but the holiday diaries brought new light to bear on the nature of this process. And in case you were wondering, yes, we did keep a diary of 2017, and it is bursting at the seams. I can imagine future generations revelling in it at some stage, not as part of a planned process of study or reflection, but simply as a result of a spontaneous suggestion or enquiry. The times on the hill, at the harbour and in the front room where we enjoyed the diaries together were all characterised by the very same therapeutic elements. Time past and time present in healthy and creative relationship.

Can You Mourn the Loss of More than One Person at a Time?

I wrote down the question that appears at the head of this article some time ago, leaving the rest of the page blank. Then on the very day that I was going to write a first draft response, I found myself in discussion with someone describing her own grief. During the conversation I shared the title with her. She immediately asked me if she could read what I had written. I confessed to her the fact that there was a problem with this: I hadn't written anything but the question at that stage. But now here it is, complete with what she shared with me over breakfast this morning.

It is possible that readers of *TTCJ* can point me to those who have addressed this question already. In the meantime, here are my reflections.

We were at the funeral of one of my close relatives. She had died having been in the bloom of health until the last few months of her life and was living life to the full. She was in full-time employment and was expecting to see yet another of her grandchildren due to be born in a few months. She was lovely and loved. And when the news of her death was shared, a wave of grief swept through the family. People said things with intensity and feeling. No surprise, you might say?

Well, that's a good point, except that many of the same people had gathered in 1984 at the funeral of three close relatives of the same family (and related to the recently deceased person), and it was patently clear that something was happening now that hadn't happened then. The difference was that we were now genuinely expressing deep feelings of loss, sorrow and anger in a way that had not happened on the previous occasion.

It should be noted that there several differences between the two events, including the fact that the three who died in 1984 were killed without warning in a car crash on a motorway, whereas this relative had been diagnosed as terminally ill for a few months. But, though aware of these, I was still beginning to home in on the question that prompted this piece. It had never occurred to me before. And as soon as I began to consider it, I sensed intuitively that it probably isn't possible to mourn the loss of two or more people at the same time in the same way as you might mourn the loss of one.

And this is why. If two or more closed family or friends die at the same time, how could you mourn one of them, while putting to one side the others? This would be to defy the deep emotional logic of grieving which by definition is not susceptible to such neat, clinically-defined boundaries. How on earth could you ration your time and your feelings in this way? Grief simply does not obey the normal categories of thought and feeling. It functions much more like a tsunami carrying all before it: no respecter of persons.

Over time it might become possible to think once again about each of the people in turn, but at the moment of loss the whole of life has become a whirl. One is in a vortex. It might be possible to control aspects of outward behaviour, and try to limit outbursts of grief to private times and places, but the inner world which is where the well-springs of grief lie, has been destabilised and is not subject to this discipline.

This led me to reflect on the feelings of children and young people who have lost or been removed from their homes and families for whatever reason or reasons. As far as they concerned it must feel at times as if they have lost everything and everyone. And there is a mass of data, evidence, material and theory based on the effects of such loss. But how much attention has been paid, I wonder, to the simple, single question: can one grieve for more than one person at a time? I suspect not.

This leads to the follow-up question for those of us engaged in therapeutic responses: given that there are multiple losses and multiple causes of grief, how can we help to provide a container that allows an unblocking of the defence mechanisms that flow from such a trauma? My guess is that there are many aspects of a therapeutic approach that lend themselves to this. One example would be to pay attention to a child's life-story. Life-story books have been de rigueur in the UK for several decades. But have we appreciated the potential they offer for a child to grieve for individuals in the story one at a time? And with play therapy and role play how much attention and focus is given to assisting the expression of grief and loss of specific individuals in a child's life?

If all this is, as they say in the field of chess, "well known to theory", then I wonder how I happened to miss it. If not, then I think we are on to something important and would like very much to work at the implications of the question.

All of which takes me back to the breakfast conversation this morning. Out of the blue the two of us found ourselves talking about the time in her life when she had lost her father and her husband had lost his twin brother at almost exactly the same time. From a geographical distance I had been trying to help her and her husband cope with their respective losses and the associated grief. And without hesitation she told me that because she was overwhelmed with her own loss and grief, she could not help him as she wanted to. And she realised that he was too affected by his own grief to respond to her and her feelings as she knew he would have done in other situations.

The thought that this was not an idiosyncrasy of her personality or his was of considerable comfort to her. She began to see some of the hidden dynamics that were going on. And, even as we spoke, we found we were able to express our sense of loss of both people, as individuals.

It obviously takes time before one can grieve at all adequately when there are multiple losses. To realise this and to find ways of assisting the expression of such grief is surely a primary task of therapeutic child care. And as we well know, the effects of this separation and loss can last a lifetime. So it is not something that is likely to have disappeared. Is it ever too late to be in touch with, and express the feelings associated with, death, physical or emotional?

The Wheel Comes Full Circle

It was a very simple ceremony. Family and friends had gathered outside the local church beside a rose-bush that was being planted, and then one by one they buried the ashes of their mother/grand-mother/sister/friend.   There were some embraces. There were some tears. The little children played, watched and engaged from time to time like butterflies. After several years of physical and emotional ill-health, Beryl (as I will call her) had died. As I tried to absorb and reflect upon the occasion and the gathering my mind went back to the time, over four decades earlier, when I first met her and her family: in a council house in Dagenham.

The person who had put the family and Social Services in contact with us at Mill Grove was a school-teacher in that area. It so happened that he also helped to run sailing holidays on the Norfolk Broads. Through these he was connected to the local church in whose grounds the ashes were being interred. When he learnt that the family was in desperate need of help he recommended that the Social Worker responsible for the case contact us. My wife and I went to see them and found a household struggling with the all too familiar combined effects of poverty, disunity, isolation, fracture and chronic anxiety. Before long the oldest son came to live with us, and a little later so did his three half-siblings: a sister and two brothers.

As is our wont, we helped the children to maintain contact with their mother and extended family for all the years that they stayed with us. Under a rare provision of the 1975 Children Act we became legal custodians of the children, and so functioned as their psychological and practical parents outside the formal state system and alongside their relatives. The children developed and grew flourishing in the comparatively secure and rich social and cultural environment that Mill Grove provided. They were good at sport, and two of them played at representative level (netball and football respectively). They were involved in Girls and Boys Brigades, went on camps. They revelled in summer holidays in North Wales and enjoyed Easter trips to Switzerland. There were predictably ups and downs, but throughout their stay with us the bonds with their mother were nurtured.

When the time was ripe each of them left to pursue their chosen lives. They went in different directions. The footballer went to Holland, where he maintained his impressive goal-scoring record. The daughter married, and her mother went to live with her in the North of England. The oldest son lived in Oxfordshire with his partner, and the other son continued to live locally and had two children.

After getting into debt and having serious problems with housing, the daughter and her family came back south to live with us (her mother included) at Mill Grove. We continued to support each member of the family as and when we could, and always remained connected. As the years went by Beryl was helped to find her own accommodation a short tube or bus-ride from Mill Grove, and she found a warm welcome and, over time, a niche in the local church. She chose to become a member and was baptised, and soon discovered that she had a gift of prayer and praying. She wrote hundreds of personal prayers, many of which she gave to the people concerned. She continued this practice until a short time before she died.

And so it was that the four offspring and their families gathered at the church to celebrate her life and bid her farewell. At the time of the funeral there were five grandchildren all told. Later in the day there was a relaxed gathering at Mill Grove. A theme of the service was the transformation of caterpillars into butterflies, and to mark this the children had butterfly badges and fairy-type wings. They played happily outside sometimes on bikes, and with lots of bubbles. Meanwhile the conversation inside flowed. There were written greetings from a sister of Beryl who had emigrated to Australia, and lots of memories of events and people were stirred. I found that my understanding of Beryl's life and extended family was considerably deepened and broadened. It became clear that she had battled against heavy odds. Our first encounter was set in a whole new context. We also learned that the teacher who had made the link between the family and Mill Grove was still alive, and that he was thrilled to discover that the introduction he had made had borne such positive fruit.

As I thought of his role in the whole process, it became clear that once again Mill Grove had functioned as a support, or rock, all through the family's life and through three generations. There had been a lot of effort, thought, care and love, of course, but the crucial thing that it was there all through for the whole family. It was a place that they knew held them in its thoughts and prayers; somewhere they could always come back to. And this longevity and continuity had allowed relationships to grow and develop with local families, churches and organisations.

An integral dynamic of this inter-generational process is that the relationships have been reciprocal. As I looked around I noticed a social worker who had befriended Beryl with resourcefulness, tenacity and sensitivity; a nurse who was in touch with her daily; and friends of different ages; her children and grand-children. The overall tenor of my feelings was not about the help that had been given over the decades in response to the initial call for help, but the blessing and blessings that we had all experienced and shared in so many places and in such a variety of ways. When the wheel came full circle, it was not a case that was completed or a case-file closed, but rather a cause for gratitude at what we had been privileged to witness and experience.

What's more, as I write this I know that one of the grandchildren is getting very excited because he will be joining us on holiday for the first time in North Wales soon. That will be just over 40 years from when his oldest uncle first began to explore with us the mountains, llyns, beaches and seas of this ruggedly beautiful adventure playground. Yet another cause for gratitude as the story continues to unfold.

[There is more information on the role of the teacher mentioned here in Section Three, Significance, entitled "Who Remembers Person-Centred Casework Nowadays?"]

The Dynamics of Community

In this column I would like to share with you in some detail what happened at Mill Grove during a recent evening. Before doing that, let me pass on some insights of Jean Vanier, the founder of the L'Arche communities that I happened to discover after the evening in question.

These helped me to understand at a deeper level something of what was going on. His observations are in his book, *Signs of the Times* (London: DLT, 2013) translated by Ann Shearer.

Describing the dynamics of the residential community of which he is part, he puts it much better than I could have done:

"[M]y life at L'Arche has brought me ... joy: each meal with my household is a blessing, a beatitude, of the sort spoken of in Luke's

Gospel. There are glances, smiles, words, laughter, events that move us; we can live a love which is neither too close nor too distant. Even moments of aggression between two people can find a place in this ample space of freedom and connection. Someone may be angry with another who touches something painful in their own history, but such tensions are tempered and made relative by the overall atmosphere and joyful shared emotions. A feeling of togetherness and of a common bonding seems to sum up this unique setting and its transforming encounters. We understand each other because relationships with ourselves and each other are at a good comfortable distance." (Pages 134-5)

Now back to the evening at Mill Grove: Ruth was in the kitchen and available to a mother and her adult child who had been around for most of the day, when a family of five, including three young children, arrived as usual. There were other members of the residential community in and around, but at that point there were eight who made up the group. I was on my way to join them as I always try to do, but on the way discovered that the family was outside enjoying the unseasonably warm February weather, and significantly that the father was playing with the oldest son (with whom I normally play before tea). I deliberately delayed my arrival to avoid disrupting this positive interaction.

When I did walk through the front door, I noticed that everyone was at that point contentedly occupied, leaving Ruth with precious time and space to get on with cooking the evening meal. To allow the dynamics to play out, I opted to go quietly outside to get the dustbins and recycling bins ready for collection the next morning. As I was doing that, another regular attender of our evening meal arrived, and told me that although it had been a better day than the wretched one about which we had shared at length a couple of weeks earlier, it hadn't been good. I joined him in the sitting room where he shared some difficult personal feelings and emotions. At this point the boy with whom I normally play came into the room and began to set up a game resembling

ten pin bowling, which he proceeded to play by himself. My friend and I continued chatting but modified the substance of our conversation.

Another adult joined us and so I suggested that he join in the embryonic game, leaving my friend and I space to round off our conversation. The game was a success, enjoyed by players and onlookers alike. Before it had finished, it was time for the evening meal. A little Swiss cowbell was rung. Another adult joined us, making eleven of us seated at two adjacent tables in the dining room. I just had time to ask how she was and learnt that she had made herself scarce in the Mill Grove community for the past few days to avoid the risk of clashes with a family that had been staying. This was her first meal back at the table with the rest of us. We each have our normal seats, so hers was still available, and my young friend was beside me with the two males I have described also at the same table as me. Ruth was at the other table, close to the youngest of the group, a little girl of four. Just as we had served the first course, I had a phone call on our landline from someone urgently needing to talk with me. I was reluctant to spend time away from the table, but at this very moment in walked another member of the Mill Grove community, an experienced teacher back from a day of work at his school. He joined my table for the rest of the meal.

This meant that I was able to listen fully to the person who had phoned me, until Ruth gently informed me that the meal was over and it was time for prayers. I terminated the call and re-joined those in the dining room, wracking my brains as to how and what to make our focus of our shared time of reflection. As we were nearing Lent, I opted to revisit the story of Peter making a complete mess of following Jesus. We read a small section of Matthew chapter 16 as an acted drama, with three taking specific parts. But despite their best efforts, the youngest was not the least engaged in what was going on. Ruth used all her experience and imagination to encourage her, but to no avail. So immediately I switched tack and asked two from my table, the visitor and the teacher, to re-enact the story, one of them playing Jesus, and the other, Peter. It worked a treat, and the little girl was soon entranced by the short unfolding drama. One or two reflected with the group on aspects of the role play before we sang a song and had a short prayer.

We then set about two sets of shared tasks: the majority helping with the washing up (we have no dishwasher), and the rest outside with me, putting out the remaining dustbins and the recycling containers. And then the rest of the evening took its relaxed course with some informal play, a game of snooker, a game of Frustration, and quite a lot of social networking.

This period of about three hours probably seems so unremarkable that it merits neither description nor analysis. And yet it is the stuff of Mill Grove life. And it seems to exemplify almost exactly what Vanier is saying. For Ruth and me, we are with our extended family; and this is our life. We see it as a blessing. Every individual involved in the meal has their own story, replete with traumas and challenges, and the dynamics are so complicated that it would be impossible to relay them to anyone else. But what makes such dynamics possible, and even also a source of healing? In addition to our joint reading of the emerging and fast-changing situation and interactions, there is a sense of togetherness and belonging. And crucially there is the "ample space" in which individuals can disagree without it spilling over and putting at risk the well-being of the whole group. There are "spaces in our togetherness" that are often not possible in tightknit nuclear families, teams or one-to-one encounters.

That sense of a safe-enough, or good-enough, place has been built up over a period of 120 years, and it may be one of the most precious resources that we have. And mealtimes are at its heart. Next week we will be having pancakes. It will be fun, but exactly how things will unfold we do not know. Only that all will be well, and some desperately hurting children and adults know that they will be welcomed, not only in their own right but as members of a group where they have their distinctive role to play in the togetherness of all, but always "at a good comfortable distance".

Ambivalence

During the 1970s a colleague of mine in the Edinburgh Social Work Department applied for a job as a specialist social worker with children in care. These were the heady days when the likes of psychotherapy, therapeutic communities, Maxwell Jones, Dingleton Hospital and R.D. Laing were forces to be reckoned with north of the border, and so, believe it or not, my friend was given an intensive two-day interview. During this process he was shadowed and, according to his version of events, was observed making a telephone call to a client or colleague. He was subsequently asked by two trained psychotherapists whether they were correct in detecting some ambivalence in him as he made the call. Being a Glaswegian, he responded with typical ready wit: "Well, yes and no". His sense of humour, which in the view of his colleagues in our team was one of his strongest suits, was not appreciated and so he did not get the job.

This is a way in to sharing with you a recent discovery that I made about ambivalence very, very close to home. It was Ruth, my wife, who proffered the word, ambivalence, to describe what I was wrestling with when trying to interpret something of the meaning of what was going on during yet another of those visits from someone who had lived at Mill Grove during their childhood, returning as an adult years later. Just in case a ready definition of ambivalence might be helpful here is one from the *Cambridge English Dictionary*: "Having two opposing feelings at the same time, or being uncertain about how you feel". It was like a shaft of light. Immediately and instinctively I knew that she was right. But for some reason I had missed it completely for over 50 years.

Finding such an insight in a single word meant that before I even began to employ it as a way of understanding better what might have been going on in relationships, situations and conversations at Mill Grove, I started musing on how it had been possible to fail to see something so basic and simple. My conclusion was that I had missed it because, like a bird in the air or a fish in water, I had always been living in this world or, if you like, this medium. Which led me to reflect how regularly I had realised that a person interviewed or consulted because they were a specialist or expert was often not the one best placed to provide an analysis or answer. It regularly happens on radio and television news, and within all professions and disciplines. One of the problems is that such people (that's you and me in some situations) are often unable to see the wood for the trees. They are overfamiliar with, possibly immersed in, the issues in hand, and so can miss patterns and evidence that is all around them if they were but able to think themselves outside their specific part of the world or perspective. However hard we may try to do this, it is an inherently difficult feat for human beings, however intelligent or willing.

With that out of the way, to my initial satisfaction at least, I started to reflect on people, events and dynamics from my life-long experience of Mill Grove. Given that I was born here, I have always been living with children who had come to stay because something had gone awry in their own families and homes at some stage and in some way.

I had often wondered (and sometimes enquired) why was it that those who had been children often left it so long before coming back? And why, when some had taken the trouble to drive a considerable distance to the street, had they not come in? Why such difficulty accepting some of the givens in their lives: such as the fact that there had been chaotic relationships in biological families, but a safe space or security at Mill Grove? Why recurrent challenges in engaging with learning at school? And so on.

In a flash it dawned on me, that the obvious and persuasive answer is that their whole experience had been one of mixed feelings and emotions. They didn't want to be here (or at

school) in the first place, and their coming to Mill Grove was traumatic irrespective of however well it was handled. They had been wrenched from the familiar, from kith as well as kin. If, and when, they experienced acceptance and kindness, they would have preferred it had it not been offered by strangers. Every act of kindness was an unwelcome reminder of the absence of their own families, relatives and friends. However positive life was at Mill Grove, it engendered a sadness because of a deep longing for home, and recurring dreams that it might be better back at home now than it had before they had been taken away.

Seen in this light, the whole place and experience was inevitably a source of, and setting for, ambivalent feelings and emotions. In this respect it represents the double-bind facing every step-parent: there is no wholly acceptable or appropriate way of responding to and caring for children who are not your own. They instinctively long for their own lost parent or the dreams that they had of them (however ordinary or even difficult they had been in reality). The novel that brought this home to me was *Other People's Children* by Joanna Trollope. But even though it opened my eyes to this dynamic, I had still missed in it my own case.

So it was that, without realising it, I grew up among those who were ambivalent (that is, had mixed feelings) about the very stuff of life, as well as its variations and particulars. Clearly a lot more was going on, and ambivalence does not begin to explain everything, but it was a vital clue in piecing together the memories and incidents that had puzzled me (not at the time when I was a child growing up here, but on mature reflection).

Did the children here want to succeed in things such as school, sport or other hobbies and activities? Some did, but often they were ambivalent. To succeed when in a situation and setting not of your own choosing was often unattractive, and strangely self-defeating.

What was their self-image? Always tinged or filtered by a lingering sense of regret that the natural or ideal setting for childhood had been taken away from them, and they were labelled,

121

or labelled themselves, as in some way "other" or "inferior". And it took a lot of time and thought to realise that this low self-esteem set in train an unconscious presentation of self as assured, confident and independent.

How did they relate to others who were in the same situation? This is interesting and important. As always in human affairs, there was a range of responses and attitudes, from the caring and accepting to despising, scapego-ating and bullying. But I think I now see that in all this there was a layer or seed of ambiva-lence.

Looking back on childhood in Mill Grove from the vantage point of marriage, parent-hood, and sometimes grandparenthood, those who lived here expressed a mixture of grati-tude for the security, boundaries, community, creativity and love in whatever combinations or intensities that they had experienced, with a sense that it was not like a real family or home.

I hope that this gives enough for the reader to go on, and I am indebted to those readers who will forgive me for missing something so obvious for so long. But what difference does it make? It has already coloured my conversa-tions, my approaches to people and situations: hopefully meaning that I am a little more sensi-tive and even understanding. I realise why my wife, who did not grow up here, saw this so clearly, and why she has acted and reacted dif-ferently to me, not just because we have differ-ent personalities, but because she was so much more aware of the subtleties of what was being experienced, felt, and sometimes of what was being said.

And of course, without venturing unduly into the world of psychotherapy, I am slowly beginning to realise that not only did I not read others with the insight that this understanding of ambivalence brings, but also that I need to re-evaluate my own memories. It is likely that there were times when I wished that I had been brought up in a normal home too. Which is, of course, yet another very good reason why I had missed the whole thing.

It is now pretty obvious to me that in all set-tings and groups where there is some form of substitute care, intervention or support going on for children, there is ambivalence, conscious and unconscious at work, probably, I would now venture to guess, in both them and those trying to help. And if so, an awareness of ambivalence should be developed as one of the first principles of intervention: hopefully, not excluding the possibility of humour being seen as a welcome resource, even for those of us not privileged to have been born and bred in Glas-gow.

The Right Kind of Space

The concept of "safe space" is familiar to all those seeking to create therapeutic environ-ments, or to intervene in the lives of children and young people by rescuing them from neglect and abuse. However, for obvious rea-sons, much of their attention is focused on the adjective, safe, rather than the noun, space. The advent of Covid 19 with its stress on "social distancing" has been a trigger to recon-sider the nature and role of space in the growth and development of children. This piece explores some of the elements that go to make up the kind of space we are looking for.

I think we all agree that it is possible for human beings to have too little or too much space. Where families are forced to live together in cramped conditions, with little res-pite or opportunity to go outside, it does not take much imagination to realise that this is a recipe for disaster. The sheer pressure of being together is bound to create friction, and feel-ings will spill over into disagreements, argu-ments and even violence. Those who are famil-iar with the London Underground in rush hour know the unfortunate social consequences of being crammed together like sardines. And those who are aware of prison and life inside know that, perhaps even greater than the loss of freedom that incarceration involves, is the fear of being trapped in a single cell with someone else, with no room in which to cool down and no opportunity to retreat.

At the other end of the spectrum, we realise that unbounded space has its disadvantages. When children are alone, knowing that there is no-one near enough to hear them cry, it's a desperate type of scenario. There are many varieties on this theme: perhaps in a hypermarket, on a large beach, or in a forest, or on their first day in a large secondary school. There comes a point where freedom to roam without let or hindrance comes to resemble the cosmic loneliness of the wanderer or seafarer.

These are the extremes, of course, but as we begin to focus in on something in between, how do we know what constitutes the most appropriate amount of space? My sense is that this is a matter of art, rather than science. Slide-rules and computers are unlikely to provide us with the right answer in terms of cubic capacity.

It was while ruminating on this during the Covid lockdown that it dawned on me how wonderfully blessed Mill Grove is with hospitable and friendly space, all through the year, inside and out, both in London and in North Wales. The process of enlightenment came as people asked me how things were going during the pandemic. I became rather defensive as I wanted to reply that we were mostly enjoying it! I tried to soften the impact of this unexpectedly good news by describing how, for the most part, and with some judicious adaptation, we were managing to thrive. As I knew that this was not the common lot of many families and groups, it set me rethinking the extent and nature of the space that we had.

In London the houses allow private space for each family and for each individual, with a variety of shared space from a small reception room equipped with internet, telephone, piano and games, to a hall large enough to contain an indoor badminton court. And there is a lot of varied space in between. And the spaces that I know intuitively are somehow more special than any other: the nooks and crannies that simply cannot be designed as such. The fact that the place was not "purpose-built" is one of its most endearing and practical characteristics.

Without it being anyone's intention, individuals and families who are resident have had no difficulty with social distancing while being close enough to be re-assured that they are not alone. There are rooms that offer varieties of ambience and resources. And there are lots of doors that can be kept open or closed depending on the situation.

Meanwhile the pre-school has opted to go fully woodland, and the orchard, playground and garden have come into their own. It has been able to function without problem, either to its own staff and children or risk to the residents. Who would have thought that the former chicken run, its inhabitants killed off by rapacious urban foxes, would in time become an idyllic outdoor classroom, their roosting area, a library, and their nesting boxes, a toilet?!

At the other end of the premises, the children with cerebral palsy and associated conditions have their own entrance, rooms and specialist equipment in the sunniest room in the house. Because they are so vulnerable to this virus they and their families need to be shielded, and this has been possible without any undue problem.

Thinking of the whole community, when there have been special events such as VE day on the 8th May, personal birthdays, or November 5th bonfire and fireworks, there has been space outside for them to work smoothly. That space is pretty much perfect: enough for social distancing, but familiar and somehow friendly.

250 miles away in North Wales, there was appropriate space for us to have our usual summer holiday in August. With a few small adjustments, the two terraced houses that belong to us were reconfigured to function as four independent "bubbles" or "pods". It was tight inside for one or two households, but most of the time we were outdoors: on the beach, sea and mountains. Here the horizons are expansive, and because we know it so well, the space was welcoming and familiar, unthreatening even during two storms, Ellen and Francis.

I know that this summary risks making the place sound like Shangri La, and that is unfortunate because the accommodation in both

London and North Wales is in many ways unexceptional and ordinary. But it helps to explain how I came to see what is now palpably obvious: since 1899, we have been blessed with just the right kind of space.

There is a literature on the dynamics of groups of different sizes, including the seminal work by Georg Simmel, *On the Social Significance of Numbers*. As a sociologist I have always found this intriguing, wondering for example what is the best size for a thriving, people-friendly city. What about class sizes? Or the number of children or young people in therapeutic residential establishments? What this reflection set in motion was an attempt to set these discussions in context: always asking about the kind of space that is available. Is the city set on a hill, for example, or beside a river delta?

We are still a long way from being able to understand how factors such as security, health, well-being, educational attainment, and creativity, relate to space and spaces available, but intuitively we know enough to realise that there are bound to be significant correlations.

Years ago, when John Major was Prime Minister, I happened to visit Blenheim Palace. Because Winston Churchill was our MP when I was a boy, I was interested in seeing where he and his family had lived. John Major had, I believe, grown up in council housing. Walking around the library, and along corridors adorned with portraits and the maps of historic battles, looking out over manicured lawns towards the lake, I couldn't help thinking how their different childhood homes might have affected their worldviews. And I have wondered about this ever since. I do not expect a definitive answer of course, but know I am on firmer ground when fearing for the welfare of children whose families are packed into confined spaces.

All through this journey of exploration, I have been trying to stay with physical space, but again and again I have been aware of how important space is symbolically; and how it seems through the eyes and imagination of children. How do they feel in the relative confinement of a tent, the cabin of a boat, or the playground of their school?

A few weeks after this article appears in *TTCJ* we will once again be celebrating Christmas at Mill Grove. It is not possible at this stage to know what the government guidelines are likely to be, but as you have probably have guessed already, it is becoming apparent that the space with which we have been blessed opens up numerous possibilities for creative activity. We are quietly confident that there will be ways of connecting, sharing, and reflecting made possible by the quality of the premises and grounds.

Is there, I wonder, a therapeutic environment (from say, Dingleton Hospital, to Newton Dee, Finchden Manor, the Mulberry Bush, or the Cotswold Community) that was not similarly blessed with the right kind of space?

When the 2012 London Olympics were planned, meticulous attention was paid to footpaths, bridleways and canal paths. During the lockdown these have come into their own: gateways for ordinary families to virtually endless varieties of parks, facilities and open spaces. The connection between indoor and outdoor space, schoolrooms and sports facilities, is integral to this whole consideration of the right kind of space.

Which reminds me: I am assuming that this Christmas 2020 in the UK carol singing outdoors, as well as family walks, will not only be allowed, but encouraged. It must be difficult for individuals and families for whom such activities are not possible. This is all about calculus or art because there are so many variables. The worst of all possible worlds is surely restricted indoor space set within oppressive, confining outdoor space. So it behoves those of us blessed with plenty of appropriate indoor space to share it where and when we can, and to do what we can by means of carols and walks to release pressure and open possibilities, not only for Christmas, but also the New Year.

Resilience Tested by Lockdowns

One of the features of life under the shadow of the Coronavirus pandemic of 2020 has been the discovery of which things carry on pretty much as before, which things have been in suspension, which things work well as substitutes, and which things don't. Though most unwelcome, it has provided an opportunity for a controlled experiment: how do things function under new conditions caused by a single variable? We have all been involved in this experiment whether we like it or not. The findings are beginning to appear and be shared. It seems that we have all found how much we miss human touch and hugs, and that there is no substitute for them.

Those who do administrative or clerical work, or study, have found that some tasks can be done effectively from home, but others such as team-building and blue sky thinking seem to require people being together and sharing the same space. Music and Zoom don't work without a lot of technical knowhow and effort, and even so, something is missing when performers and audiences do not share the same moment and space. One of the surprises for us at Mill Grove has been that consultations and mentoring seem to work a lot better than we thought they might at the outset of lockdown. There are some different dynamics, but consultations of two people, or three at the outside, have functioned rather well. For me this has included student supervision, mentoring sessions and regular times with a consultant psychotherapist.

Meanwhile within households dynamics have changed, and it has become apparent that there is a range of reactions and effects. Some have thrived and even enjoyed it (although it is not good form or sensitive to let this be widely known), while others have struggled. The purpose of this piece is to share some experience of, and reflections on, dependency and resilience. Lockdown interrupted many patterns of life and interactions with those for whom we

care and have supported long term. We know the importance of these reliable and predictable rhythms. They help to provide secure boundaries and shape daily life so that there is something to look forward to. Implicit in the relationship is a form of inter-dependence or dependence.

As we began to cancel weekly visits and meals with individuals and families, we became anxious about possible effects. In a few cases we found it hard to imagine what might be going on households, and how long it would be before things exploded or imploded. In some, the dynamics were chronically fraught and dysfunctional. And others, living alone, had come to see their visits to Mill Grove as an extension of family. We were aware of the mounting data indicating growing concerns about mental health and the examples of those close to us was consistent with this.

We immediately adapted to support in other ways. Regular contact by phone and text was one of the key features of this. We organised some Zoom gatherings so that members of the extended family of Mill Grove could connect on special annual occasions such as anniversaries or Christmas. And it was possible at times as guidance and regulations permitted to have times outside with a limited number of children and adults. We purchased a fire pit so that we could have barbecues during the winter. But we still feared that there might be serious deterioration in relationships and the emotional wellbeing of individuals.

It is far too early to draw conclusions about long-term effects but, in the interim, there has been one very significant and reassuring trend emerging. Most of the individuals and families have been more resilient than we had expected. With families living together 24/7, three or four young children in combined spaces, home-schooling, no garden and virtually no accessible outside facilities or resources, the prospects seemed bleak. But only this week we had a phone call from a mother of three (she had lived with us as a child). She rang to tell us that, after months of applications and re-applications, the youngest child had finally been given a place at the school the two others attended. Meanwhile she had been home-schooling him along with his siblings. (For those who are regular readers of these columns, the little boy has figured from time to time.) We shared our excitement with her and with him. There was no denying the struggles of daily life, but months after the start of lockdown, and the interruption of the regular times of support, the family was intact and even looking ahead purposefully.

When we took some birthday presents and food to another family, socially distanced of course, on one of the children's seventh birthday, there was a similar sense that somehow things were holding together. Not only had they not given up: there was a sense that things would be OK.

On the single occasion when an individual member of the Mill Grove family came to meet us outside the conversation was animated and positive. Pre-Covid she would have popped in several times a month and spent large parts of the day with us.

I have pondered the nature of resilience over the years. Although I have seen it in evidence again and again I fail to understand it in any depth. It is probably a characteristic or quality that will never be adequately analysed, or perhaps even defined. Like a compost heap, it seems to be far too organic and complex. But during a consultation session (yes, you've guessed it, by Zoom!) when we mused on these cases, a few common threads emerged. There was in the children an innate looking forward, and hope. They were growing, and in the normal course of events there were things to work towards, to anticipate. The school

place for the youngest child in one household was a case in point. But in the other, when we handed over the birthday presents to the girl who was seven that very day, a younger member of the family reminded us that her birthday was next! Such hope is not a sufficient explanation of resilience, but it is necessary.

Then there was the fact that Mill Grove was still there for them, and that we held them in our minds although we were not physically present. What this means and how it works is difficult to fathom, but it involves a two-way process. Resilience somehow recognises and draws sustenance from this reality.

And finally, for now at least, the families had all experienced Mill Grove and its way of living, its patterns of life, and its values. The consultant reminded us that this should not be underestimated, because we had not even considered this element of the process of survival and growth. Whatever else might be said about Mill Grove, after 121 years it is palpably resilient. Sometimes there have been unexpected and unusual pressures, but despair or giving up have never been options. This is not something talked about: it is embedded in the very nature of things.

As I write there has been another, serious spike in the spread of the Covid 19 virus, and the future is uncertain. We are under no illusions that pressures will mount, and there could still be serious fallout in the lives of individuals and families. Even so, what we have learned so far gives us cautious grounds for hope. And meanwhile they know that we are looking forward very, very much to the time when we can be together again.

Mill Grove and Topsy

In his introduction to *Living with Children*, the second volume of articles from *TTCJ*, David Lane describes Mill Grove as a most unusual place which "for the purposes of statutory registration is unclassifiable". This is right on the nail. Some decades earlier, R.J.N. Todd, an

inspector from the Home Office, wrote in one of his reports that it is "not like any other home", and Bob Holman used this as the title for his history of the place. Because it has been my home for most of my life, I am in some ways the least well-placed person to describe it, unable to see the wood for the trees. And what I take for granted may well be exactly what someone trying to fathom it needs to know.

What I would like to do in this piece is to describe a few features of what is going on today, and then to suggest some of the reasons why it has developed differently to most other places that started with similar aims, and that were in former times classified in roughly the same way.

On roughly an acre of land with premises that have 90 rooms, from broom-cupboards and nooks to a spacious dining room and indoor badminton court, between 20 and 25 people live at any given time. There are seven or eight independent living spaces, and these are occupied by families or individuals who have turned to us for help. On occasions pregnant mothers have come to live with us, but more often, families with very young children. There is no leaving age, and we make a commitment to those who come that they can stay for as long as they feel it is the most appropriate place for them to be. This means that there are some individuals living in what we think of as the core of the residential community, and it was only when trying to explain who they were and why they lived here that a penny dropped for me.

So let me share with you a little about four of them; how they relate to each other; and what part they play in Mill Grove and its story.

The first is the granddaughter of someone who came to live here as a young girl in 1928. She represents continuity on a grand scale because her mother had also lived at Mill Grove for part of her childhood following a family tragedy. She has two grown-up children and is separated from her husband.

The second is the daughter of a boy who came to live at Mill Grove with his two brothers in 1980.

The third came to live at Mill Grove as a very young boy in the 1960s, along with three siblings. Like them he moved on, but 30 years later he was struggling with work, housing and citizenship. In response to a call from his older sister, we welcomed him back home.

The fourth is an adult who came to live at Mill Grove as a girl and who has lived here ever since. (In recent months she has moved into one of the independent living spaces.)

What these four individuals have in common is a long-term connection with Mill Grove and what is commonly known as the "Mill Grove family". When people use this term, they are thinking of a global network of those who lived at Mill Grove, or whose parents or grandparents did, and who still identify as part of this extended family. Connections are maintained in all sorts of ways. There are guest rooms, for example, for those who wish to stay for a break or a special annual event. There has been a yearly newsletter, *Links*, since 1901. There are informal networks of relationships. For each of them Mill Grove functions as home. To get a sense of what this means, it is important to take in the fact that their connections with the place go back nearly a century and span four generations.

One other feature of Mill Grove that needs to be included in any attempt to understand it is the development of several local initiatives such as the Pre-School, the Rose Walton Centre (for children with cerebral palsy), a community association, a badminton club, music lessons, keep-fit sessions and Thursday lunches for senior citizens in the neighbourhood.

There is a lot more to it than this, but this is probably enough to indicate the shape or contours of the place as it has become today. What started as a "Home for Motherless and Destitute Children" (these are the exact words), has become a residential community or extended family, a centre or hub of a neighbourhood. In 1975 it deliberately chose the name Mill Grove as a way of avoiding any such labels or labelling, then or in the future. If you really want to get to know what it stands for or what it is, then come along and find out. Even sociologists have been at a loss to find a generically accurate or appropriate description, so if you do turn up, it is worth keeping an open mind.

Since 1899, like Topsy, Mill Grove has developed into something that seems to be rather unique, not because it has sought to be different, but as part of a process best described as organic rather than planned. Many voluntary children's homes like say Quarriers, Bridge of Weir, Barnardo's, Fegan's, the Children's Society, National Children's Home, Muller's started at roughly the same time as Mill Grove, but all have taken different paths or trajectories. So what I wonder might some of the factors be that have caused Mill Grove to take a road less travelled, and become what it is? Here are a few reflections.

The same location and buildings. The land and the buildings are in the same place, and most of the buildings, though adapted and extended, are recognisably Victorian. The address and telephone numbers have never changed. This means that there was never a revolution when the place was demolished or relocated, and something "purpose-built" erected. Changes have been mostly incremental and responses to emerging needs, requests for help or insights.

The same family. The person who started Mill Grove was Herbert White, my grandfather, and like my grandmother, Edith, he lived here until his death. My father was born at Mill Grove and became responsible for the place and family, until he handed over to myself and Ruth. We lived at Mill Grove with our family until they were grown up. Members of the White family were part of, and helped and supported, what went on all through. So, whatever else it might be it is in fact a family home.

An independent charity. At no point has Mill Grove ever been part of a larger body or organisation. This means that there has never been a corporate decision taken elsewhere that interrupted or influenced its development. Like ordinary families there has been a remarkable degree of independence.

A faith commitment. The story of how the place started and the way it has operated only makes sense with reference to the Christian faith of those who set it up and maintained it, and the wider Christian community who have supported it.

A growing body of knowledge. Over the years, and notably since 1968, there has been continuous reflection on what is going on, informed by insights from psychology, sociology, community work, residential and group dynamics.

Interaction with context. This is implicit in the idea of an organic process, in that no organism exists out of context. In this case the community has developed with reference to local area, neighbourhood, local government, national trends and global movements. This has happened not least because it has become a global family.

Individuals. The story cannot be told or explained without reference to those whose characters helped to shape the development of the place. This includes the founder and carers, but also those who came to live at Mill Grove as children. Several of the latter have written and published their own life-stories.

North Wales. Since 1984 Mill Grove has been blessed with two houses in a picturesque part of Snowdonia. And three generations have now enjoyed exploring this part of the United Kingdom. Holidays spent on its beaches, seas, rocks, rivers, lakes and mountains are part of the shared experience and story of all who live at Mill Grove. And as with many families, holiday memories are some of the most treasured and enjoyed.

It would be interesting to hear what others think. Meanwhile the unique dynamics continue to play themselves out. For example: between the time I started this piece and my conclusion here is an incident from last Saturday morning. I was mowing the grass when a family of four arrived from Swansea. The father of this family was one of the three boys who came to live at Mill Grove (from Nigeria) in 1980. He, his wife and two daughters had come to see his eldest daughter, the one currently living at Mill Grove, before they all went off to see his brother and family.

We ambled round outside the buildings taking an occasional photo, and his daughter recalled the times when she came to Mill Grove as a young girl. She paused at the door on a balcony where she used to come in to join us and our Labrador dog, called Drake. The way she spoke it was obvious to us all that these were eagerly awaited times of great enjoyment, and memories started flooding back. Concurrently, her father was recounting some of his childhood memories of North Wales.

So it was that there were seven of us united by over 40 years of shared life and experience.

A Place Where Things Are Mended

It was the Spring Bank Holiday, and with Covid restrictions still in place, we couldn't go with our usual custom and practice and have a barbecue with an open house. So we opted to be around and let things happen: no plans, except for having a pizza or two in reserve.

As we were welcoming two new residents to Mill Grove during the week, Ruth had quite a lot of practical preparation to do, and I spent the morning clearing out a garage so I could gain access to one of our Mirror dinghies and begin to get it and the trailer ready for the summer holidays. It took me the best part of two hours to clear away dozens of roofing tiles, a bunk bed and assorted wood and junk that had accrued over the past couple of years. I was joined by one of the Mill Grove family (she had come as a child and, now in her mid-thirties, is still living with us). We chatted about old times, and because there was time to spare and no pressure, I introduced the subject of her relationship with her younger sister.

In other articles I discuss the subject of the long-term effects of separation and loss on the relationships of siblings from the same family. These two sisters had never been able to manage their fraught relationship without a lot of support, nurture and patient encouragement. But I was able to comment that we knew they were fond of each other, even though they did their best to disguise the fact, and usually preferred communication through a third party. For the first time that I could recall she didn't enter denial mode. She made no comment, but at last the truth could be spoken. Although

None of this was planned: it was a natural outworking of the story. And, as we chatted plans, were bounced around for the coming summer and other anniversaries and events. There is little doubt that the story is set to run for years, possibly generations yet!

they had never resolved issues around the reason for them being taken into care in the first place, they were always concerned about each other, though separated by over 70 miles and not having seen each other since before lockdown in April 2020.

It sounds a small thing, and it was an incremental step in a long process, but it is part of the mending of their relationship. Ruth and I know how much they mean to each other, and so do they at one level, but anyone else would have difficulty gathering enough concrete evidence that this was the case. A relaxed time on a bank holiday Monday had created the space for this sharing of a deep truth.

Then two of the Pre-School staff joined me in the orchard (where the garage is situated) taking time out from an online First Aid course. Before long we were joined by another resident of Mill Grove, and when the staff left to resume their training, she and I were left alone talking about her plans for IVF treatment, adoption or fostering. It was one of the most difficult, personal and far-reaching decisions of her life. With the old pear trees shading us from the sun and with time to spare, she began to sketch out the issues, choices and her anxieties and hopes. It is part of a long process of mending from the time her marriage ran into difficulty and she separated. She was still without the hoped-for long-term partner, and time was ticking away. Now she had just received the news that she would not be able to use her own eggs in any treatment. Being with us was part of a delicate journey of mending her life.

I had just got the lawnmower out of the shed to cut the grass in the orchard when a family of five arrived. The mother of three had lived with us at Mill Grove as a child and had come back with her partner two decades later.

When the accommodation we were able to offer became overcrowded she and the family had moved into council accommodation nearby, where we continued to support them. They had had a great morning together watching *Peter Rabbit* Two at the cinema and having had a takeaway meal before arriving by bus. They revelled in being with us with space and time to play, ride bikes and chat. There was some football, basketball and bike riding, and the youngest one helped me (as always) with cutting the lawn, putting the cuttings on the compost heap, and eventually putting the mower away in the shed and locking the door. Neither of the other siblings is the least interested in this, but for the two of us, it is part of what we enjoy doing together.

We all had a game of cricket in the playground using a dustbin as a wicket. The six of us had very clear boundaries, not only to mark fours and sixes, but roles, tasks, fielding positions and the order of batting and bowling. It was a brief game, but each was involved and played well. We enjoyed it. Compared to the first time we tried it together, this marked a considerable improvement in relationships all round. We went in for an evening meal of pizza and melon followed by a prayer time involving one of two songs with actions that the children asked for.

While this was happening a mother and her child arrived and sat outside the dining room on the grass that we call the bank. Another resident and her adult son arrived with a rug and pizzas. They were celebrating the sixth birthday of the boy. Mother and child had lived with us before a chronic health condition resulted in them having to move a short distance away. We had celebrated his fifth birthday during lockdown in June 2020, outside, in just the same place. Ruth and I had no idea that this was the plan on this bank holiday Monday.

I opened the window and began to play Happy Birthday on my guitar. As we all joined in the birthday boy beamed and came to the window thrilled that the same group were around a year later. We finished our meal and prayer time and joined the families on the bank. Before long the children were playing an imaginary game using the climbing frame as a base, possibly a house, while the adults chatted. Another resident came to join us. He had come as a little child, and then come back to live 50 years later.

The mother of the six-year-old and I started talking about a poem she had written describing her feelings about Mill Grove. We had shared it at her request on our website and I wanted to thank her in person for such a touching piece. Here it is.

Mill Grove

The sound of joy,
That spreads out with children's voices,
In the orchard, across the sky,
Children now and children no more,
Handed me down, patched and darned with care,
Mill Grove is handed to the children.
Who watch the fireworks,
With a woosh and ahh …
Of something glittering in the sky,
That's like an angel.
With an ahh and a wish,
That things will be better now …
We look down in prayer …
But we should look up,
At the bricks and the mortar
And the stories that hold a place together,
That gives …
And does not ask in return.
A place where absent hearts
Have grown again like new
Seedlings in the garden.
And the stories that join us
When dark falls on this place
I'm sure even the wildlife knows.
Broken things keep getting repaired:
I noticed that.
They are mending kettles and gates,
And people all the time.
And friendships form, which is part of the mending and borrowing,
And chopping of wood and quieter moments,
When there is a deep knowing between friends
that times are hard
Or times are good.
The knowing you find with

Brothers and sisters.
With a family.
Tonight the sky looks full over Mill Grove.
And if the sky should empty…be wanting?
We all know we will have shelter.
Children now and children no more,
Handed me down, patched and darned with care,
Mill Grove is handed to the children.
Who watch the fireworks,
With a woosh and ahh …
Of something glittering in the sky
That's like an angel.
With an ahh and a wish,
That things will be better now …

It was the lines:
"Broken things keep getting repaired: I noticed that.
They are mending kettles and gates,
And people all the time.
And friendships form, which is part of the mending and borrowing …"

that really moved me. And she confirmed in chatting with her friend that they both felt this was how it was. They had become part of an extended family and this connection would remain wherever they lived. It had been a place of mending for them both.

The following day I was talking to her friend and recalled the first day that I had met with her and her son. I commented that he was obviously full of resentment and rage at the way the rest of their family had treated his mother. She confirmed that she had felt awful: rejected and alone. And that Mill Grove had become a place of healing and mending. I replied that it was so good to see her son growing, relaxing and playing contentedly with others much younger than him during the previous evening.

And so it was that an unplanned and unscripted bank holiday had been rich with conversations, play, celebration … and mending. People of three generations connecting with a deep knowing … the knowing you find with brothers and sisters. With a family.

I don't understand the dynamics. As a matter of fact, they become more a of mystery by the day. But I have come to realise that it's true. It is a therapeutic community where healing comes in its own way and time.

What is Your Favourite Colour?

Recently, during a Golden Wedding anniversary celebration, there was a surprise impromptu version of the TV game, *Mr and Mrs*. (For those unfamiliar with this, the idea is to find out how well a husband and wife know each other.) On this occasion, the questions were kindly and helpful, so we both scored perfectly. The only moment of doubt came when I was asked Ruth's favourite colour. As far as I know she doesn't have one, always preferring subtle tones that are set in a context of other colours, rather as Cezanne in his landscapes. But given that I had to offer a single colour, I ventured to suggest that her favourite colour was gold. She replied without hesitation: "It is today!" Perhaps 50 years together have helped us develop such shared survival mechanisms.

It so happened that a short time earlier, I had been asked a similar question by a child, which came to mind for obvious reasons when you know my reply. She asked me my favourite flower. In this case there was no doubt in my mind at all. It is the Tormentil. Yes, the lowly, diminutive cruciform shiny yellow plant that grows on the hillsides.

Its Latin name is *Potentilla Erecta*, which seems ironic in that it often appears at the level of the grass growing around it. None of the children or young people had heard of it, and so I explained that I would show them one on our next mountain walk.

We were on to the slopes of the nearby Moel-y- Gest, with the Snowdon Horseshoe coming into view, when I asked whether any of the group had seen one yet. No one had. I explained that they had been walking over them and occasionally treading on them for several minutes. In fact, if we knelt down right now, we would see them under our noses. We did. And there they were. Each four-petalled flower growing seemingly by itself, though actually connected by low-lying runners. Very soon each child was looking at one. They were everywhere. And immediately they seemed to understand why I was so fond of them.

Focusing on the specimen nearest me, I told how when I was climbing mountains alone I sometimes stopped and stooped to take in the deep shiny yellow of a Tormentil. It was a companion in the vast silence of the mountains. And I ventured that, more often than not, I was the only person who would ever see this particular plant. It made the encounter that much more significant, even poignant. How remarkable that such lavish attention to detail should have been given to something so small and so seemingly insignificant, that might never be seen or remarked by anyone else.

After a while we followed the path that led over a stile and through fern-covered rocks to the crags at the top of the mountain. We had a great time exploring various routes up some of the slabs. I thought we had left the topic of my favourite flower behind, but it cropped up in a variant form as we had a picnic while sitting on some rocks at the foot of the summit crags. We began to notice the lichens and mosses growing on them. Often overlooked, these rather strange, hybrid like species hold the key to life on land. They represent a transition between bare rock and what will eventually become grasses, flowers and shrubs.

It is one of the great joys of our holidays in North Wales that we have the opportunities and times to notice and discuss aspects of the natural world that tend to escape the notice of most people. And that we do so in their natural habitats.

I have never been fully attracted to or persuaded by gardens, and it's likely that a colour defect involving reds and greens doesn't help my appreciation of complex and colourful borders and flowerbeds. (I can't see poppies in a green field for example unless they are pointed out to me.) But a little Tormentil or lichen draws me intuitively to pause and admire it and evoke a sense of wonder, even awe.

Perhaps unconsciously I am reflecting the sort of humility, the coming down to ground level, that is integral to respecting, understanding, playing with little children. Perhaps the lichen represent childhood: that stage between the early phase of life on earth, the basis of the growth and maturity that follows.

Whether this is so or not, there were two associations stirred by reflecting on this walk on our local hill. One concerns Donald Winnicott and an incident recalled by my dear friend Simon Rodway. He told how on one occasion he observed Winnicott meeting a child for the first time for a preliminary assessment. Simon told how Winnicott took off his jacket, got down on the floor and did nothing but play with the boy, spontaneously, and at the boy's pace. That was all he did, commented Simon. As I knelt down on the hillside with the children there was a similar dynamic. If we are ever to begin to glimpse any understanding of the mystery of childhood, surely it will involve some form of stooping or coming down, not as a gesture or procedure, but because that is the only way to get to know each other genuinely, as we interact with nature, toys or transitional objects.

The other association is the tectonic shift going on in the way children and young people understand and interact with Planet Earth. I am completing this piece during COP26 in Glasgow, and it is no coincidence that Greta Thunberg speaks for so many. They relate to the natural world differently to many of previous generations, including my own. Human existence is fragile, contingent on a careful and respectful relationship with the environment. This is not primarily about statistics and percentages. Respect for the Tormentil and lichen goes hand in hand with a strand in the new way of living that is emerging, or being re-discovered. These species have developed over seasons, years and geological eras. Had they not existed nor would we. And yet, now our shared future lies in our hands.

Can there be any excuse for seeking to "educate" children and young people, without creating a therapeutic milieu in which we take off our jackets and get down to ground level with them in wonder and awe? What are one or two of your favourites among all things bright and beautiful, I wonder?

The Roots of Hospitality

On a beach near Borth-y-Gest during August 2021 a visiting family greeted us as we arrived by sailing dinghy. Once we had disembarked and stowed our buoyancy aids and lunch, the adults struck up conversation during which we discovered that our new-found friends had roots in Poland. Meanwhile one of the young girls in our family, and one of theirs, began to play in the sand together. Without the need of any language, they engaged in constructing some sort of miniature dwelling, possibly part castle, part enclosure, part home. My hunch is that we were experiencing something close to the roots of hospitality. It was a spontaneous human reaction or interaction, assuming common values and without any need of introductions or planning.

Months later, on Easter Day 2022 (as will become apparent, this was the Western, rather than the Orthodox Easter, the latter coming a week later) there was another conversation also involving someone from Poland. It was several weeks into the war resulting from the Russian invasion of Ukraine beginning on 24th February 2022, and I was wearing a small Ukrainian flag. Over a cup of tea before Sunday lunch at Mill Grove, I was chatting with one of the residents: the Polish mother of two. By that time, while the first refugees were arriving in the UK with all the challenges of visas and administration, well over two million refugees from Ukraine had been welcomed in neighbouring Poland. Given this meant that a very high proportion of households and communities were likely to be involved in offering some degree of hospitality, my question was what the Poles might be feeling in their hearts. What motivated or prompted them to respond so generously and spontaneously?

After a pause for thought, she replied: "We all know how they felt. Every one of our families in one generation or another had experienced a similar invasion, so all understood what it is to leave your home at a moment's notice, having to leave nearly everything behind, while fearing that you might never be reunited with belongings or home. When someone in that predicament is asking for help, it's not something you think about or weigh up: it is a response from the heart."

This reminded me of the time some decades earlier when one of the children living at Mill Grove had asked me with a good deal of feeling whether I really wanted to be there caring for her and others. It was the beginning of a lengthy period of introspection, when I was forced to confront a range of emotions and identify and address all sorts of defence mechanisms. It was certainly not a simple matter, and I was rattled by the natural testing of a young person who was seriously probing my motives and commitment.

In a while we were sitting down with others in the Mill Grove family to a traditional English lunch and, while we were enjoying the meal, a couple of other residents were playing football just outside in the playground. (For the record, and not because it matters, one supports Liverpool, the other Crystal Palace.) With a relaxed meal inside, and contented play within earshot, it was a pleasing and uneventful time, and I was acutely aware that many in Ukraine would have envied the predictability and safety of our life together, not to mention the freedom to play outside and the ample meal on the table.

This is when our Polish friend continued by making a link with what she had said earlier. "Mill Grove is a welcoming place", she commented. "And life is different here. It is not part of the rat race." I asked if this was something she felt, or whether it was a more objective reflection. She responded immediately that she had experienced and warmed to this acceptance and alternative way of life. Pondering the possible connections between the summer play of the little girls on the beach, this current observation and the generous hospitality of people in Poland, I reflected on how welcoming this woman had been when a mother and young child had come to live at Mill Grove. She was gracious and patient, accepting and encouraging of them both. And when they had needed to leave due to the mother's ill-health, she had kept in touch. More recently she had assumed something very close to a proxy mother's role to another resident at Mill Grove.

At the end of the meal, we opened Kinder Eggs and played with the little toys and gadgets inside. After another cup of tea, we painted eggs and watched this mother and one of her two sons engage in a traditional painted egg contest, which she won easily. She then invited us to join her at the church where she worshipped the following week (the Orthodox Easter). They were hosting a meal and celebration for Ukrainian refugees in London. Ruth and I were already committed that day, but the resident of Mill Grove who had been "mothered" by our Polish friend did go. This was no small matter, as she had not attended church of any kind for a decade or more.

Something was going on that touched or affected us all. Mill Grove is an extended family, or residential community, that has welcomed well over 1,200 children (including some Hungarian refugees in 1956) since it began. It is manifestly a place of hospitality and is committed to operating in a way that is more inclusive than most nuclear families, institutions and organisations.

There are lots of factors involved and a history of nearly 125 years but, as I came to realise during the time of introspection I mentioned earlier, at its heart is a genuine empathy: rather than an "us" and "them", or "we" and "others", there is a tacit understanding and acceptance that beneath the surface and distinctions such as ethnicity, gender, status, age and culture, we have the same DNA.

It has often been remarked that young children accept others without question, but that as they grow up social and cultural distinctions begin to take shape and harden, stereotyping and labelling leads to the "othering" of those perceived to be different. Without suggesting a

sentimental understanding of the worldview of children of early years, we have observed that this does seem to be the case more often than not. There is the obvious and necessary specific bonding and attachment between a very young child and her significant other, but this does not affect the general principle of welcoming and accepting others.

And it may not be incidental that with very early children it is by play and without words that this acceptance, this hospitality, takes place. For words and language by their very nature embody social, cultural and ideological traditions and carry much baggage including stereotypes.

Before completing this piece, I discovered that one of our nearest neighbours, who has just arrived, is a refugee from Ukraine. On meeting her for the first time it was not long before tears welled up in her eyes as she saw my little Ukrainian flag and two larger flags in the front window of Mill Grove. She couldn't say any more. It was just too painful. And that is a similar dynamic: hospitality, acceptance and welcome does not depend on analysis and definitions: there is "something understood" and shared between human beings. What unites us is deeper and more significant than differences.

This is not a matter of feeling or preference: it is, at a certain level, a fact however you want to define it. And young children need no introduction to this truth: it is part of the very nature of things, who they are and who others are.

Which leads me to a final thought: I wonder whether such "hospitality" between those who welcome and accept each other across social, cultural and ethnic divides is somewhere near the heart of therapeutic care and therapeutic communities. There will be assigned roles within such settings but, when all is said and done, isn't it about recognising our common humanity and shared roots? Somewhere in the life-story or family history of the carers there is the recognition of that which connects us to those we are seeking to understand and help. It is about person-centred dynamics, growth and healing, rather than a programme, manual or technique.

INTRODUCTION TO THEME FIVE
Creativity

The articles in this section are predictably playful, reflecting the way creativity and imagination provide resources for the growth of love, and also how creative thinking and action is in turn inspired by love.

There are thoughts on politics, team sports and competitive games, imaginative responses to the Covid lock-downs, social media, silence, a wheelbarrow, snails, and educational philosophy that is attuned to play, love and reciprocity.

Still the best ready reckoner of healthy group dynamics is spontaneous humour and laughter.

Two of my favourite pieces are here: "The Silence" and "The Gardener and the Boy". Both are descriptions of creative interaction, one between human beings and the other how a trusting relationship provided the context for the self-expression of a young boy.

While the final piece, "Snails and Comenius", is a reminder that, having spent 25 years researching philosophies of education, I have only just discovered one of the great pioneers. It feels as if I am arriving at the place where I started, with perhaps just a glimmer of recognising that place for the first time.

Brexit and Young People in Care

It has dawned on me fbelatedly that there is one subject even more taboo than religion in residential and foster care settings, and that is politics. Scanning the 200 or so articles that I have written for *TTCJ* and *ChildrenWebmag* I find for example that I have never devoted a single piece to the subject. And looking at the books on my shelves dedicated to child care I find that, apart from one or two by the late Bob Holman, which are about community action and community work rather than residential care, all steer well clear of politics.

So here we go! Perhaps there is something to do with referenda as distinct from elections that engages with people of all ages and cuts across some of the predictable dividing lines in a society. I was not able to visit Scotland during the 2014 Independence referendum but even from a distance it was palpably obvious that deep emotions were stirring. In households, schools, clubs and in pubs and community centres conversation was unusually deep-seated and fresh. I haven't heard from residential and foster carers, but I would be surprised if they were exempt from such a lively national conversation.

And now the UK has held its Brexit referendum, and very deep feelings have been touched and laid bare. Apparently the two post-Brexit days at Glastonbury were like a wake: and this had little or nothing to do with the customary mud! We have regularly discussed aspects of the subject at the meal table at Mill Grove for weeks, and a few days before the actual vote my oldest grandson asked me what I thought about Brexit. I can't remember exactly how I replied then, but his question stayed in the mind. The result is that I have just posted a letter to him explaining how and why I voted as I did.

I can't imagine writing a 3,500-word letter to a grandchild about more general politics or economics, but this seemed to be an historic occasion that merited serious thought. I told him that I voted strategically with his future, and that of his sisters and cousins, in the forefront of my mind. And as I wrote I realised that he would be well placed to see how accurate my analysis and forecasts were, long after I was no longer around to test them for myself! It was rather cathartic to point out that I might be quite wrong!

But as I say, perhaps referenda could be a special case. If so, what about everyday party politics in residential and foster care? Clearly there are reasons why we have trod so carefully around so potentially contentious an issue. For some there is the spectre of radicalisation (Ayatollah Khomeini: "Anyone who will say that religion is separate from politics is a fool; he does not know Islam or politics." *Tahrir al-Wasila* Vol. I). We are understandably wary of airing our political views in professional settings and contexts. The current shadow chancellor of the UK, John McDonnell, was in residential child care for several years, and although he has well-known political views now, I am not aware that he made them known to the children and young people for whom he was responsible.

What possible guidelines or code of practice would or could be drawn up? I thought I would have a go, just to get the ball rolling. With citizenship education on the agenda, it might be worth professional bodies having a go.

There needs to be space created in which political (and that includes ethical and economic) issues can be discussed without awkwardness or fear. The idea of no newspapers and no news in a residential or foster home is a sad one. But which papers and which channel? Who chooses? For years I have encouraged both the *Guardian* and the *Daily Telegraph* at Mill Grove, as a way of demonstrating the fault-lines in British politics and society.

Theoretically the professionals in these settings would remain politically neutral, but why should that be? If young people ask honest questions about what we believe, should we not respect them enough to answer them?

I guess we could rule out homes functioning as wings of political parties.

But what if candidates appear on the doorstep? Why not invite them in for a chat?

What and how do we go about discussing history and current affairs around the world? Surely it is not appropriate to remain agnostic about the relative merits of Stalinism, Maoism, Nazism and, say, the European Project? If historical questions never arise, then there is something suspicious about how a home engages with the personal and social development of a young person.

And what do we say about the importance of voting in a democracy? Is it not appropriate to encourage young people to see how the system (however imperfect) works, and to encourage them to vote? Involvement in politics at whatever level is surely part of personal and social development.

This leaves the thorny issue of whether a professional should reveal how he or she has voted (in an election as distinct from a one-off referendum). Is there a convincing reason why not? Perhaps a person chooses not to reveal this to anyone including close members of their own family, but if someone is happy to share with others, why not with those in care?

I am in an interesting and possibly helpful situation as far as this is concerned because no political party in the UK remotely represents my political views. They don't fit. On the one hand, more radically love-communist than the most ardent left winger; on the other hand, sympathetic to the conservative political philosophy of Edmund Burke. On the one hand, pragmatic; on the other hand, enthusiastically green. The elections I like best therefore are those when I have more than one vote. With a careful allocation of my handful of votes I can spread them with just a hint of what I would like to see as a good government, local or national.

But if a professional is a member of a radical political party, should he or she withhold this information from young people in care? Perhaps the person would not have been appointed in the first place were their views known.

How different is this, I wonder, from what happens in ordinary families?

You will have noticed that the questions keep spilling out, and there are many more waiting in the wings.

But it is a start. And if readers of *TTCJ* really wanted to know what I wrote to my grandson about Brexit I might just be willing to consider sharing that letter with others!

Learning Together

There is a poem which describes my philosophy of education beautifully. It is called, "Child Though I Take Your Hand", and is by Jane Clement.

> Child, though I take your hand
> and walk in the snow;
> though we follow the track of the mouse
>   together,
> though we try to unlock together the
>   mystery
> of the printed word, and slowly discover
> why two and three makes five
> always, in an uncertain world –
>
> child, though I am meant to teach you
>   much,
>
> what is it, in the end,
> except that together we are
> meant to be children
> of the same Father
>
> and I must unlearn
> all the adult structure
> and the cumbering years
>
> and you must teach me
> to look at the earth and the heaven
> with your fresh wonder.

Two days ago it was as if the poem came to life. I was in Auckland, New Zealand, with two young members of the Mill Grove extended family. I will call them Abel and Samuel, boys aged seven and five respectively. They wanted to take me up one of the 50 or so volcanoes in the city area. This one is called Mangere. After I had packed a very small snack in my knapsack and they had provided two plastic bottles of water, we set off. I had no map and so was completely in their hands. They knew the approach to the mountain like the back of their hands and we were soon on the grass-covered rim of the crater. So far they led the way, but at this point I suggested a turn to the right that was new to them. After some discussion they agreed to this. (The reason for my suggestion was that I wanted to conserve contour lines rather than go a more direct route which involved descent and more ascent.)

It was a little steep and narrow in one or two places and the younger brother took my hand. On reaching the summit of Mangere Mountain, marked by a triangulation point, the learning together really took off. We had 360-degree views of Auckland, and that meant city landmarks, bays, bridges, islands ... and, of course, volcanoes. They pointed them out and named them with unerring accuracy: Mount Eden, Mount Victoria, St. Johns, North Head ... and frankly I was amazed. For a start some of them looked pretty similar to me, and secondly how did two small boys know them anyway? They played on the trig point as if it were a climbing frame (which it might just as well have been designed for), and then as we descended a short way a question arose about the colour and nature of the rock or scree on which we had been walking. Samuel picked up a piece and we inspected it closely. (I had my climbing anorak complete with compass and magnifying glass.)

It was, unsurprisingly, a rusty red colour as befits lava, and there were traces of black ash. But it was set on a path that had some sandy-coloured material. I explained that it was probably sand that had been blown to this point over the years and compacted by the elements. At this point things started to get exciting. And I mean exciting because there were broad smiles accompanied by small dances of joy. We discovered some large rocks on the rim which were of a grey, whitish colour. They hadn't a clue why this was, or what it was that was

covering the rocks to give them this hue.

So I invited guesses as time stopped still. Paper was one of their many suggestions. After several minutes I ventured the idea that it might be a kind of plant. They were sceptical, and eventually asked me to tell them what it was. I told them it was lichen and began to explain something of the nature of lichen with its symbiotic combination of two species of plant, its many varieties, and most importantly its unique role in geology and biology: that it grew on bare rock where nothing else could take root. They queried the last of these assertions by pointing out moss and grass on the same rock. "They are growing on the rock" they said in unison. "Good point" I replied, "but which came first, I wonder?" And the penny dropped: it was because of the prior existence of the lichen that the moss and grass could survive.

Well, we might have arrived at the South Pole or the summit of Everest if you were to judge by the excitement. With more lamb-like skips of joy and occasional pauses with the magnifying glass we jumped from rock to rock, discovering different kinds of lichen, white and yellow. It was as if we had found the secret of life (which in a way we had), until we came across broken shells on the path around the rim. They had no idea how seashells could have got up this high. I ventured that they were probably from birds who had carried their sea-food to a safe point and then crushed the shells before enjoying a snack. This provoked smiles, but did not remind them at all of our own snack. In fact we never had time to think about that, and they never once mentioned food or water in our two hours together on the mountain.

We continued around the rim and came across a herd of bullocks standing astride the path along the rim. The boys followed me quietly through them and then we saw a heron (variety not known to me) which was clearly eating something, probably a fish. They quickly made the link between a sea bird and the rim, which helped to confirm my hypothesis about the seashells now some way behind us.

Believe it or not we were pretty much alone on this wonderful adventure playground called Mangere Mountain, until on the edge of the rim there appeared a school group led by a knowledgeable Maori who sat the pupils down and told the story of the core (tholoid) of the volcano and how a single man had lived there, and cut his body, shedding blood as part of the sacred process and belief that connected heaven and earth, past and present, ancestors and future generations. The two boys stood at a viewpoint silently as we eavesdropped on the questions and answers that helped us understand the story of this place. It was as new to me as to them.

Moving on and finding time running out (I was to meet one of their uncles at the airport) we ran past a couple of ancient Maori dwelling places (marked by distinct rectangular-shaped dips in the ground) until we found a display that described how the volcano had formed in five stages. I don't know how long we spent at this spot, but both boys were absorbing the diagrams as they checked the pictures with what they could see in front of them,and what we had discovered on the trip so far.

As they did so, one statement of the Maori teacher dominated all other considerations. She had said that we should not climb the plug (tholoid) out of respect for Maori tradition. The problem was that as we stood looking at it, someone (not from the school party of course) was doing just this. What would happen, they wondered?

And so it was that we were left with a very big question as we started running down the slope to get home on time. We came to some low wooden posts that were designed to prevent cars parking on a grassy verge, and I suggested that we might pretend we were on snow and doing a downhill slalom. Abel led, and Samuel and I followed. It was a perfect mock-slalom course, and served to aid our speed of descent.

We arrived back at the house late for lunch and with me needing to leave immediately for the airport. As I did so I wondered why the boys weren't at school like everyone else (uniforms are prominent in NZ). Then I realised that they were home-schooled. So our adventure was part of the learning process, and presumably I had been experiencing something of how they learnt things and why they were so absorbent, particularly the older brother. "Can you write down the name of that special volcano you talked about in the Philippines," he asked, "I want to google it". So I wrote down the word "Tagaytay". And the next day when we met, he told me how beautiful it looked with the little volcano in the middle of the huge volcanic lake. As it happened the next day we explored surfing, shells and chess together, but that is another story.

Rarely have I followed the track of the mouse together in such a literal way. Is there any way of learning that is not together? And, with all this in mind, what are schools for, I wonder, and why?

Unblocking a Log Jam

I am not sure whether the term "log jam" has been used in, or applied to, counselling and psycho-therapy alongside familiar concepts such as resistance, defence mechanisms, blocks and blockage, repression and denial. But it came to mind some time ago when we were trying to describe the nature and dynamics of a situation in which a mother and her family of three generations had been trapped in for over 20 years.

The "logs" which combined to create the jam included the deep-seated and chronic problems in the childhood of the mother that were not known to most of her family; the reactions of the mother (usually now termed Obsessive Compulsive Disorder – OCD) which had dominated and shaped the whole of her life, habits and behaviour; how she struggled with actually living in any sort of accommodation; the effects of the mother's condition on her children throughout their childhoods and still a pivotal factor in how they relate to her and she to them, despite the fact that she has shared with them the nature of her sad and difficult early years; the strained relationships with the rest of her extended family who do not know about what she suffered and endured; physical ill-health, inappropriate life-styles and diet; the inability of the mother to undertake any paid employment or to engage in consistent voluntary work or parenting; the absence of any sense of hope when contemplating the future; a deep sense of defilement and contamination that prevents normal interaction with others outside the family; and a belief among the other members of the family that the mother should "snap out of it" assuming that her condition relates to other traumas in her life that they have known about for years.

By any standards this is a formidable list, or to use the term in question: a pretty comprehensive log jam. Over the past two decades the mother has received various forms of help and treatment ranging from psychotherapy to behaviour therapy, but there have been few improvements detected by most of her family or acquaintances. One unfortunate unintended consequence of this treatment is that she has come to accept the labelling that has been involved in the process as her script for life. She sees herself as a victim, powerless to question or move beyond this ascription and status.

We had been alongside and supporting this mother and her children for many years as extended family and resourceful friends. But despite one or two very specific and limited improvements, the mother's condition and the family dynamics have remained stubbornly resistant to change: log-jammed! Despite so much engagement with professionals in mental health over the years there has not been a course or programme of treatment that could break the log jam in which mother and family found themselves.

And then it happened. When we described some of the changes that had taken place within a matter of days to our consultant psychotherapist, she used most unusual and very dramatic language to describe what she was hearing. "It seems as if a bomb has gone off," she said. I questioned why she had used such an extraordinary term or metaphor, and she replied that the effects were so significant and dramatic that they called for something that indicated such a startling cause.

Normally, of course, bombs going off are not a cause of celebration (at least to those among whom they have exploded), and it was at this point in the consultation that I realised that J.R.R. Tolkien had coined a phrase to describe another dramatic event that called for new, shocking language. In trying to find a word opposite to "tragedy" in drama, he realised that there was nothing appropriate to describe the consolation of a happy ending in fairy stories. So he offered the word "eucatastrophe": the sudden joyous turnaround when it dawns upon the consciousness that there is deliverance from the seeming inevitability of catastrophic defeat. He saw the resurrection of Jesus as good news beyond human imagining: that which gathered up every longing in art and legend. (J.R.R. Tolkien "On Fairy-Stories", *Tree and Leaf*. London: Unwin, 1964, pages 60-63)

Unaware of Tolkien's proffered term, our psychotherapist had seen deeply enough into the nature of the log jam to understand that anything dismantling it was likely to be packed with unusual power, if not dynamite.

It is just possible by now that you are wondering what it was that caused the change signified by the word "bomb". So here it is. The grandmother of the mother of whom I am writing died. That's it.

So how could the death of an elderly relative possibly come to have such a comprehensive effect? Here are some of the repercussions (ricochets, perhaps?) of this event.

The grandmother lived in the house where the abuse had taken place (completely unbeknown to her or anyone else at the time except the perpetrator and the victim), and although the mother had said that she would never enter that house again, she did.

For those familiar with the novel *The Shack*, there are distinct echoes of the re-visitation of the exact place where suffering has occurred: the place one seeks to avoid at all costs. (William P. Young, *The Shack*. London: Hodder and Stoughton, 2007. The book has been made into a 2017 film of the same title.)

All sorts of changes stemmed from the decision to face the unthinkable, and it isn't possible (as with a bomb) to work out how they are related: it has been an explosion with results and effects here, there and everywhere, seemingly random in some cases.

The mother discovered photos in this house: precious family photos. She shared them eagerly with family and close friends of her mother and family.

Her father, himself widowed at a young age, had found it hard to know how to relate to his daughter (the mother in my account) and her visit and the photos established a new line and form of communication between them.

He was the executor of her grandmother's will, and the mother took responsibility for arranging the funeral. He provided her with a hand-written tribute, crafted with sensitivity and attention to detail and potential audience. He handed this tribute to my wife and myself, and later in the day I went round to his house and had the longest conversation we have ever engaged in, heart to heart. Until that moment we had been distanced by the chronic intra and extra-personal struggles of the mother and the refraction of everything through her experiences, feelings and fears. I came to realise that he was still grieving the loss of his wife (the mother's mother), so that there were limits to how much he could become vulnerable enough to share in the suffering of his daughter (the mother).

I was with the mother when she visited the minister taking the funeral, and to see her taking decisions and responsibility for an event as significant as a funeral was so unusual and unpredicted, that it was a source of something like wonder. She was in regular contact with others in her family about details of the service and reception, as well as with the minister and the funeral director.

But then there was the matter of her separation from her husband. Although this had taken place over 20 years before, it had never been formalised by a divorce. It was all too much for her before, but now there was a very practical dimension: whatever the will contained, she wanted to make sure that the legal position was clear. Alongside her father and her son she went to an appointment with a solicitor to begin legal proceedings aimed at securing a divorce.

How and what the timescale for the further dismantling of the log jam will be, one cannot say. But water is now flowing downstream (to continue the metaphor) and it is gathering pace. It could well prove irresistible, as the first one, and then another log is moved.

Perhaps I will be able to revisit this continuing story in a future column, but for now there are just two interim reflections.

First, no amount of therapy, treatment or counselling have had anything like this effect. Life itself (and that includes death which is such a natural part of it) has within its powers the potential for healing. Times and seasons are vital to healing and growth: we cannot and should not act as if we can assist the healing process without respect for the nature of life itself. The wisest psychiatrists and counsellors will always be attuned to the context of their encounters with those they are seeking to help.

And second, we see once again the remarkable wisdom of T.S. Eliot when he wrote *Little Gidding: The Complete Poems of Plays* (London: Faber, 1969, page 192):

"... what the dead had no speech for, when
    living,
They can tell you, being dead: the
    communication
Of the dead is tongued with fire beyond the
    language of the living."

A Wheelbarrow

Years ago, when I lived in Scotland, I remember a senior residential worker passing on to me the insight that people like gardeners and cooks were often best placed to be alongside children and young people in situations and at times when genuine exchanges might take place. I have borne this in mind ever since, and it seems to me to be true. One of the great advantages of a residential setting, over say counselling or formal treatment, is that it offers the in between times and spaces, when there are opportunities to say things or listen to someone who just happens to be there. It's not about anything formal, or a person fulfilling a role. It's more like two human beings relating to each other spontaneously.

So it is that I share with you about a wheelbarrow. Just to set the scene: at Mill Grove, one of my roles is that of gardener. I am responsible for the trees, the bushes and the grass, so it is not uncommon to find me with a lawnmower or pushing a wheelbarrow. The pre-school children rarely come across me in any other role, so it shouldn't have come as a surprise when one of the four-year-olds asked me, "Uncle Keith, do you sleep in the big garden?"

Most often I push the wheelbarrow only when I have specific tasks to do, but on one occasion recently I had just learned that a son of one of the pre-school staff had died in tragic circumstances the day before, so I wanted to be alongside and available to all the staff. As everyone was outside in the playground and orchard on a cloudless spring morning no one seemed surprised to see me appearing behind the wheelbarrow. This meant that I could push it around, getting alongside first one, and then another of the staff. They were all in a state of shock, so there wasn't much to be said. It was simply a case of being there with them.

As we stood and chatted, the children carried on with their activities, which included riding on trundle toys, kicking and throwing footballs, playing around the allotment paths and reading in the outside library. The normality of their play and interactions was somehow reassuring. It was a visible reminder that life carried on come what may. One of the staff told me that she had been thinking how fortunate she was to be alive following a serious brain tumour. Another told me that she had lost her two sisters at an early age, and that this event brought it all back. It had taken her something like six years to begin to come to terms with her loss. And then another of the staff looked to me for a hug: she had lost one of her own sons in not dissimilar circumstances less than two years before.

I had some grass cuttings in the barrow and, as several children gathered around, I enlisted their help in getting the contents to the compost heap. We managed to push it up a plank together and unload our cargo, and then I offered a ride to one of the helpers. We imagined that it was a steam train and made appropriate sounds as it drew up beside two other locomotives (that both looked distinctly like wheelbarrows)! Had there been time we would have made lots of trips in the wheelbarrow turned train, but a visitor had arrived to see me, and so my time was over.

Just a day later I had completed email correspondence, the first draft of a paper, and some minutes of a board meeting, in time to greet one of those in the Mill Grove family who calls me Grandpa. I told him that I would appreciate some help cutting down a tree. He was delighted to have been asked and so we walked hand in hand down to the orchard where he jumped into the wheelbarrow as we set off for the big garden. Once again, we imagined it was a train, and I asked him to be the driver alerting me to any hazards ahead. We stopped at the garden shed to collect some cutters and a bow saw which he held carefully as we continued our journey to the area behind the leylandii where we store branches and brushwood ready for our November 5th bonfire celebrations.

I asked him if he could see an elderberry tree that was growing uninvited, but he told me he didn't know what it looked like. We found it together and saw that it had a very different trunk and leaves to the leylandii that towered above us. He handed me the tools and then jumped out of the wheelbarrow as we set about dismantling the rogue tree. I cut the branches and handed them to him. He placed them neatly alongside the garden wall, each one parallel to the wall. He did it meticulously. Time was running out because it was nearly time for our evening meal, but we managed to finish the job by cutting the main trunk down just above the ground.

Then the train drew out of the tunnel formed by the leylandii, past the newly-appearing rhubarb near the spot where the bonfire is located each year. We hung up the cutters and saw, when his sister appeared with the news that the meal was indeed ready. On seeing her brother having a ride she wanted to jump on board too. He was happy about this, so she joined us as we set off with all the right noises of a steam train towards the orchard.

As we did so we reminisced about our summer holiday the previous August in North Wales. One of the memorable days together had involved a ride on a steam train from Beddgelert to Porthmadog. And there were lots of photos of the two of them on both platforms,

as well as on the train. They said that they hoped they could go to Wales again this year.

Having alighted, we went inside, washed our hands together and re-joined the rest of the family, including their new baby sister, born the day before! We had an enjoyable meal during which we chatted about Mr. and Mrs. Fox who I had mentioned during the wood-cutting.

It was, you might say, an uneventful time together with little of note. But I am inclined to see it as a time when our relationships continued to develop, when past and future were connected, and when brother and sister shared happily together, and when we enjoyed teamwork and doing a job well.

But it probably seemed uneventful to everyone else, and that's just the point. We hadn't planned to do this: it just happened in the normal course of events in the life of a gardener. I reckon lots of teachers and social workers would have given their right arms for that sort of opportunity. Having a burger together in McDonalds, either with the pre-school staff and pupils, or these two members of the extended family, wouldn't have been the same at all, however hard I might have tried!

Like a Child

It so happens that I have been having a rather concentrated spell of time working on PhDs: from initial discussions about possible questions through to comments on final drafts. Because it is possible to have enough of a good thing, it came as a joy (as well as something of a relief) to find a quote in one of the manuscripts that prompted me to reflect in this piece something of what happened last night at Mill Grove.

The quotation was from Karl Barth who, acknowledging the impact that singing simple songs about Gospel events and acting them out as a child himself had upon his spiritual development, wrote: "Yes it was very naive, but perhaps in the very naivety there lay the deepest wisdom and greatest power." (*Church Dogmatics*, IV/2 112-13)

Holding this in mind, let me describe what happened at Mill Grove. It was Monday and we were enjoying our evening meal. There were 14 of us sitting at two tables. This occasion was special in that it was the birthday of a mother who spends each Monday with us, usually accompanied by her teenage daughter who joins us directly from college.

The youngest person present was a pre-school girl. She loved every minute of the meal, eating her food with enthusiasm and not a little skill. After the lighting of the candles on the birthday cake, she joined in the singing of Happy Birthday with gusto, and then without a moment's thought blew out the candles before you could say "Speech!"

The next youngest was her primary school-age brother who relishes every part of the pattern of Monday evenings with us, from games and projects to snooker and the putting out of the dustbins and the recycling containers. (He has thankfully not yet reached the age when he distinguishes between work and play as far as the joy and fun are concerned.)

We concluded the meal with ice cream, custard and portions of the birthday cake, and then I suggested that we sang a chorus before I said a prayer for the mother whose celebration it was. The words of the chorus, *Two Little Eyes to Look to God*, are written on the assumption (as were those referred to by Professor Karl Barth) that they will be accompanied by actions, and most of us knew both words and actions. For some reason it is one of the most popular action songs we sing.

But then the brother offered to sing as an unaccompanied solo a song he had been learning at school: *The World is a Wonderful Place*. He sang it especially for the mother, with confidence and evident satisfaction. It drew a very warm round of applause.

Over the weekend there had been mixed emotions in London with another terrorist attack occurring not long before the Manchester memorial concert for the victims and relatives of the attack in that city. And on Sunday there had been associated arrests just down the road in Barking. Traffic had been gridlocked in our area as a result. This meant that we were celebrating against a rather depressing backdrop. The Queen later referred to the mood of the country as "sombre".

In this context the words we sang and listened to were simple, naïve you might say: Happy Birthday; Two Little Eyes; and The World is a Wonderful Place. But the presence of these two little ones and their part in the proceedings brought some "wisdom" and "power" into our midst. There was a genuine sense of joy unaffected by (because unacquainted with) the political and social context. And there was a taken-for-granted hopefulness. With words and actions their presence warmed the hearts of the rest of us present. Simply by being children they were a blessing among us: not because they were wise or knowledgeable beyond their age and expected ability.

Several of the group sitting at the tables struggle with issues of anxiety, depression and poor mental health, and I was reminded yet again that being part of a community is of itself of considerable value. I have written before how I am regularly asked whether Mill Grove is a therapeutic community. The answer comprises two complementary strands. It is not a residential community with specific and planned therapeutic alliances, strategies and interventions. But it is a place where the patterns, rhythms and dynamics of everyday and seasonal life have benefits that can appropriately be called therapeutic. Caring relationships develop in this setting, and seasons and annual events such as birthdays provide the stimulus for part of our shared life together.

The rest of us (including the mother whose birthday it was) were blessed by the presence of the two little ones in our midst. But what of the little ones themselves? Let me speak of the brother who was, as usual, sitting beside me throughout the meal. He is experiencing difficulties both at school and in his family. It is early days for us (and other concerned professionals) to find a way of understanding, let alone describing, what he is going through. But it is already clear that he finds much of his family life unpredictable and bewildering. He has taken to creating a fantasy world in which he hopes he will feel safer.

If this takes time and careful thought for resourceful adults to decode, it is downright puzzling and frustrating for his peers at school. On one occasion he stood outside our window in the twilight, and when I went out to be with him, he told me that he had been "thrown out" by his family, that he was cold, and that no one was at home. We chatted for a bit, and then I ambled with him to his family home. All the members of the family were there, and his mother's description of and reaction to the situation did not resonate for me with the feelings he was articulating. There wasn't a way of trying to build a bridge of understanding between these two worlds. And my guess is that this happens more often than not at school too.

We are considering carefully how best to be alongside him and his family as we seek to help. But in the meantime he looks forward eagerly to Monday evenings with us. And what makes it so enjoyable for him is its patterned predictability and reliability. He knows that he is welcome and will never be "thrown out" (whatever he meant by this). He knows that there are shared values, behaviour and accepted ways of doing things. He knows that he is respected as an individual, while at the same time expected to take on board the norms of the group. In short, he finds Mill Grove a secure base within which he can thrive, and from which he can explore ideas, games and exploration.

He offers to help in practical ways (inside and out) and is always inventing new games that he is happy to play himself, or to share with others. And so, despite all the inner confusion and turmoil, something else is going on. And his rendering of The World is a Wonderful Place could not have been more pertinent or poignant in all the circumstances.

A Question of Sport

After we had dealt with the dustbins and recycling on a Monday evening, four of us decided to have a friendly game of snooker: two against two. The youngest member of the group, who is still at junior school, chose me as his partner. Our opponents were both adults. We knew each other well and, as we broke off, there was no needle and much mutual encouragement characterised by friendly banter.

But from the very start things did not go well for my partner and me. I missed a couple of sitters, and my partner even missed the cue ball. We managed eventually to pot a few balls between us and set up a snooker or two, but the result was never in doubt. Inexorably the gap between the two sides grew on the scoreboard. And as the game wore on my young friend grew more and more frustrated, until he said he wanted to quit. He handed over his cue and made for the door. It took quite a lot of gentle persuasion from all of us to keep him engaged until the end. But when the game was over, and the final score announced, he left the room in a huff saying that he wasn't going to play again.

I know how he felt and why but, as far as I can recall, it had never occurred to me, however young I was, to quit a game of sport, or any other game for that matter. I write as one who took the playing of sport for granted: I never knowingly turned down an offer to play with other children whatever the game happened to be, and that included games like Chess and Draughts. Most of the play was friendly with no record kept of the results and nothing tangible to show for a victory. But in time I became involved in leagues and cups in several sports including football, cricket, table tennis, tennis, athletics and rugby, with my main sport being badminton. In the process I managed to notch up a few modest medals and trophies. I have always attributed this love of sport in part at least to the fact that I grew up at Mill Grove where there were always enough of us to make up the necessary teams. But the fact is that both my parents played sport and they modelled it for me and, at senior school and then university, there was plenty of opportunity to play in excellent facilities.

My friend's experience and attitude raised a fundamental question for me: what advantages are there in playing competitive sport? Put another way, how does sport help to shape a person's character and inner world for good? He was very young and let's hope there is plenty ahead of him, but he is not being taught team sport. His parents have not introduced him to team games and are not modelling together how to cope under stress. I hope that over the years it will be possible to nurture this in a game or games of his choice.

You can see that I need to distance myself from my own experience even to begin to work out what a person is missing if they never play competitive sport. As I have reflected on this it turns out that it seems to be a good deal. Sport mirrors life in certain ways, and it is, like play in young animals, a way of developing and honing skills that will be used later in life. There are reflexes, and the coordination skills of hand, foot and eye. There is the discovery of what teamwork entails, including leadership and following. And there is the need to recognise and assess the qualities, strategies and tactics of the opponents. But a key thing, common to all sport, is that you often find yourself playing in conditions not of your own preference and choosing. And losing is always part of the experience.

I still recall my very first representative game of sport. It was a football match against another school, in Harlow. I was ten at the time. We lost 8-0. The opponents were older and bigger than us. The pitch was sloping. The wind seemed to be against us all the match, the rain was in our eyes and the ball was too heavy to kick more than a few yards. But there was never a thought of quitting, and after the dispiriting game our coach assured us that this was par for the course. Within a season the tables would be turned. And his words were proved right. The very next year our team, consisting of exactly the same players now considerably more experienced and battle-hardened, won the double in our local area.

A key attitude that develops in the whole process is that of continuing to do your best for yourself and for the team when everything seems to be against you. Any sportsperson could list dozens of times when things were going badly. I am not sure if this is what was meant by the saying that the battle of Waterloo was won on the playing fields of Eton, but from what I know of the battle it did not go well for the allies for much of the time and was a close-run thing. Sticking it out and not giving up was a necessary condition of winning.

Now we know that life itself, real life, is also like this. We all operate, by definition, in conditions not of our own making or choosing. And the question is how we function in adversity. Are we able to rise above the conditions, not just for our own good, but crucially for the benefit of others in our family and group of friends?

In therapeutic care we are trying to find ways of preparing children and young people for real life when many, if not most in our care, have experienced the traumas associated with real life going so badly that it has already hurt and scarred them deeply. And there are many ways in which we go about that process. I wonder how much serious attention we give to the question of whether team sport might be one of the keys in the process for at least some of the young people we seek to help. I really don't know and would be fascinated to find out more. What I do know is that those alongside young people in difficult urban situations often find sport one of the ways in which they can relate to such people, and with sports such as boxing, basketball and football, teach them some of the basic physical and emotional skills that equip them for life. I am not sure if this is equally true of boys and girls and would appreciate any data or reflections on gender differences.

Over recent decades the term resilience has become significant in the assessment and understanding of young people. Has there been research on resilience and sport, I wonder? And are there other activities that have a similar effect? As I write this I realise that music has been used and beneficial in just such a way. I remember instantly Russell Burgess and the Wandsworth School Boys' Choir in England, Gustavo Dudamel and the Simon Bolivar Orchestra in Venezuela, and Daniel Barenboim in the West-Eastern Divan Orchestra in Palestine. All deliberately chose and used music as a means of developing character, belonging and teamwork.

We know of play therapy, art therapy, drama therapy, role play and so much more, but have we given sufficient attention to the benefits of team sport? Isn't one of the ways we can conceive of sport as a form of role play that embodies or replicates certain features of everyday life and relationships? And if confidence building is critical in self-esteem and development, then we need to identify those who may have the necessary abilities and skills to build that confidence in games of their choice.

Which reminds me, in closing, of an evening at the Newton Dee Camphill Community in Scotland. Staying as a guest, I had offered to help with a session of basketball in a nearby gym. I found myself responsible for picking one of the teams, with nothing to go on except appearances and kit. One I chose to be part of our team looked every inch a superb athlete, and he was dressed impeccably. However, when the whistle blew at the start of the game, he retreated immediately to the wall outside the court, and spent the whole game running round it. Not once did he grace the court with his presence or even encourage his team-mates with a cheer. Meanwhile on the other team there was a small, rotund person with Down's Syndrome. He was dressed in the same clothes he had used when gardening during the afternoon. He never moved throughout the game, remaining rooted to a single spot. It wasn't long before I realised it was not a randomly chosen place. It was exactly where penalties are taken from, and whenever the ball was thrown to him, he lobbed it using two hands, and without looking up, got it into the net every time (perhaps my memory has glorified his achievements unduly). We lost the game, and I was just a little wiser.

I am obviously not arguing that team sport is for everyone, but on the other hand, I think its therapeutic potential may have been underestimated. It would be interesting to hear what others think.

Social Networking and the Education of Children

There can be little doubt that the internet and social networking are transforming our lives individually and collectively. As individuals there are opportunities to decide and revise our "identities", and socially we are all potentially globally connected. It will be for future historians to assess what effects this is having, how profound and how lasting they are. But already there are pressing issues for western democracy and elections. There are questions about personal privacy and what is shared with third parties of various kinds. There are rising concerns about harassment and bullying on social media. And as I write this, there is a growing fear that social media combined with YouTube are fuelling gun and knife crime among children and young people in London.

Against this backdrop I would like to consider a single matter: the impact of social media on the education and learning of children and young people. When Tony Blair was Prime Minister of Great Britain and Northern Ireland, he saw himself as an arch-moderniser, and one of his many pronouncements was that every class in every primary and junior school would have computers. At the time it was seen generally as a good thing: just as the replacement of slates by exercise books, and blackboards by interactive white boards had been in bygone eras. But already some deep questions are being raised. And it is both interesting and very significant to note that in the vanguard of those posing the questions are some of the very people who know most about social networking.

On 10th February 2018 *The Times* carried a piece about tech-free schools. And the message was that digital pioneers, including Alan Eagle, Director of Communications at Google, a chief technology officer at eBay, and senior executives at Apple and Yahoo, were all concerned about the effect of social networking on children's brains. Sean Parker, an early investor in Facebook, admitted that they had made it as addictive as possible. He is then reported as saying: "God only know what it's doing to our children's brains". Tim Cook, Chief Executive of Apple, said he did not want his nephew (who is coming up for 12 years old) to use social media.

It seems that many of this breed living in Silicon Valley are choosing to send their children to Waldorf Schools based on the educational philosophy of Rudolph Steiner. As a matter of principle, these places of learning do not use electronic media. Instead, they value physical experiences and tasks, the use of imagination, problem-solving (rather than consulting Google for an answer), and collaborative skills.

Now it would be easy to see this contrast in black and white, binary terms, and to identify with a nostalgic view of the past. This is not how I see it. All technological innovation offers new opportunities, accompanied by new challenges and problems. One aspect of the challenge is always how to use them appropriately. And one of the very practical problems is the universality of social media: across all cultures, classes and ages. Take just the variable of age: what if one needs adult experience and maturity before one can use them responsibly and properly?

I go with Sean Parker in wondering what Facebook and the like are doing to children's brains. I fear that they are undermining basic skills and qualities such as concentration, problem-solving, critical thinking and analysis, delayed gratification, hand-eye coordination, imagination, reading and purposeful or playful physical exercise.

I am informed by the cognoscenti that the future of computing lies with quantum theory. This will replace the Boolean binary system that has been with us from the birth of computers. It is not about speed and capacity, so much as the subtlety of thinking and calculation. And this gives me cause for hope, because it may well be that human beings will need to be smarter in their interactions with computers. We shall see. But meanwhile households, schools and therapeutic communities would do well to think carefully about the boundaries that need to be constructed and placed around access to social networks. If a child is bombarded with advertising aimed at distracting her from the task in hand, and is reduced to pressing a button indicating "Like" or "Dislike", with no guiding frameworks of the sort offered by geography, history, religion, philosophy, literature, grammar, mathematics, physics and the like, then I cannot see how she is learning to think and act appropriately.

This is a very practical and pressing challenge for a residential community such as Mill Grove. We are not (for the most part) a formal place of education, but our philosophy is that it is in everyday life, relationships, patterns, rituals, seasons and activities that learning is always taking place. So let me share with you the simple rules that we have devised as a family at Mill Grove when we go on holiday to North Wales. (This period of vacation is packed with exploration and learning of every kind. In fact, it is a pity that it gets interrupted every year by the need to return to schools and colleges!)

Smart phones and computers are banned from communal living space, from meals, and from times spent together on beaches, seas, lakes, rivers and mountains. Instead, we talk face to face, we make our own music with guitars, recorders and singing, we make our fires for cooking, use the wind for sailing and paddles for kayaking, learn together to scramble, make dens together, use art, poetry and prose to record what we do in diaries and scrapbooks. It's a conscious shared way of life, and it seems to me to be self-evidently superior to one in which people are glued to little screens connecting us with others and the world by means of electronic imaging.

This does not mean that we have turned our back on the benefits of digital communication and storage. We are grateful for weather forecasts and global information, and these inform us in our shared living and activities. It is not a Luddite approach to technological advances, nor is it a way of harking back to a golden era in the past. But it does require discipline and shared values and ownership of this way of life.

Perhaps a way of introducing these challenges and dilemmas to young people is to ask them to consider what they would want for their own children. And it is this very question that seems to have been the deciding factor with the leaders of electronic technology: not how can I make money, or how can information be shared most speedily, but what would be best for my children?

Historians will be able to tell future generations whether ours had the courage and determination to follow where this simple question leads. Societies generally are rarely able to make informed, conscious radical choices, but households and communities can. Is there a role here for therapeutic communities existing to help children and young people might take a lead in this? Waldorf Schools are among those that have begun the process. Who is ready to join them?

How to Say "Thank You"

I was facilitating a day course on the book, *The Growth of Love* (Abingdon: BRF 2008) with a team from a Pre-School, and in the process, we focused on one of the most common practical challenges of daily interaction in this environment. In my experience it is a conundrum not just in these early years settings, but in any therapeutically-aware interactions with children and young people wherever they occur. So, let me begin by describing it. A child comes into the setting and the first thing she does is to show you her new shoes (or coat, or ribbon, or lunch box or anything else that she is wearing or carrying). Sometime later she brings you a piece of paper which she has covered with brightly covered paint (or some Lego she has assembled, or a construction involving egg-boxes, cardboard and some stickers). Or perhaps it is something that she has found (a leaf, a stone, or a ladybird). I hope this makes the scenario clear and leave the reader to imagine where it occurs most often for you.

The question is: how should you react? Now we can dismiss the obvious inappropriate responses immediately. No responsible or sensitive adult is going to ignore or turn their back on what the child is bringing or showing them. And neither would they be critical or dismissive of it. So, what is the problem? It doesn't seem difficult: one receives the object with a smile and by praising it? Well, it's not quite that simple. Let's go back a stage or two. The purpose of the setting is to provide a secure base (safe space) in which a child can develop the trust, confidence, social skills, encouragement, acceptance and affirmation that constitute the elements of love. I take it that this (that is the growth of love) is the overall objective. How can we possibly settle for less than this? (This may require some digestion, but in the meantime, I move on.)

Where love grows, and for love to grow, there will be lots of creativity in activities and relationships, so shaping, making, wearing things is integral to the growth of positive relationships. Who could imagine a courtship in any culture or stage of history, for example, without the gift of a love spoon, a card, flower, poem, ring, bracelet etc.? In a setting for young children nothing could be more normal than a child sharing with a significant adult something that they value. But, and here's the rub: how can you react and respond to the proffered object without reinforcing the problematic dynamic that you value, not the child for and in herself, but rather because of what she does, wears or makes? What if the interaction is prompted by the child's chronic sense of insecurity, lack of self-worth and desire to gain attention or to win affection? Such commonly-learned behaviour could be anywhere on a spectrum from a conscious act to something completely unconscious on the part of the child.

With this possibility in mind, the nature of the adult's reaction both in a particular case and in general, over a period of such interactions, becomes critically important. Clearly there needs to be acceptance and valuing of the object, but not at the expense of finding a way of showing the child that our attention, commitment to them and our affection and love for them do not depend on such acts.

To give lavish and ecstatic praise every time is both inappropriate and self-defeating because it is likely to prompt more such gifts at the expense of the affirmation of the identity, person and significance of the child in and of herself. It risks the search on the part of the child for more striking clothes, and more exceptional gifts or creations.

One of the group, trained in Montessori educational philosophy, offered a remarkably well-honed and practical observation. She reminded us that Maria Montessori recognised that this was a dynamic common in all interactions in an educational setting, and that it required careful thought. There were two key elements to it. First was getting the right language; and second, what is for me the crucial dimension, of taking time with the child as part of the response. Let's take each in turn. First, it is vital that what is said to the child is wholly appropriate: commensurate with the object and situation in question and said with complete integrity. Overblown language, including those meaningless adjectives that dominate the airwaves such as fantastic, brilliant, absolutely wonderful and the like, are nearly always going to be out of place. Preschools are not bursting at the seams with Leonardos and Shakespeares at their mature best (however promising every child may be). And what language does that leave for the deeper responses to the child as a person?

So possible alternatives suggested during the training were these: "That's an interesting/good/colourful creation ... would you like to take that home, I wonder?" "You know, I think that your mummy would really like that. Shall we show it to her?" "That's an unusual colour: how did you make it, I wonder?" "Where would you like to put it for the rest of the morning?" "Look how the colours are running into each other: that's cool!" The list can, and should be, extended as the adult considers carefully their honest and thoughtful reaction to the actual object in question. If, as happens quite often in my interactions with young people, you are playing snooker with them, and if the child or young person begins to start a celebrity-footballer type of routine expressly designed for the television cameras, I remind them that this is snooker, and the best players react in this way when, and only when, it is deserved. The first element therefore is a careful, considered and commensurate response.

But my sense is that the second is the one that may be of most significance: it is that the adult deliberately takes time to be with the child while reflecting on what is being given or signed. Time in relationships is a priceless commodity. It is ultimately about recognising and offering the child our presence: we are at that moment present for them, and tangibly with

them. If love is to grow, this matters more than any words, however carefully they are chosen. So the very process of considering what to say is the means of offering something more precious. Without words we are honouring and respecting the presence of the child, including their gift, but not simply because of it.

Perhaps there will be times when what the child has showed us or made deserves not only our consideration, but our wonder: "You know, I don't think I have ever seen anything quite like that! Have you?" "I didn't think those colours went together, but now I realise they do!" And there is just the possibility that the time together results in a conversation about the child and her relationship to home, family, kith, allowing the subject of the focus to shift from the object to the person. And this will be enhanced if in between the display of objects, we take the initiative so that the child has no thought or need of engaging our attention: we are already there for them.

As so often tends to happen, such an insight is, for me, coupled with a real-life example of the very issue in question. On Easter Day at Mill Grove, we were as usual hand-painting eggs ready for a display. Without any planning I found myself interrupted in my own very unimaginative first strokes on the brown egg assigned to me, when I was joined by one of the youngest members of the Mill Grove family. We have done a few things together, but this was a new venture. I offered my egg and brush to him and asked him what he would like to do with it. He pointed to the box of poster paints indicating the colour, white. So it was that we quickly established a working method: I put the colour on the brush, and he painted it on our shared egg with his left hand.

After a time and surrounded by others who were getting caught up in increasingly colourful and imaginative creations (a foetus on the outside of the egg; a garden of daisies; the representation of a broken egg and so on), I enquired as to whether there might be another colour he would like to use. I am not sure whether he ever heard this question because it was becoming evident that his sole aim was to cover the whole egg in thick white paint. So we did. We put it in an egg cup and placed it on the windowsill to dry. At that point he was outside in a flash, playing football with a few others who had finished their eggs. (In case you were wondering, he kicked the ball consistently with his left foot!) When he came back inside again, our egg was dry, and I asked whether he thought it was finished, or whether we should add some stickers that my wife had graciously provided for those of us differently-abled when it comes to painting. He opted enthusiastically for the stickers, and once again we immediately found a method of working as a team. He pointed to a sticker he liked, and I put it on the plain and neat white surface of the egg where we agreed it should go. He seemed not to notice what I did on the surface of the egg, because he was so engrossed in choosing the next sticker. I had to work very fast! And within less than two minutes, before he headed out to play again, we had created an egg that had a lace-like girdle around its circumference, and tiny eggs and flowers arranged in curves on the rest of the surface.

With that, it was placed with eleven other eggs in a tray and handed over to the judges. We had some egg rolling and an egg hunt before the time came for the announcement of the winner, runner-up and third-placed painted eggs. The judges had no idea who had painted what, and so there was no allowance for age or ability. The winner was the egg covered by elegant and well-spaced daisies. But can you imagine our surprise when our distinctively white-based egg was selected as the runner-up? I am not at all sure whether my young partner understood what was going on at the time, but he soon did, when I let out a whoop of joy. This was the first time I had ever won any prize for something drawn or painted, so I was over the moon with the accolade, and he was mighty pleased with the Easter Egg he received on our behalf (for the record, I never saw or heard of the prize chocolate egg again!).

We engaged in high fives and found others around us applauding. The response to his labours was spontaneous. And I have a hunch that we will as a community revisit this story and achievement over the years. It will enter our mythology and folklore. And the next time that he sits on the lawnmower while I cut the grass (this is something we much enjoy doing together) we will remind ourselves of it. Not every creation evokes such a response, but it has the hallmarks of what Montessori was looking for: a commensurate response, and shared time.

And as far as I can recall he has never seen fit to show me or offer me anything else: to this point in time, and thankfully, he just seems to accept that I welcome and value him as a person.

Being Together

To preserve anonymity, I won't locate this factual narrative in time or place …

The young boy in question is growing up in a dysfunctional family. His parents are not married, and it's not clear what commitment they have to each other. The family has chronic problems with debt; with obesity; and with poor housing. The father has been off sick long-term with a form of anxiety/depression that means he struggles to control his outbursts at the boy. The boy has been bullied at school, where he has been constructing a fantasy world as a defence against the chaotic unpredictability of the boundaries of his experiences in the real world. Children's services have been alerted, and following an assessment, a social worker was given the brief to help the whole family through "intensive intervention".

I think that's enough to be going on with, and hope you get the gist of things. On this occasion, I became involved when a very anxious mother phoned me to say that after a blow-up at home, the boy had walked out, locking the front door and taking the keys with him. After walking around the block and seeing no sign of him, she then knocked on my door, with a look of desperation verging on panic. To her palpable relief it was then that we both saw her son, kicking a ball around nearby.

I agreed to speak with him, and the mother returned to her home (with the keys that I had requested from him). On coming alongside the boy, it wasn't long before he had warmly accepted my invitation to have a meal with Ruth and myself. I saw this as the most practical and natural way of calming the situation down and trying to prepare him for returning to his family should that be appropriate. Before the meal we had a hot drink together and then sat down in comfy chairs in the lounge/reception room (where he and I often play games together). From the time of his mother's phone-call, when I first learned of his absence from home, I had been toying over how to react and respond when he had been found. As a matter of interest, I never doubted that he would be somewhere nearby, and in confirmation he volunteered the fact that he had hoped to find me so we could be together. So how, I wondered, was I going to play our interaction? What were the key issues, and what might be the possible outcomes?

The first thing was to make sure that he felt secure in the sense that I was there for him and with him. And within this safe context to seek to understand from him what had been going on in his household, and the feelings and behaviour that had led him to walk out with the keys. This objective wasn't at all difficult because he was just where he wanted to be. And he explained without hesitation that he felt angry because his parents "wouldn't let him do anything". He also said that he was hungry, and they "wouldn't let him eat". I had no other information to go on, so guessed that the social worker in her intervention had been stressing the importance of boundaries in his life, and that he was on the receiving end of aspects of this strategy, in addition to the effects of the very poor family dynamics in overcrowded accommodation.

It wasn't long before it was obvious that he wanted to be with me, but not to talk. He didn't say this, but rather communicated it by other non-verbal means. And that made complete sense, because this was far from an isolated incident and touched deep raw nerves

about a whole range of issues, relationships, feelings and fears. Deep down what was at stake was whether he was wanted and loved at home. He had a very low sense of self-esteem and was chronically depressed.

I suggested that we might play some sort of game together, and his relief was immediate. My sense was that this reaction was not only about the anticipation of playing together, but also that we were avoiding going too near psychologically sensitive places. As I said, when we first saw him, he had been kicking a football around, and on other occasions we would have had a kick-about. I was going by instinct/intuition, when I suggested a game of marbles on the carpet in the room where we were sitting. This meant we didn't have to move anywhere: it was cosy and safe. It was inside and resonated perhaps with the warmth and acceptance that he lacked at home. My idea was that we were close enough to continue our conversation at some stage should this continue or develop.

He sprang up and found the familiar tin containing the marbles. He knows where the games are kept and that they are there for him and others who are part of the extended family of Mill Grove.

As usual we played a version of the game that we have invented ourselves. The rules are based on bowls but with each of us having five marbles and playing from opposite ends of the carpet (rather than side by side). I can't remember who won, but it was competitive and close as it always is. And there was not the least hint that anything else could or should be said about the incident that had brought us unexpectedly together.

By this time Ruth had prepared a meal for us and, as we ate together, we chatted about geography, the news and a bit of sport. He absorbs an impressive amount of information from the television news coupled with Google searches.

At the end of the meal, I mused with Ruth in his hearing about whether it might be time to re-establish contact with his family. Something in his reaction assured us that the time was ripe. And so it was that he and I made our way to the front door of his home, and we spoke with the members of the family who greeted us. Not a lot was said, but clearly the atmosphere had had time to settle. I felt that everyone wanted to be together once again.

And that was it. In some ways it might seem rather like a non-event. Throughout the time that we were together there were no emotional fireworks, and certainly nothing remotely resembling therapy or counselling. But on the other hand, it called to mind two insights. The first was from Rev. Dr. Sam Wells, the Vicar of St Martin in the Fields. He has written extensively on the concept of "being with", as distinct from being for, or working with, or working for someone. And his primary point is that being with is of value in and of itself. It needs not further justification or motivation. As human beings one of our deepest fears is of loneliness, isolation and ultimately the void which is represented by death itself. Yet we have become so used to disguising this primal fear that we are in danger of overlooking the cardinal value of simply and solely being with someone, of being together and enjoying one another's presence.

The other insight came several years ago from a child psychologist at a hospital in Cardiff. He told a conference that roughly a third of the children referred to him were looking for nothing more than someone with whom they could kick a ball about. Whether at home or school they did not find anyone who valued them enough to simply be with them and play together.

So it is that the two of us were together and played. I have no mobile phone to distract me from togetherness in such situations, and the nature of Mill Grove is that being with someone trumps all other demands on our time. So perhaps it would be fair to say, as he knew and found it to be on the occasion, that it's a place where there is time and space to be with each other. And, of course, the space means not just the physical setting, but the emotional commitment that reassures each child that they are intrinsically valuable and have no need to display virtuosity or need: it is enough simply to be, and to be together.

· ·

The Silence

It's obviously a challenge, if not downright foolhardy, to write about silence. But in this case, I believe there is no alternative. Some weeks ago, a person who had lived at Mill Grove as a child came back after a gap of over 20 years. He is now a trained psychotherapist and prison chaplain. It was while we were together that "the silence" took place. After he took into both hands a document relating to his admission to Mill Grove, within a short time I became aware that something significant was going on. It was nothing to do with movement or words. He didn't move … at all. And I knew that the only attuned response for me was to remain motionless too. As the minutes passed and the silence deepened, I realised that I would need to stay so perfectly still that there was no way I could even look at my watch. For this reason, I will never know how long we

remained together in that mutual silent stillness.

After a while, tears began to well up in his eyes before beginning a slow journey down his cheeks. But still he remained silent and without the hint of any other movement. Then at last he indicated by a gesture with his hands and breathing that he wanted to communicate with me verbally. I can't remember the exact words that he spoke because I was still held in thrall to the deep quality of the silence. But he uttered the word, "So", and this was followed, slowly and emotionally, by his indication that in this moment there had been a revelation: everything he had believed or taken for granted up until that moment, reinforced by what others had said, had been overturned, or turned inside out.

His stay at Mill Grove as a little boy, which he and others had assumed to be the saddest and bleakest part of his life, was nothing of the sort. It had been more like the period, possibly the only one, in which he had experienced security and love. And now, that is in this very time and place, having come back, he was experiencing this truth afresh. He said little more because there was nothing more to add. This was an overwhelming experience which I was privileged not only to witness, but also of which I was a part.

When he eventually left, I reflected deeply and often on the nature of the silence in which I had participated, but whose depth I had intuited rather than grasped in any way that could be put into words. I tried to process things by writing down some of my feelings and shared them with others who I knew would understand something of the profundity of what had been at stake and might have been going on. But its essence remained a mystery, about whose significance I was in no doubt.

Then he contacted me and asked if he could make a return visit from the North of England where he lived. He arrived on time and took the very same seat in which he had remained motionless for that period of shared silence. I then chose to sit in the seat that I had occupied previously. I had no idea why he had come again or what he wanted to talk about. So, because there were just 15 minutes before lunch, I mentioned to him that I had still not got over the experience of being with him on the last occasion. I knew something unique and psychologically momentous had been going on in his heart, mind and soul. But apart from the fact that it had positive connotations, I remained in the dark.

I went on to share with him how I had written and talked about it several times since as a way of trying to fathom what was going on. And it came as no surprise to learn that he had done the very same thing, both in England and America, when he had been teaching and lecturing. So it was that we began to explore it together. One of his key concepts was of life as a "road-map", by which he seemed to mean something close to an assigned "script" (as, for example, with gender or class stereotyping). On his road map he was destined to be a victim. And there was no space or room for moving beyond victimhood. What's more there was absolutely no possibility of love. Yes, he really did use this, often neglected, word!

Yet, he went on to tell me how in sessions with a therapist some years ago, he discovered that there was what he called a "hot spot" in childhood, that he would one day need to revisit. And as I understand it, Mill Grove was this hotspot, or covered the time and processes in his life associated with it.

At this point words began to fail once again and I recall his pronounced and repeated hand movements. He placed them together and pointed them downwards from in front of his face towards his feet, and then moved them upwards again. I responded by musing with him about the depth of his feelings and how I had wondered whether the tears had come from his feet. He said that they came from a much deeper source than that: in "the silence" he had been connected deeply with the earth below his feet.

Now I am conscious that this might sound rather "new-ageish", but for some reason, it didn't feel like that at all. It was earthy and matter of fact. He pointed around to encompass the whole of the time (the moment) and place (and its context). Love was being experienced again. And as far as I could gather this was not restricted to an event or a particular person, but to something that comprised both people and place, his inner and outer worlds.

When he had visited previously, and on discovering that he was a therapist and counsellor, I gave him a copy of The Growth of Love. And he now spoke of how he was experiencing afresh the sense of primal acceptance and security that he had known, relatively fleetingly, at Mill Grove. (His mother had taken him away from Mill Grove because she wanted him back with her.) This helped to make sense of both, that connection to the earth with its likeness to a stable foundation, and his insistence on speaking of love (which is premised, I believe, on primal security of some sort).

It wasn't long before he started his long journey home, and I have been musing since, as no doubt he has done. The branches of my thought multiply all the while. But prominent among them is the reminder that security can be found in some unlikely places and seemingly unpromising periods of life. He wasn't the only one to have found it in what is sometimes termed "substitute care". For some children this means that "primary care" has not been experienced elsewhere. Then I recalled how he and his younger sister were with us for just two years or so. Was it possible that something so profoundly significant and lasting could take root in such a short time? Once again, the testimony of people's lives over the years have confirmed that it is indeed possible. One should never underestimate the potential and power of a single, sometimes brief, relationship or experience.

Then what if he had not come back or, if on coming back, he found that the place and its people were no longer there for him? How much of the meaning of the past had been discovered, perhaps even unlocked, by his recent visits after several decades? Healing and self-knowledge always intersect in and through time in unpredictable ways. A road map or script can be transcended years later, and the healing works back. But perhaps the converse: the healing was there, but not realised and appropriated until years later.

And would any of this have been possible without "the silence" and the fact that we had shared it together? I recall a psychotherapist describing a session during his training in which he and his supervisor had spent 55 minutes (that's the whole session) in silence. Neither the student nor his supervisor felt under no compulsion to say anything. And I recall the late Dame Cicely Saunders saying to me that those who are dying look most of all for someone who will watch and pray with them: not offer them words of advice or comfort.

There is, of course, a time and place for words. But as Job discovered to his cost, the words of "comforters" can have the opposite of their intended effect. In counselling and therapy, as in music, silence is integral to the whole process. Whatever "attunement" means, it will sometimes be best expressed and received in and through silence.

"Remember what peace there may be in silence," go the ancient words. And we might venture to add, "and remember what healing there may be found in that peace."

Necessity and Invention

Necessity, as we all know, is said to be the mother of invention. And this has been confirmed by the technological and social innovations spawned during wars. This line of thoughts leads on logically to the question of whether this is true in, say, times of plague. I am not sure what creative ideas came out of the Black Death (1342–1353) and Spanish Flu (1918–1920), but it does seem as if Covid 19 is spawning quite a lot. With this in mind, I thought it might be worth sharing a few examples from this neck of the woods, in the hope that readers of *TTCJ* will be forthcoming with what they have discovered over the same period, and under similar conditions and constraints, wherever they happen to live around the world.

We have found that management, board meetings and supervision have been able to function using platforms such as Zoom and Microsoft Teams. Attendance has been good, and by and large they have worked well. It's not the same as being together face to face, but certainly better than not meeting at all. Serious or sustained discussion or debate do not work, but provided everyone has the relevant papers beforehand, you can get a sense of how the majority feels and make informed decisions.

One great serendipity has emerged from the first online sessions of our centre for children with cerebral palsy. These are conducted from the usual, dedicated classroom at Mill Grove, for one or more children and families in their own homes. Prior to these sessions, each family had been provided with the necessary specialist equipment. The idea then is to get the best of both worlds. Up to a maximum of two children/families can attend in person at Mill Grove, while others join in via Zoom. There is interaction between everyone, whether at home or in the training area. By rotating who attends week by week, each child gets the feel of being present, as well as finding out how things look from either end of the camera.

The added value of this arrangement is the engagement of families in their own homes, so that they can continue activities and exercises as much as they wish after the sessions have finished. The feedback is that some children are making more progress in this way than before. I checked this out with a physiotherapist at Great Ormond Street Hospital, and she confirmed the potential of this form of distance learning.

To make enough safe space available for these sessions, the Pre-School at Mill Grove has migrated to its outdoor classroom and made this the site of all its operations. And it's working a treat. I have been sampling the atmosphere and have found that both children and teachers are lapping it up. Parents applaud seeing some of the adventures and experiences that their children have been enjoying, admitting that they were denied some of them when they were a similar age. And to see everyone caked in thick mud after a session dedicated to water play gave real evidence that they were not outside as a substitute venue: but rather up to their waists in the real thing! Mud, mud, glorious mud: on a very hot day there's nothing quite like it for cooling the blood!

Meanwhile we have been able to celebrate the birthdays of several of the younger members of the extended family of Mill Grove, by having them outside and appropriately socially distanced. There are sometimes challenges in trying to light the candles, but with facilities for football, Twister, basketball cycling and water play, the celebrations have gone with a swing.

Each year in the early summer we have an annual gathering of the Mill Grove clan from around the world. This year it had to be completely re-thought. We recorded a service devised and executed by the youngsters, followed by a two-hour Zoom session joined by people from places as far afield as Ethiopia, the USA and Switzerland. Our website was brimming with clips and greetings. It looks as if

such gatherings will never be the same again. Many connected this time who would otherwise have been unable to do so. We missed refreshments together of course, not least the barbecue!

Several of the families whose children are at the pre-school, or who are part of the extended community of Mill Grove, have been struggling to make ends meet. And this has brought our food store into its own. We are given harvest produce from 40 or more churches and schools each autumn, and with produce carefully stacked and kept in date, it meant that we have been able to supply these families with exactly what they need, without any fuss or stigma. We have been conscious that a number of organisations such as restaurants and pubs have food and drink that has been at risk of passing its sell-by date, and we have been able to make sure that this doesn't happen to ours.

One of the things we support in a nearby village is a junior school assembly each Monday morning of term time. When the school had to be closed, we started up the assembly by Zoom. There were some teething problems, but before long they began to take on a life of their own. A huge bonus is the fact that we are communicating with parents and siblings in the households taking part, and that increases the community that we are seeking to support.

These are a few examples to kick-start what I hope will be a sharing of ideas from other residential communities.

This process of reflection has led me to wonder how much analysis there has been of virtual therapeutic communities worldwide, before and during Covid 19. I sincerely hope that one or more Erving Goffman-type sociologists will emerge funded and resourced to explore this phenomenon.

Meanwhile my interim conclusion is that there could well be some new hybrids emerging. No one is seriously imagining that face-to-face relationships and community will become a thing of the past, but creative new possibilities are opening up. And would you believe it, as I was writing this piece today, I heard a rendering of Thomas Tallis' *If Ye love me* by the

Kings' Singers. It was a performance of the highest quality, made by six individuals each in their own home, and using Zoom. Of course, it requires musicianship beyond most of us, but these socially-isolated individuals formed an ensemble of exquisite harmony and timing. If this can be done with such demanding music, then there must be scope for groups seeking quality communication in word, and perhaps even body language.

What will the new normal look like for therapeutic communities I wonder?

The Roots of Research

For this issue of *TTCJ* with its focus on research I intend to go back to the very origins of research. To do this it is necessary to connect the educational philosophy of Friedrich Fröbel with studies of plants and marine biology.

First Fröbel. I came across his educational theory when researching in India. Fröbel's methods and resources are based on original and primary research that he undertook into the way children develop. He did this by observing very young children (and their mothers) at play in the open air. (By doing this in public spaces he overcame one of the fundamental challenges of any social research, which is gaining appropriate permission to observe and analyse what is happening.) One of his key discoveries was that physical movement was one of the primary features of, and triggers to, learning and discovery. Children are designed to move, to engage with the natural world and its movement (say through running water; clouds; the distinctive behaviours of insects, animals and birds; leaves and branches; through the growth of fruit and shrubs; through active interaction with wood and other materials, reshaping and combining them).

The toddler who has just begun to move of her own accord, even to crawl, stand and walk, has unknowingly set about the most important and strategic research of her life. Movement will bring her into contact with every aspect of the natural and social world, earth, air, fire and water, involving any number of bumps and scratches, and endless discoveries and connections. It is a mind-bogglingly complex project which is the origin of all research. It is not an option, but integral to human being, survival and growth. To make sense of the natural and social world in which we find ourselves we have to find ways of understanding and naming its constituent parts, their characteristics, and how they interact with each other and respond to our engagement with them.

Armed with the evidence of his research, Fröbel went on to model educational methods, tools ("gifts") and environments in which children were encouraged to move, even to dance as part of the whole process of all learning including subjects such as maths and grammar. This was in sharp contrast to prevailing methods of formal education that assumed children would be seated, sitting still and learning by rote, listening or writing.

Now for (scientific) research into the natural world. Here I would like to cite the sea squirt as one of the very best examples of how physical movement relates to the brain and intellectual development. It is such a common feature that we may overlook the significance of the fact that, whereas no plant has a brain, all animals do. Why is that? The evidence suggests that it is because animals move (albeit at different speeds and in different ways and mediums, including air and water). And that movement requires constant checking of coordinates, calculation of the substance of materials ... or to give it its usual name, research.

The sea squirt is a remarkable proof of this. In the early part of its life cycle, it swims around like a tadpole, its movement requiring and made possible by its brain and nerve cord. But when it matures, it fixes itself to a rock, where it then stays in that one place like a plant. Now here comes the exciting bit: because it no longer moves, it has no need of its brain, so it digests its own brain and nerve cord! I came across this example in the book by

Joe Griffin and Ivan Tyrrell, *Human Givens* (Chalvington: HG Publishing, 2018, page 6), but the data can be found in any encyclopedia.

Putting educational philosophy and marine research together it seems that we have evidence of the roots, the DNA, of research. Of course, research comes in many shapes and forms, and can be of considerable quantitative complexity but, in essence, it is about movement, about growth, about change and modification, size, numbers, substance, the dynamics of groups. And children who thrive are encouraged not only to move physically (without the worrying advice accompanying every move: "Be careful"), but to allow their minds to wander and their imaginations to dream.

In his seminal book, *The Act of Creation*, Arthur Koestler argued (with many examples) that the great breakthroughs in scientific research came through something very like play. Einstein imagined how things would look from two different model trains travelling alongside each other. There are stories about Newton and an apple, and Archimedes and an overflowing bath. However apocryphal these may be, there can be little doubt that such breakthroughs did not come about by observation, linear thought or number-crunching. And you will have noticed that the three examples, chosen at random, all involve physical movement.

I would like to conclude this piece by referring to some of the seminal research in child development which shows how observation of movement plays a critical role.

Much contemporary child development theory draws from the research of René Spitz and William Goldfarb and John Bowlby done in the 1940s and 1950s. There were several types of studies done, but a theme in all of them concerned observation of how children moved (or remained stationary). A major variable in the samples was between children who were in residential institutions (orphanages, camps or hospitals) and those who lived at home or with foster carers. There are harrowing films that demonstrate the distinctive and divergent reactions of each category of children to the presence or absence of an adult or carer.

Those who have seen them never get over the sad rocking of children constrained within cage-like cots or beds. Visits to zoos confirm a similar pattern in some animals that are restricted and kept from their natural environments.

Carefully studied, these movements indicate something deeply significant about the feelings and emotional state of the children that paved the way for much understanding of separation and loss. Dan Hughes developed his therapeutic work with children who had not experienced secure attachment on these insights, and significantly one of his contributions to practical therapy concerns attunement, and what he refers to as the "dance" between parent and child. We are back to physical movement as a way into much, much more.

A parting reference to the research of Piaget. His experiments focused on how children at different stages of development conceived and understood the relationships between shape, size and space. Could a child imagine for example how things appeared to a person situated in another place? It doesn't take much thought to realise how important this is to any, and all, human relationships: discovering how "the other" sees and feels about things from another perspective.

Not only are these examples focused on movement: they also show adult researchers observing and learning from children. It's not obvious how they could have arrived at their conclusions without the assistance, conscious or otherwise, of real children.

If we could as a society see how the very best form of learning is all about enabling children to do research, and to gain confidence in exploring the world including human relationships for themselves, there could be the seeds of a gentle revolution, not only in education and schools but in the way we understand human development, and go about parenting, therapy and care … not to mention research!

The following poem, that seems best to capture the essence of learning together in the natural world, is by Jane Tyson Clement, and imagines a teacher and a child in some sort of educational setting:

Child, though I take your hand
and walk in the snow;
though we follow the track of the mouse
together,
though we try to unlock together the mystery
of the printed word, and slowly discover
why two and three make five
always, in an uncertain world –

    child, though I am meant to teach you
      much,

what is it, in the end,
except that together we are
meant to be children
of the same Father
and I must unlearn
all the adult structure
and the cumbering years

and you must teach me
to look at the earth and the heaven
with your fresh wonder.

The Gardener and the Boy

It all happened as we were getting ready to walk back to our house from the beach we tend to think of as our own at Borth y Gest. We have been holidaying here since 1976, and there must have been a huge number of different sandcastles and sand creations on the beach since then. Most are of stereotypical castles, boats, cars, with a few mermaids, tortoises, alligators and crocodiles appearing from time to time. And there are tide fights and canals and embankments associated with the stream near the dunes, and the sandbanks between the two outcrops, Garreg Cnwc and Garreg Wyn, that constitute the outer boundaries of the bay. But this one was of a different order. In the light of the evening sun there was a beautifully executed array of walls, castles, bridges and steps moulded around a limpet-covered slate rock.

Several onlookers associated it immediately

with the Great Wall of China and it certainly deserved such a comparison, but as one who has visited mainland China it struck a deeper chord for me: it was about human interaction with the natural world, where there was the deepest respect for existing geology, geography and biology reflected in creations that revelled in the uniqueness of micro-landscapes and adapted ideas to harmonise and interact with them.

The boy was one of two people involved in the project: the other was a hirsute middle-aged man, who I took to be a relative of the child. In conversation it turned out that this was not so. The man, whose job was that of a gardener, and who had studied Philosophy at Cardiff University, had embarked on the creation himself, and the boy had come alongside and joined the endeavour. He was part of an extended family based nearby on the beach. The philosophically-minded gardener was not only open to such assistance, but eventually left the work in progress entirely in the hands of his apprentice.

As I was studying the intricacies of the stairs and arches in the walls a lady noticed my interest and came alongside. The boy was completely engrossed in his work, so much so that had it not been for the incoming tide I think he would have been lost to the world until nightfall. The lady was either the mother or grandmother of the boy, and when I congratulated her on such a gifted and creative child, she told me that he had been very late in learning to speak and was way behind at school. He had been diagnosed on the autistic spectrum. In his early years he seemed to express himself most naturally and fully through Lego.

This made perfect sense of what I was witnessing: as the gardener had discovered, this was a talented boy indeed, fully engaged in and centred on the task in hand. So much so that I do not recall the boy's face: I am not at all sure that he turned round, despite my conversation of ten minutes or so. The child's adult relative was clearly overjoyed that the boy had found such an inspiring and welcoming friend.

It so happened that at the time I was re-reading one of my favourite books, *Mountains of the Mind*, by Robert Macfarlane. Not an easy work to categorise, but I think of it as a philosophy of human relationships with mountains over several centuries. It was mountains that had drawn us to North Wales in the first place, and from a child, like Macfarlane, I was drawn to them irresistibly, developing a love affair with them while living in Scotland. There are symbiotic relationships between beaches, rocks, sand, castles, walls and paths, and the gardener and the boy seemed to me to epitomise the best of interactions with this aspect of the natural world. Their model fortification followed the contours of the sloping slate perfectly, and they used the quality of the sand (rough with plenty of friction) together with the limpet-covered surface of the rock to make narrow and intricate walls and staircases that appeared to defy gravity and the ordinary laws of nature.

I don't want it to sound as if there is a moral to this story, because the purpose of sharing it with you is to pass on something of the satisfaction and joy that I found in admiring such a beautiful work, while discovering the unique and complementary nature of the relationship between the gardener and the boy. But I hope it doesn't seem out of place to reflect on the potential of the natural world, both for human exploration and creative expression and the healing properties of such spontaneous play. It has been my privilege to have children and young people alongside me in North Wales for most of my life, and to engage with them in enjoying the natural world from snorkelling in sea and rivers to hill-walking, scrambling and rock climbing on local crags and mountains. What the gardener had done, both with his hands and his acceptance of the boy, epitomised all that I seek to do and to be: one who loves the place and seeks to inspire in others the same love; to encourage them to develop their natural skills and talents; and to be blessed by their natural enthusiasm and imagination.

I think it goes without saying that this feels a long way away from conventional school and education, counselling and social care. I knew that this evening on our beach I was privileged to be witnessing a rare process of acceptance and teamwork where, as far as I could gather, there was little or no need of words, and certainly not of books or instructions. The next morning there was barely a trace of this creation, and I have not seen the gardener or the boy since, but they have caused my spirit to sing. It was singing today as little ones with me on the very same beach played with and explored the same beach and rocks. As it happened, they haven't yet seen my photos of this work of art, and they were making volcanoes of the best sand and using dark, estuarine mud for the lava. In case you were wondering, they too were wholly engrossed in their spontaneous endeavours, and they are growing and maturing.

The thing that they each had in common with the little boy was that their start in life was not auspicious, so this activity alongside us, and with our encouragement as and when appropriate, is part of the healing process in their lives, in a therapeutic milieu that combines the security and acceptance of Mill Grove with the infinite varieties of possibilities offered in this uniquely varied part of the world.

Snails and Comenius

The inspiration for this piece was an unlikely combination of recent rain and Melvyn Bragg's BBC Radio 4 programme, *In our Time*. It was the rain in East London that brought out the snails, and Melvyn Bragg who introduced me to Comenius. Let's start chronologically … with Johan Amos Comenius (1592–1670). If, like me, you didn't know of him until now, this might just be the moment to start finding out more! How I had not come across his life or work before listening to that radio programme I find it hard to fathom. I am insatiably interested in how young children learn, and my PhD had as one of its main themes the educational philosophy and practice of Friedrich Fröbel, someone who drew deeply from the writings and methods of Comenius. Since my belated discovery of the "father of modern education" many things have been falling into place. Much of what Fröbel advocated and modelled, and most of my life and work with young children, is based on the pioneering analysis, philosophy, beliefs and vision of Comenius.

Comenius believed among other things that any textbooks should be pictorial (he produced one, *Orbis Pictus*) and in the child's vernacular language as well as Latin; that learning was a life-long process sensitive to the growth and development of the child, and the context of the process. This was sometimes termed "education according to nature", and started with physical objects familiar to the child, rather than a focus on literacy and numeracy. This approach, which is sometimes called pansophism, aimed to introduce the child to the whole of her environment, from the inner world and the smallest creatures to the galaxies and outer space, by means of an integration of all the senses drawing from, and drawing together, scientific, social, religious and moral discourses or ways of seeing and understanding things.

Crucially for the purposes of this article, and for Fröbel, play was the key to learning, rather academic study, work, didacticism and tables;

it should be available to all irrespective of gender, status, ethnicity or ability, and it started with very young children. He wrote a text for mothers, *The School of Infancy*, in which he encouraged them to introduce their children to subjects, activities and types of experiment or reflection that they would encounter later at kindergarten and school.

Which leads us to the snails …. On Monday evening (that was just four days after I discovered Comenius) Ruth and I were, as usual, with one of the families who make up the extended family of Mill Grove. They come round after school, and although the children call us uncle and auntie, it feels much more like a grandparent-grandchild relationship to me. Before a meal there are different games and activities in which the young children choose to engage. But on this occasion there was only one subject or activity in sight: snails. Outside there were so many that it was difficult to walk more than a few steps without risk of stepping on one. Before long, the two children had begun to rescue some.

This involved finding a suitable "home" for them (this was the word that they used) comprising a container and a variety of leaves. This was placed on a coffee table, and the snails were duly named and labelled with roles in the household (for example, grandpa, mum, baby …). Soon it was decided that they needed some exercise, so they were taken out of their home and placed side by side on the table, as if it were the start of a race.

You may find it hard to believe that the girl was wearing a pendant presented to her at school earlier in the day, bearing the message: the "Race for Life". What happened next was a surprise to us all (I was now part of the project): some of the smaller snails did not move ("they are sleeping", said the little girl), while two of the bigger ones set off at snail's pace in different directions until they both reached the edge of the table … and fell off. They were carefully picked up ("rescued" again) and placed back in the safety of their home.

All the time we were engaged in discussion: the number and size of their feelers, and whether they could see or hear. At some point I introduced the thought that a snail might not think of home as we do, given that they carry their equivalent of a home with them, but as far as I could see, this was irrelevant to the children's understanding of what was going on and how they were trying to help the snail family (they were activists with no time for sociology or psychology). As happens with spontaneous projects like this, time tended to slow up, even stop still. But the time for our evening meal was approaching and I still needed to get some petrol for our mowers. I asked the young boy if he was happy to come with me to buy some from the local garage. and whether his sister could cope with the snail household on her own.

A brief interlude was negotiated, and we had soon stored two full cans of petrol in the mower shed. But as you might have gathered, the trip outside only reinforced our awareness of just how many snails there were. The two of us brought back a flowerpot full of additional refugees, and they were immediately introduced to the existing family. The enlarged household was placed carefully outside, while we humans sat down for a meal.

Afterwards the challenge for Ruth and myself was how to bring some kind of non-traumatic closure to the project. The family would be going home on a bus, and although the little girl was quite sure that a snail household would be welcome on a London double-decker, it was not obvious how they would be able to cope with such a large extended family of snails in their own flat. So it was that we identified a sheltered spot at the back of Mill Grove where the snails would be safe, with plenty of food close by.

My guess is that next Monday life for the children will have moved on, and the snails will have found a way of coping without the patient attention and care of the two children.

But, of course, I may be wrong. Which is part of the fun of the learning process.

Hopefully readers will spot a connection between what we were doing and the theory and practice of Comenius. If so, they will have identified what makes up most of my time alongside children. Mill Grove is not a school, and my role in the eyes of these two small children has nothing to do with teaching. What we are doing is being together, eating together, exploring together, doing jobs together (such as mowing the grass or cooking), and playing together.

One of the ways societies and languages categorise activities, professions and roles is to see "learning" as part of education, and the responsibility of teachers and schools (including nurseries), while "care" is part of family life and home. Comenius was observant and bright enough to see that this misses one of the most important aspects of life: that play is common to every stage of life, to every period of history and to all cultures. And that without it, childhood is impoverished and learning, whether personal, social or cognitive, is put at risk.

A problem with the label "father of modern education", as applied to Comenius, is that worldwide, education is still mostly set within schools, and associated with work rather than play ("homework" as distinct from "playtime"). Finding ways of integrating and connecting home and school, learning and care, parenting and teaching, and little creatures like snails, with the great galaxies in space, seems as far off as it was in the sixteenth century.

But for those who see the point and have the freedom to devote time to a project wholly chosen and owned by children, as Comenius did, life with little children could not be more fun, surprising and challenging. Which reminds me, have you any sense of whether snails have a concept of home, I wonder?

REFLECTIONS

Part TWO

Reviews and Other Pieces

INTRODUCTION
Reviews and Other Pieces

Just two of these articles were written and published as reviews (*Nobody's Child*; *Shaping Children's Services*). Eight other pieces took the form of reviews as I wrote them. And two were commissioned for other purposes. "With Thanks to Barbara Dockar-Drysdale" was part of an issue of TTCJ featuring her life and work. The "Introduction" to *A Finchden Experience* was a piece that I had agreed to write when discussing the publication with Alan's widow, Claire.

References to other books pepper the whole collection, but it seemed appropriate to highlight some of the writings that have offered me substantive insights as I have wrestled with deepening questions arising from my life alongside children.

One of the practical reasons is that those living or working in various forms of therapeutic setting are unlikely to have come across some, if not most of them. They reflect the catholic character of my own reading: drawing help and resources like a magpie from wherever they may be found.

They confirm a growing conviction that it is novelists, poets, writers and artists who have most to offer when it comes to matters of love and how it grows. For whatever combination of reasons, the professional writings are often defensive, even silent. Those working in the realms of the imagination, stirred and prompted by the vagaries of real life experience, have no such inhibitions.

A Child Possessed

R.C. Hutchinson
(London: Geoffrey Bles, 1964)

Thankfully those of us who live alongside, and try to understand, support and care for children, whether as parents, teachers, counsellors, therapists or social workers, know that there is a rich variety of sources of knowledge and wisdom available to help us. Such resources are over and above our own intuitions, common sense and experience. They include professional writing and training, legislation, cultural traditions, religion and scientific findings. But one source that can be all too easily overlooked, even dismissed, is literature in its various manifestations from poetry and drama through to novels. Over the years it has become apparent that some of these writers, blessed with extraordinary powers of observation, empathy and imagination, have often arrived at insights about children and childhood long before the so-called specialists in the field.

On reflection this should not be too much of a shock: there is a huge breadth and depth to the questions that drive poets and writers. So no wonder that drama has provided some of the basic categories of, say, psychoanalysis (e.g. "Oedipal Complex") and models of how loss and trauma are worked out in human experience (e.g. *Hamlet*); novels have long explored aspects of the development including the abuse of children within and outside familial contexts (e.g. *We Need to Talk About Kevin*); poetry has handed beliefs about children (e.g. *Ode: Intimations of Mortality*); not to mention the vast field of children's literature itself.

In this article I would like to share some of the wisdom gleaned from the writing of the best-selling novelist R.C. Hutchinson (1907–1975) in his novel, *A Child Possessed*. Hutchinson wrote 17 novels between 1930 and 1975 and was shortlisted for the Booker prize but, for some reason, though highly rated during his time, he is now little-known. The reason that his work is on my mind is that I have been re-reading some of his novels in preparation for meeting one of his children soon: in this eagerly-awaited conversation I hope to learn more about his own story, background and influences.

The book centres on a child, Eugenie, who was born both brain-damaged and disfigured. Her mother is a successful actress and her father a radical Russian who has become a lorry driver in Marseilles. Early in the child's life she was placed in a residential institution in Switzerland that specialised in the care of such children and persons. Her parents separated, but did not formalise this with a divorce. So when a surgeon proposes to operate on the child's brain, it is necessary to get the permission of both parents. The father refuses to give his assent to such radical medical treatment, choosing the alternative of having his daughter live with him in his digs. His work means that she travels with him in his lorry on trips, whether local or farther afield.

The child's mother continues to hope that Eugenie will be placed in more suitable, specialist care. At the end of the story the child dies of a respiratory condition, but in the process both her father and mother have come to know themselves better than ever before and are drawn closer to each other once again.

As a genre the novel is probably best described as a love story of an unusual kind. It is not primarily a novel of ideas, but as the narrative unfolds a number of troubling questions arise and are explored with considerable tenacity and rigour. One of them concerns how far a child who cannot speak or care for herself can be described as human. What is the essence of human being? Eugenie is not "useful" in the sense that she can make any tangible contribution to her family or community. Her father argues that this makes no difference: "She's a child of God, she has the same value as all the rest of us." This prompts the response from a friend: "Indeed? One can only remark that God now and then goes in for rather startling progeny" (page 113). This is tested out with troubling intensity when she is compared with a herd of goats (138-141), and Coco, a pedigree dog (268-277), respectively.

Another way of considering her essence is to think of what might happen if she were to have brain surgery that transformed her intellectual ability unrecognisably. Her father reflects in a letter to her mother: "She might be able to rehearse the works of Hume and Heidegger without a mistake, and solve problems in the calculus of variation – she might even develop the mind of another Pascal. But she would cease to be the Eugenie who has come into the world through you and me" (187). Body, mind, spirit are inseparably interwoven in a particular person with a unique life-story.

In time her father, Stepan begins to realise that through relating to his daughter and trying to understand her by putting himself in her place (impossible though this seems to be, both to him and to others), he is starting to see the world in a whole new way and light. As he begins to focus his eyes "to smallness" he discovers through her that he is no longer simply an observer of nature, but a link in creation: "and he realised that he owed to her existence this fresh delight in the marvels of life about him, the enchantment of small, created things ..." (136).

If this sounds at all sentimental then be assured that the novel is anything but. Stepan realises over time that there is an unbridgeable gulf between him and his daughter, and that she lives in dreadful solitude (192). But this takes him back to his own time in prison as a political radical, and particularly when he was in solitary confinement. In his helplessness, enforced solitude and darkness he saw the essence of things with startling clarity, and part of this was that God "can only work by means of His creation ... even the degenerate and the feeble" (184). His journey of discovery leads him to see that he is closer to her than he can describe. All through, he redoubles his efforts to find ways into her way of seeing (to stand in the place of "the Other").

On one occasion he was walking with her on a Sunday morning when he squatted so that his eyes were level with hers. He narrowed his field of vision to make it correspond with hers and moved his head from side to side as she did habitually. This resulted in him becoming weirdly confused as "yellow lettering on a kiosk, the pink legs of a woman passing, the splashboard of a bus, swung to and fro before him" (191). He marvels that with this puzzling information from her senses she has any power of identification. (Those who have read Mark Haddon's The Curious Incident of the Dog in the Night-Time will recall the harrowing experience in the train.) He realises that he has to get rid of assumptions and clutter in order to stand any chance of understanding her at all, and in the painful process he gains insight into his own inadequacy as a person and in relationships.

One of the most remarkable insights concerns the relationship between Eugenie as a person and Marseilles as a city! Stepan begins to realise that his daughter and the city of Marseilles are quite remarkably connected ... and similar. To devote an extended passage to the similarities between a coastal city and a brain-damaged child is an act of creative daring: but it is convincing (194-205). It is not possible to summarise this chapter, but it helped me to see that there are limitless resources that come to our aid if we are genuinely, passionately and unconditionally committed in our desire to understand an "other". I readily confess that I had never considered the nature of cities as one of these resources before.

Towards the end, having been seriously injured in a crash, the paradox which comprises both the gulf between them and their identification, has intensified to the point where Stepan reflects: "... I see it now – now that I'm helpless, now that my eyes have got like yours, wandering and clouded. You and I are out of touch with the rest, perhaps we could never have learnt to fit ourselves to other people's ways. And now I'm no use to you any more, stuck here with a body too weak to do what I say. But in the end it makes no difference. We have both to be patient, for a time we have to make our own ways in the dark. In the end our dullness and our feebleness don't matter – God's love will find us and our only business will be to reflect his love." (336)

Whether in such a short piece I have been able to convey anything of the quality of this novel I rather doubt. After all, a piece of literature is sui generis, and it cannot be replaced by any other form or a summary. But I hope that this brief flavour of Hutchinson's work will encourage those alongside children who are struggling to understand, empathise and help them, by reassuring them that there are probably innumerable additional resources in that process waiting to be found.

I have spent most of my life reading literature, starting one Saturday morning in a local library with *Far from the Madding Crowd* and the description in the first paragraph of Farmer Oak's smile. Since then I have been surrounded by books. And I have spent even longer living with and among children, most of that time at Mill Grove. From time to time I have read something that enriches my understanding, challenges my assumptions, stirs my heart and encourages me on my journey. *A Child Possessed* is one of the most precious discoveries I have made, and that is why I commend it to others.

A General Theory of Love

T. Lewis, F. Amini, R. Lannon
(New York: Random House, 2001)

In the autumn of 2018 I exchanged emails, as we do from time to time, with my friend and colleague, Jerome Berryman, the founder of Godly Play. He is a polymath who worked at the Texas Children's Hospital and Houston Child Guidance Centre, was Adjunct Asst. Professor of Paediatric Pastoral Care on the clinical faculty of Baylor College of Medicine 1979–1984, and headmaster of a Montessori school for 250 children from 2-14 years of age in Cleveland Heights.

For some reason we exchanged book recommendations. I proffered Yan Martel's novel, *The High Mountains of Portugal*, while he suggested that I read *A General Theory of Love*. The reason for his offer was that he knew I had been working for some time on a fundamental reconfiguration of Child Development Theory, and that I knew that it had to have somewhere near its core the concept of love. Readers of my columns in this journal may recall that I have sometimes wondered how different things might have been had John Bowlby stayed with the word "love", rather than the more specific terms, bonding and attachment. Jerome had assumed that as the author of *The Growth of Love*, I probably knew of *A General Theory of Love* already.

I am still not sure whether Jerome has read Martel's book, but I have devoured his recommendation, and am profoundly grateful to him for introducing me to it. When I realised that its three authors, all formerly practising psychiatrists and academics, acknowledged the significance of Blaise Pascal's insight that "le coeur a ses raisons que la raison ne connaît point", I knew I was on to something dear to my heart. But little did I know how dear, or how challenging for my mind. The basic argument of the book is that human beings are wired for relationships and intimacy: interdependence and love. The bonds and ties that develop from before birth affect and form the way that our brains are structured and function as strongly as the medication and drugs that are the staple diet of most invasive mental health treatment in our time.

Now because both Jerome and I are familiar with the writing and research associated with what has come to be known as children's spirituality, we have both witnessed the way in which little children make connections with ideas and concepts that transcend everyday interactions and learning. The plasticity of their neural networks means that at the very earliest stages of life they have the potential to connect with virtually everything in the universe and beyond. But what I lacked was a theory that helped to explain why this should be and how their brains develop and operate.

Based at Mill Grove for most of my life, I have been privileged to be alongside children, young people and adults whose attitudes and behaviour have clearly been affected and shaped by experiences in early childhood, and mostly some time before I got to know them. I was familiar with psychotherapeutic and psychoanalytic history and theory, but I could not begin to get a coherent understanding of how they functioned as whole human beings in relationships that included their brain development (thinking and processing) and patterns of behaviour. And I was puzzled and saddened, because I could not understand why they replicated sameness even when this led them continually into difficulties, anxiety and sometimes despair.

Lewis, Amini and Lannon, the three retired psychiatrists who combined their long clinical experience to write this book, propose reasons for this. The basis for their argument is a simple map of the human brain. Like Gaul, it is divided into three parts: reptilian, limbic, and neocortical. The *reptilian* part is located at the top of our spinal column and is responsible for our bodily functions and reactions. It provides the fundamental "background tone to our emotional life" or temperament (pp. 47-48). The emotional circuits in the reptilian part of our brain create a broad behavioural disposition, including the most common binary reflex reaction: fight or flight. This is given for the most part, in the sense of having been formed early on, and is almost completely outside our control.

The reptilian brain is encased by the *limbic*. Its primary function is to monitor and regulate the relationship between external and the internal worlds, fine-tuning physiology and what the body sees, hears, feels and smells. A crucial part of the body is the human face: it is a primary communicator of expressive signals, and the limbic part of the brain both processes what it learns from the faces of others, as well as shaping the muscles in the face of its owner. The way it does this can cause the reptilian brain to change its cardiovascular function (heart rate and blood flow), depending on whether it detects hostility and threats or not.

The last part of the brain to develop in the evolutionary scheme of things is the precisely-named *neo-cortical*. It is where language, abstract logic, mathematics and problem-solving are done. It is not the seat of emotions as we have seen, but it does have a role in moderating them. The differences between the left and right sides of the brain are well charted. The left side deals with the decoding of signs, data and language, while the right side is where the emotional interpretation of signs and speech are read. Emotional literacy, as distinct from raw intelligence, depends heavily on the right side of the neocortical brain. It is worth bearing in mind here the role of emojis in electronic communication: symbols that add emotion to the words on the screen.

The human baby is skilled from the earliest days in reading the mother's face (it is usually, though not always, the mother), and this is not a one-way process. There is constant interaction between the child's expressions and those of the mother. Limbic resonance is the attunement of the emotional states of parent and child. And this is necessarily patterned, or wired in the child, with neural patterns and pathways developing unconsciously. We have here the territory in which John Bowlby worked, influenced by the data and studies coming in from those observing children separated from their parents and living in orphanages or prisons.

Emotional wellbeing depends on the instinctive bonding between mothers and their children. This shapes the limbic region where the congruence and balance between the internal and external worlds of the child are regulated.

There is much more, and I propose to share more of my discoveries in subsequent articles for *TTCJ*, but this is the basis of the argument. And as the title indicates the authors are intent on using the word love to describe what is going on. The growth of love in a person is dependent on a healthy limbic resonance, and yet the limbic region is beyond the reach of consciousness.

So, where there has been insecure attachment and where unhealthy emotional and behaviours and reactions occur, what can be done about them? We are in the territory so memorably set out and described by Dan Hughes, *Building the Bonds of Attachment: Awakening Love in Deeply Traumatized Children*. It is not just a case of seeking to repair bonds of attachment, because they are not there to start with. They have to be built. Here is the heart of much psychiatry and therapeutic care.

This is what I have been about at Mill Grove, along with many others in a range of therapeutic settings. Psychiatry in the UK recognises much of this brain research, which is why drug treatment is so prevalent. Changes in the brain and the way it processes data, feelings, dreams and emotions is necessary, and drugs produce changes, so QED! Except that they operate without reference to experience of the real world, to other human beings, to relationships and to love. For the model of treatment by medication assumes a single brain, and particular drugs and doses. But if we are wired for relationships, the person treated is being deprived of what is necessary for human growth and development.

Which is where love comes in. For consistent and healthy long-term relationships are another way of seeking to build bonds of attachment. It is not an either/or, but drugs alone deny the very nature of what it is to be human.

Since reading the book with its analysis of the way the limbic region functions, I have been re-thinking all sorts of labels, dynamics and processes: autism, Asperger's syndrome, cognitive and behavioural therapy (which deliberately eschew emotions and love), the role of poetry and fiction, religion and fantasy in the developing life of children. And the trajectory of modern western "society" with its stress on human autonomy and individualism. I thought of the demise of marriage and the rise of short-term cohabitations. And of educational theories and institutions which proceed without reference to emotional intelligence and attunement.

Recently I was at a conference of Christian Social Workers, and several remarked that they were not sure what social work was about nowadays. A generation ago we believed in relationship-based engagement and knew of Felix Biestek and his seminal book, *The Casework Relationship*. Today there were "pieces of work" and specific interventions and tasks. But where is long-term relationship and love?

Ruth and I have devoted our lives to specific children, adults and families, and to staying with them, alongside them and for them. This book has given us encouragement and hope. While others pursue different methods, *A General Theory of Love* has reminded us that there is a valid place, possibly a unique and essential one, for love.

Thank you, Jerome. Thank you very much.

- -

A General Theory of Love

Further Thoughts from Work in Progress

Since writing the previous article on *A General Theory of Love* (New York: Random House, 2001) by the three psychiatrists, T. Lewis, F. Amini, R. Lannon, and then re-reading the book, my mind has been teeming with a mass of thoughts, questions, and ideas. And gradually these have been getting sorted out into what a chess player familiar with the teaching of Alexander Kotov might term branches that make up a "Tree of Thought". Now that I realise that the book describes what most call neuro-science, it is obvious that I am catching up with what many therapists and carers already take for granted. So, if you are one of these, please forgive me a beginner's excitement.

Just to re-cap. These three retired psychiatrists and academics brought their combined wisdom and case studies together to describe what they believe to be a better foundation for psychiatry and psychotherapy than Freudian psychoanalysis, Skinner-dominated behavioural psychology or the use of medication respectively. There is a simple description of the three primary parts of the human brain: *reptilian* (wrapped around the top of the spinal cord); *limbic* (coming between this and the third part), and the *neo-cortical* (which is the outer part). The first deals with self-protection and regulation of the body functioning largely by means of reflexes. The second comprises patterns of neural networks established unconsciously early in a child's life and shaping how the growing person sees, processes and deals with the challenges of the stream of knowledge, data, experiences and emotions that accompany human life in the real world. The third part is where practical decisions, language, logic and mathematics are concentrated.

Attachment theory is taken to be at the heart of how the limbic patterns of thought, reaction and processing are learned and established in the earliest years of a child's life, including the time in the mother's womb. And the trio argue that love is not only a valid word, but the only one that will do, when seeking to understand what genuine therapy and therapeutic care are needed, when a person is struggling with their emotions, feelings and fears, as a result of childhood traumas, separation, loss and insensitive and inappropriate relationships with parents and/or significant others.

With that summary in mind, here are some of the branches of my thought.

The unconscious in human thinking and emotions is, for me, axiomatic. The evidence is, as I have seen and witnessed it, overwhelming. Freudian theory has helped establish this, but is profoundly suspect and generally held to lack an objective and verifiable foundation. The concept of the "shadow" in Jungian theory and practice has been rather more helpful in my own practice, and I wonder how it might relate to the limbic patterning of neural networks. (There is a tantalising sentence on page 192 of the chapter entitled A Walk in the Shadows which hints at a possible connection without developing it: "Every solid object casts a shadow, and the architecture of the human mind is no exception".)

This leads the authors to consider what they call "culture". They are critical of contemporary American norms and expectations (although much of what they describe applies more widely in the world), but do not discuss how this relates to the Jungian idea of the collective unconscious. It seems to me that such an exploration might provide a fruitful way of enriching our understanding of limbic functioning. As someone who has taught cross-cultural courses

in child development, I have been struck by both the differences and also the commonalities between unconscious (taken for granted) assumptions around the world. If it takes a village to raise a child (well), then there is a lot of data worldwide on villages!

I wondered too whether many of the syndromes and conditions that we now speak of commonly, such as Autistic, Aspergers, ADHD, Dementia, Alzeimers and so on, have been studied with reference to the way neural networks have been established (whether genetically, culturally or in development within family and community). Please understand that I am in a stage of overload, and hoping that others will come to my aid with chapters and verse!

I have long been sceptical of behavioural psychology, not in the specific areas in which it can be shown to be relevant and effective, but in those deep-seated, often subconscious conditions and patterning where it cannot. To seek to modify conscious thoughts and behaviour while leaving limbic mal-functioning (the writers are willing to talk of "bad" parenting) unattended, has always seemed to me to be at best wilfully ignorant and, at worst, a dereliction of professional medical duty.

And the same goes for medication. In my experience it clearly has a role to play in a number of psychological conditions. But if limbic functioning is to be addressed it will ultimately require longstanding and unconditional love, whether in family or professionals. I recall giving a paper when I became president of the Social Care Association in 1984. I talked of Korczak and the way his sacrificial concern for the orphans in his care in the Warsaw Ghetto challenged me. More than one member of SCA spoke to me afterwards to say that they felt this was going too far in a professional organisation. But, if it is at times necessary, surely we cannot simply deny it? And if professionals cannot commit themselves to love a client appropriately, then this means that they must redouble their efforts to identify, encourage and nurture those who will.

A General Theory of Love refuses to sit on the fence (this is often the blessing of the writings of those who are retired!): humans are wired to give and receive love, and yet contemporary cultures and professionals seem too often to offer almost anything but love. They write that the unimpeachable verdict of research is that "love matters in the life of a child" (page 199). And in saying this they are aware of the role not only of parents and the nuclear family but of kith, kin, community, peers and culture itself. What for example might be the difference if our culture genuinely encouraged to "love our neighbours as ourselves", I wonder? When unsatisfied, this inbuilt longing (need) that is hard-wired into us all will seek out, both consciously and unconsciously, substitutes. They include gangs, sects, companies and corporations (this is a very interesting section in the book, (pages 214-219), and the acting out of despair and anger in self-harm and the injury and killing of others.

This leads me, at this embryonic stage of my development in this whole area of thought, to consider what practical steps parents and carers with a therapeutic understanding and intent might take to apply the arguments of the book. There have been many on offer and in evidence through the ages, and across cultures. But those that come to mind most readily here and now mostly seem to occur in my book, *The Growth of Love*. It is just that now so many new links have been forged, and reasons emerged. So let me suggest that we settle for nothing less than love, and therefore using the word "love", in all talk about caring, healing and teaching. And that quasi-scientific ("empirically-demonstrated" and "driven") language is tempered with the humility appropriate for the partial knowledge and understandings that we have of the human heart (the limbic patterns). The poets, the musicians, the artists, the mystics have opened doors for us that we do well to look through, even if we cannot enter.

Shaping Children's Services

Chris Hanvey
(Oxford: Routledge, 2019)

This is such a thoughtful, insightful, balanced, well-informed and seminal book that this review will be in the form of a conversational response. My review copy is so heavily annotated that it is obvious that Chris Hanvey has challenged and stimulated my thinking and imagination considerably.

In 128 pages, which include an appendix and index, the author surveys the scene of children's services (mostly in England, but with reference to the rest of the UK and Europe), concluding with a recommendation as to how they might be re-shaped fundamentally in order to build a "first-class integrated child-care service that fully recognises the role of all the professions and fully engages them in looking holistically at the needs of children and young people" (page 119).

The prose is clear and unobtrusive, but with some fine touches when Hanvey draws from literature or history. A good example is the stunning quote on page 114 by Helen Seaford, which I came across for the first time in this book: "The child moves through Whitehall growing and shrinking like Alice: in the Department of Health she is a small potential victim, at the Treasury and Department of Education a growing but silent unit of investment, but at the Home Office a huge and threatening yob." Could anyone have put it better, I wonder? It is to the author's credit that he has found it and allows it to speak for itself.

The analysis is set in historical context starting for the most part with the 1899–1902 Boer War and Charles Booth's and Seebohm Rowntree's studies on poverty and nutrition. Key points in the story are the 1942 Beveridge Report, the 1944 Education Act, the establishment of the NHS in 1946, and the 1948 Children Act. There is a useful summary of more recent major changes, including those in health, education and juvenile justice.

The descriptions of interventions and initiatives between 1997 and the present day include the Troubled Families Programme, the Social Exclusion Unit, *Every Child Matters*, *Working*

Together to Safeguard Children, the CANparent scheme, *Putting Children First*, *Adoption: a New Approach*, CAMHS, Education Action Zones, Connexions, and the Youth Justice Board. (They came so fast that it is useful to have an aide-memoire!) Examples of initiatives in integration that are discussed in a little more detail are Total Place, Extended Schools, the Children's Fund, Children's Centres and Sure Start.

By the end of chapter two Hanvey has concluded that one of the endemic problems in England (and the UK) is short-termism, "blown by the winds of expediency and political preference" (page 46). It is also clear, because of the history, that much intervention is a "knee-jerk" reaction (page 49) to crises, notably tragic deaths of children (such as Maria Colwell or Victoria Climbie) where the system has failed. He suggests that it needs at least 20 years before a fundamental change can be effectively implemented and evaluated (page 46).

When the quality of childhood and child care in the UK is assessed alongside European and UNICEF data, in chapter 4, the conclusion is salutary: "could do better" might be a simple way of putting it.

Chapter 5 is a brave attempt to find a way of analysing what is spent on looking after children (across the full spectrum of services and departments) in the UK. Readers will be grateful to the author for providing the workings out that lead to his conclusion: "we do not know with any accuracy what we are collectively spending on children" (page 75).

In chapter 6 there is a focus on the roles of the voluntary and private sectors in providing services for children. This charts a massive shift in children's residential homes, for example. Before 1948 the voluntary sector had been a major provider; after this they were increasingly run by Local Authorities. By 2016, 66% were run by private sector and private equity firms. Any attempt at integrated services for children must find ways of including the hugely diverse voluntary sector (dominated by national organisations such as Barnardo's and Action for Children), the private sector, local and central government.

The case for integration is made in chapter

7, and it is difficult to imagine anyone disagreeing with the concept in general, however much they might question specific elements of it. Examples given include Multi-Agency Safeguarding Hubs (MASH), the Greater Manchester Combined Authority, and a very useful list of international initiatives (pages 97-99). The principles underlying such integration that Hanvey finds particularly helpful are those of the British Association of Community Child Health (BACCH), and these are spelt out on page 100.

The ground is thus prepared for the author's recommended way forward, given in a chapter entitled "Building a World Class Children's Service" (pages 103-113). It revolves around the creation of local Children's Services Teams (CSTs). These have a comprehensive and shared referral and assessment process, pooled budgets, a common database, a triage system and a "Named Person" who is given the "lead professional role". The CST would be responsible to a Local Management Board. Eight case studies provide examples of how such teams would operate.

Hanvey identifies three major challenges that need to be overcome if such a scheme is to become a reality: avoiding more disruptive short-term re-organisations, and taking the time to develop a shared culture; political consensus, such as there was in welfare (1942), education (1944) and health (1946); and a vision that involves lifting eyes beyond narrow domestic and professional agendas.

On reflection it is remarkable that Chris Hanvey has managed to squeeze so much information and analysis into such a slim tome. I can pay no higher tribute than to remark that several times his writing reminded me of the clarity, fairness, breadth of knowledge and wisdom of the late Professors Roy Parker, and Jean Packman. Strange that they, like Chris, had roots in Devon! But like them, Chris' lifelong experience in children's work and services gives him a wealth of insights drawn from a range of perspectives from the local to the regional, national and international, as well as across professional boundaries such as education, social work and health. He is in a unique position to describe and assess things as he has done and we owe him a debt of gratitude. And it is to Routledge's credit that they have seen fit to amplify his voice.

Those seeking a conventional review can turn off at this point, because here is where I seek to engage in conversation with Chris and hopefully other professionals for whom the welfare of children is a paramount concern. I do so as one who finds that this book provides a historical backcloth to much of my life alongside children. Just to identify how much, here are a few strands and episodes. I studied the history of residential child care in the UK, with an analysis of the period of the Children's Departments in Scotland and England between 1948 and 1968, visiting and staying in 20 homes in Hull and Edinburgh between 1969 and 1971. I was a trainee social worker in the newly-formed Edinburgh Social Work Department, based on the housing scheme in West Pilton, before becoming a community development officer with the Scottish Council of Social Service. From 1975 Mill Grove has been my home and the crucible of my life, work and study. In passing I recall that one of my books about Mill Grove, *A Place for Us*, had a preface by the Rt. Hon. Patrick Jenkin who was soon to become Secretary of State for Social Services. It helped me to see that living at Mill Grove between 1947 and the present provided a rather unusual window on children's needs and children's services. Two of those who helped me to look more intelligently through this window were trustees Bob Holman and Derek Spicer.

I was also a member of the Barclay Committee charged with re-thinking Social Workers' roles and tasks. My PhD was done in India focusing on a radical philosophy of childhood, gender, care and education as represented by the life and work of Pandita Ramabai (1858–1922). I became involved with the Social Care Association, the National Council of Voluntary Child Care Organisations, a number of bodies in the London Borough of Redbridge, and also Frontier Youth Trust. Since 1978 I have lectured in Sociology and Child Development. And all the time I needed to write as a way of trying to make some sense of the lives of the children and families we were seeking to understand and help, and to conceive of better ways of responding singly and in partnership with others. One role was on behalf of NCVCCO when I edited three volumes of essays and articles, including some by senior civil servants as well as representatives of the diverse voluntary sector: *Children and Social Exclusion, The Changing Face of Child Care, Re-Framing Children's Services*, respectively. I apologise for the length of this background, but it all seems relevant to what follows. Chris Hanvey has been writing about something that matters hugely to me, and I hope part of this at least helps to explain why.

So what would I like to say to Chris and to others gathering around an imaginary table having read this seminal book? A starting point might be that we have a fundamental problem in the England (and to a lesser extent in the rest of the UK), in that we do not have any time or place for philosophy. This is far from an arcane or academic point in relation to this book, because a coherent political, professional and moral case for integrated children's services requires an agreed understanding of childhood, the village it takes to raise a child, the purpose of education, the limits and boundaries of the market, state services, familial care, the ethics of medicine and much, much more. And the fact is that we will never agree on this because that is not the way we see or do things. Some pride themselves on our educational system for example, perhaps with Oxbridge in mind, but the truth is that universal education in England has always been pragmatic in nature and practice. We have little or no time for the likes of Fröbel, Montessori, Pestalozzi, Illich and Freire. And who but a small band are inspired by therapeutic, holistic communities such as Mulberry Bush, Caldecott and Cotswold?

Given this it is no surprise that the landscape of children's services is littered with short-term initiatives and changing guidance targets and standards. There has to be something to fill the moral, ethical and philosophical void in which we operate. To be busy gives as the reassurance that we are at least doing something which we hope might be worthwhile, while refusing to acknowledge the futility of spending money and energy on that which we will never (remotely) be able to assess and evaluate.

A second line of discussion might be to do with timescales. Patrick Jenkin, a child of his time, referred in his foreword to a "cycle of deprivation". The term is no longer in use as far as I know, and comes with much problematical political baggage. But when we use terms like "early intervention", referring to the age of a child, should we not also acknowledge that this is likely to be very late intervention in the life of the child's family? All the evidence seems to suggest that poverty and poor parenting have inter-generational family, class, communal and cultural roots. Put at its crispest, an early intervention in the life of a child at risk is likely to be a late, possibly re-intervention in the life of the child's parent or parents. For this reason among others I would suggest a 40-year timescale for assessment and evaluation of the impact and effect of strategies, well aware of the immense challenges that this poses, but encouraged by the NCB study, Born to Fail?

Then I would like to begin to explore some of the familial, communal, religious resources (some have talked of social capital) that make up what we might think of as the informal voluntary sector. That is the vast pool of people, acts of unremembered kindness and networks of relationships that go to make up the village that it takes to raise a child (apart from the formal state, local authority, private and voluntary organisations). In trying to describe and analyse provision for children this represents a massive challenge, and yet we risk skewing the conclusions if we ignore it on the grounds that it is so difficult to calculate. A practical implication of this will follow.

Next comes an observation of changes that are common among professions and professionals. One of these is the way in which practice and meetings have become dominated by targets, forms, tick-boxes, pieces of work and time-limited interventions. This has been at the expense of what used to be called, in one profession, "person-centred social work", but which can be applied across the board. Face to face contacts which develop into relationships have been replaced by bureaucratically-influenced processes and practice. This has negative implications for everyone (professionals and clients alike), but in the case of children it is potentially very damaging. Young children are looking for attuned adults and faces. We all know that.

On reflection, I wonder if we ought to think harder about the "Named Person", both in terms of role, and also identity. The description that Bob Holman used in his landmark work in Bath and then Glasgow was that of a "resourceful friend", which sums it up for me. Each child needs a trusted adult who will be there for them long term. Given the likely career paths of professionals, we need to think very carefully of those who might fulfil this role, including those in the extended family and community, as well as in faith communities, sports clubs and groups, alongside professionals who are able and willing to give such a commitment. It is a thorny pint, but if we aspire to a world-class service then it needs to be grasped.

Part of the issue surrounding the identity of a Named Person (resourceful friend) is the matter of choice. Many of the recent developments in say health and education (both significantly universal, not specialist, services) centre on the issue of choice and purchasing. But the reality of children's services for the poor and at-risk children and families is that there is little or no choice. Which is why being able to choose who you put your trust in for your well-being is so crucial. Can we defend giving child and family no choice? If so, how and why?

With still more fermenting in my brain just now as a result of reading this book, I will bring the imaginary conversation to a close with a comment about locality and place. I mentioned being part of the Barclay Committee, but I was in fact one of three members who produced a minority report entitled "A case for neighbourhood-based social work and social services". Unsurprisingly I read Chris Hanvey's book through this lens. After all, the whole of my working life has been spent based in one residential community and neighbourhood, and those whom I have admired, like Bob Holman, Janusz Korzcak, Pandita Ramabai, and Jean Vanier, have done the same.

The word "localism" is used in the book (for example, pages 104-5) and the location of CSTs is carefully considered (pages 106-7). But we need to take immense care at this point. Talk of integrated services and "one door" must not disguise the problem from the child and family's point of view. It needs to be a door that they can get to, that they wish to enter and, crucially, where they receive a welcome. When Social Services (Social Work) Departments replaced Children's Departments they were, in organisational terms, unified organisations, but for many children and families there was no such one door.

It so happens that since 1899 hundreds of children and families have entered the door of Mill Grove, and also professionals in health, education, social work among others. Long before Sure Start and Children's Centres, we functioned effectively as just such a thing. Communication between generations is normal (not an exciting new venture). We are trusted by many neighbours as resourceful friends. Assuming we are not alone, where do such places figure in the vision of integrated children's services, I wonder? And would there be a place for the likes of Bob Holman?

· ·

Nobody's Child: The True Story of Growing Up in a Yorkshire Children's Home

G. J. Urquhart
(Cheltenham: The History Press, 2020)

Gloria Urquhart was born in 1946 and her story of life in a Yorkshire children's home is set mostly in the period of the Children's Departments in England from 1948 to 1971. There have been many studies of this era, including Bob Holman's *The Corporate Parent: Manchester Children's Department, 1948-71* (London: NISW, 1996). But this autobiography may well prove to be in a class of its own.

GJ (her nickname during this time) evokes memories of life in this post-war era for those who were struggling to make ends meet, as well as in middle-class households. Music included recordings of Bing Crosby, Vera Lynn and sacred songs. There was *Children's Hour* on the BBC Home Service, and *Mrs. Dale's Diary*. Bedrooms were cold in the winter; clothes were washed with carbolic soap before being put through cast iron mangles and hung out on wooden rods suspended on pulleys. Church attendance was common for many children, and Sunday-best clothes were worn. Sunday breakfast featured boiled eggs and Sunday lunch included roast beef and Yorkshire pudding. Grace was said before meals. Treats included home-made scones and jam. Caps and berets were part of the school uniform. Schools had assemblies each morning, and the corridors and classrooms smelt of disinfectant and plasticine.

There were blankets and eiderdowns on beds. At home clothes were hung on wooden stands in bedrooms. There were mats on polished wooden floors. Sitting rooms were heated by coal fires. Furniture was handed down through the generations. WCs were usually outside for those living in older terraced houses. Children played outside as a matter of course, swung high on swings and made daisy chains. Christmas decorations were home-made streamers.

Visits to local department stores, and restaurants like Betty's, were treasured delights. Children's feet were looked at through X-ray machines when new shoes were purchased. Clothes purchased were wrapped in brown paper packages tied up with string. Local markets were alive with colour, humour and every kind of food or household product, notably material for dresses and clothes. National events like royal weddings, funerals and the ascent of Everest were watched in cinemas on Pathé News. Scrapbooks and stamp collections were a focus for activity and attention in many households. There were lots of people in army uniform at stations and, in Yorkshire, coal miners walking to and from the pitheads. There were outings to local coastal resorts.

All this is described as the story unfolds: part of the background, and the stuff of everyday life. But for Gloria there was a darker side to life: sometimes unspeakably and chillingly dark. Aged three years and ten months, she was separated from the kith and kin: most painfully, as far as she was concerned, from her younger brother, Kevin, as she entered the local authority care system. What follows is a remarkably measured, vivid, insightful expose of the vagaries, extremes, culture, hierarchies, pervasive control, and power dynamics of that system. Any engaged in social work or substitute care (adoption, foster or residential care) could do little better than to listen to, and inevitably cry with, this poor little girl.

The narrative is gripping and were it a work of fiction it would have been deemed to have been contrived because of so many coincidences of place, proximity and characters. It is a telling reminder that the truth can often be stranger than fiction.

The first part of this review focuses on the nature of the system as experienced by one of those for whom it was designed to care; the second, on the resilience of Gloria.

There were basically four parts to the care system: social work and family support; adoption; foster care and residential care. All are to be found running through this book. Residential care and adoption are the bookends of substitute care and in this account both feature prominently, though for different reasons. Gloria spends most of her childhood in children's homes (including an assessment centre), while her brother Kevin is adopted. Each experienced separation and loss, with all the loneliness and anxiety, anger and depression that are associated with them. Towards the end of the story, we learn that Kevin had struggled in his relationship with his adoptive father. Gloria had sought after him from the moment they were separated, and her search for him runs through the narrative. They are eventually reunited, but then tragically Kevin, aged 27, committed suicide. Gloria was never adopted, although it had been considered at one stage. She suffered in residential care but, as evidenced by the book, she survived emotionally. In this way we are required to lay aside neat formulae and prescriptions, and to listen to the experiences and voices of the children themselves.

The local authority care system, as represented by Children's Departments, emerged from the shadows of the Poor Law. This was reflected in remnants of Poor Law culture, notably in the way those with "less eligibility" were treated. Gloria tries to understand the motives of those responsible for her "care", but there is no plausible reason other than that society at that time seemed to conceive of them as "the Other". As part of their birth families, they were seen as incompetent, lazy, parasitical, or even bad. The large Victorian Poor Law buildings were still standing, and local authorities often adapted them into residential homes for children or the elderly. In other parts of Europe, such as, say, Denmark, the Second World War marked the end of previous systems, and prompted a complete overhaul of the philosophy and practice of child care, but in England, although there was a rethink represented by the 1946 Curtis Report, there was not such a clean break. Small children's homes were among the options recommended, but it took time for suitable places to be identified or built, and in the meantime existing buildings were used.

The ultimate power or authority resided in a Children's Officer along with a children's committee, and this was devolved to senior field workers. The farther you were from these, whether residential or foster carers, parents or children, the less information, choice, agency and rights you had. In this case, those in power took decisions that proved to be manifestly against Gloria's best interests. They held sway over those who were trying to help her and knew her best. Sometimes the resulting mistakes or errors were covered up by a wall of prevarication or misinformation.

As with all systems, there was good and bad

within it. Gloria is careful to point out and praise individual carers, a particular small children's home, along with social workers who showed understanding and empathy. But sadly, there were some who were incompetent and lacking insight, and some who were downright wicked. Foremost among the latter was a Miss Silverwood, head of Rothwell Children's Home. She bullied, beat and abused children routinely and mercilessly, including Gloria. The book contains two letters from Gloria (chapter 12, pages 82-88) written when she was an adult, one to Miss Silverwood, and one to the reader. These documents alone stand as a withering indictment of a system that somehow appointed and allowed such people to abuse children with such impunity.

In the first she asks Miss Silverwood whether she had ever read the Children Act. This legislation envisaged substitute care as safe, secure and protected. Gloria says she would have preferred a continuation of the neglect and abuse in her own family to that meted out to her in Rothwell children's home: "hell on earth". Because of the repression and torture inflicted on her, by the time she was six she wanted to die. She then contrasts the absolute safety of being cuddled in the arms of her friend and foster carer with the time Miss Silverwood smashed her face with ferocity and continued to thump her head when she fell to the floor in a pool of blood.

But the excesses of such vindictive individuals should not be allowed to detract from the major flaws in the system considered as a whole. Not only were the slapping and beating of children rife, but there was a culture of silence that meant Gloria was never told, and could not find out, some of the basics of her life. From the time she was stripped of all contact with her family, and every piece of clothing and possession, she was haunted by insistent questions. Why was she in the care system at all? Was her mother dead or alive? Who was the old woman she had been taken to see (it was her grandmother)? Where was her brother, Kevin, and why had they been separated at the very moment she entered the children's home? Year after year the system not only refused to answer, but forced others who tried to help her, including supportive friends, prospective foster and adoptive carers, to collude with the local authority in hiding the truth from Gloria.

One of the tragedies of her story is that a couple who wanted to adopt her, and with whom she had begun to bond, were prevented from doing so (she only found out years later that it was because they had moved out of the local authority area). And that two sisters who fostered her for a time, and were committed to her until they died, were also prevented from fostering her through to adulthood.

The nett effect of all this was a deep sense of shame, that she was in some way to blame (a bad child), and a deep and lasting sense of rejection and loneliness. Like other children, she cried herself to sleep. There were no comforting arms, no cuddles and no love. Little children adopted predictably sad behavioural patterns, such as rocking on their beds, banging their heads on walls or furniture. Gloria describes one girl literally pulling her hair out until she was quite bald, and another child aged eight cutting herself with kitchen cutlery. In time Gloria suffered anxiety and depression. She acted out her anger and resentment, was locked and pinned down in a room in the children's home, and later placed in a padded room in a mental hospital.

All the time children appeared or disappeared from the home without explanation. All this would not have been out of place in the middle of the Poor Law era. With this comparison in mind, it can be added that there were mice in the buildings, mice droppings in the breakfast cereal, staff eating preferentially, heavy tasks and jobs to be done every day by the children under threat of punishment. Washing facilities were shared and the children slept in large dormitories. Meagre personal belongings were kept in lockers. Communication with the outside world was carefully monitored and usually forbidden. Siblings were routinely separated within the same complex of houses.

So much for the system. But somehow Gloria survived, and in time came to thrive. Though the physical and emotional scars have accompanied her through life, she did not succumb to the self-pity of permanent victim status. So what were the elements and factors that seem to have contributed to her ability to withstand such a system?

It is obvious that she was an intelligent and determined child and young person. She showed tenacity and inventiveness in finding ways of coping with and sometimes outwitting the system, even at the cost of reproof and punishment. But how was her inner world nurtured over all these years? One factor is the understanding and care of other children who were also subject to the same system. Much of the truth about her life, as well as life in general that she learnt, came from them rather than from adult carers or social workers. And this remains a challenge to British philosophies of child development and care, which privilege individual rights and agency over the potential for children to empathise with and care for each other. There were children who bullied and took out their feelings of anger and resentment on her. But taken overall, the children proved to be a more reliable resource than many of the staff.

Then there were carers in the system who genuinely sought to understand, help and support her. Often they were aware of the abuse meted out by colleagues (such as Miss Silverwood), but could do nothing to prevent it. There was also a small children's home run by an Irish person called Miss Smith. After Rothwell children's home this proved to be something of an oasis, or haven. There were social workers or welfare officers whom she respected, too.

But the heroines of the story are Auntie Agnes and her sister Auntie Cissy, who gave all they had, including sharing their home with Gloria. From them she learned not only acceptance but also the nature of love and many practical skills. They taught her ways of coping with anger and the painful necessity of forgiving others. They were also among those who introduced her to the social world outside the system: shops, parks, markets, churches and friends.

The natural world, not least the parks in Leeds, provided solace, space for thinking and dreaming, and also reminders of all that Gloria had not only with nature but with other human beings. She revelled in the beauty of trees, flowers and the sociability of pets.

But Gloria attributes much, if not most of her resilience, to her Christian faith, and the "Unseen Guest", which was her name for Jesus. This is something little written about in the professional literature of child development and social work in the UK. But to those who have read the stories of children who have suffered trauma and abuse it will not come as a surprise. The reflections of the psychologist Dr. Robert Coles on Ruby Bridges should be compulsory reading for any seeking to understand or help children suffering loss or abuse. At the time that Gloria was part of the system, some form of Christian church attendance was obligatory, but there was of course a disjunction between words and actions. Outside the system, notably the prospective adoptive parents, a Baptist minister and his wife, and the two sisters, both Christians, one belonging to the Salvation Army, Gloria found integrity. They walked the talk.

Understanding resilience requires a willingness to listen to the experiences and stories of those who have gone through the fire and come out the other side. Quietly but insistently Gloria, in prose and one or two poems or hymns, describes how her faith kept her going when nearly everything else was pulling her down. And the way she came to understand the pressures on those who sometimes failed her, and sought to stand in their shoes, shows how her concepts of empathy and forgiveness worked in practice. When reading her story, it comes as no surprise that in time she proved a good nurse, wife, mother and grandmother.

A final thought. It might be supposed that with the system having failed Gloria so comprehensively, a sensible conclusion would be that local authorities cannot, and should not, be corporate parents. Also that children's homes should be disbanded in favour of increased family support, and where necessary foster care and adoption. But all through the stories of those who have been separated from their families there is a thread that records the considered preference of some children for children's homes rather than familial care. Gloria experienced much that she appreciated in both Miss Smith's small children's home, as well as in the foster home of aunties Agnes and Cissy.

History does not allow us to form conclusions as to why things happened, only evidence on which to base pertinent questions. And this book leaves us with a question that Gloria does not pose: who was served better by the system, Kevin or her? The problem that Kevin and many other children have faced with adoption is the isolation, not only from kith and kin, but also from other children and from people like a person Gloria came to call "Dad Dean". Other children in care, along with "uncles" and "aunties" who are not blood relatives, are often the ones who help to nurture resilience. It seems that Kevin lacked them.

If one is looking for some sort of moral from the story (and Gloria is certainly not) it might be that it takes a village to raise a child. Villages are so varied and organic that they defy dogma. A friend and colleague of mine, David Lane, has suggested that there might be something like "corporate families", where children in care could derive and give mutual long-term support. My experience is that something like this happens informally already. Whatever the nature and shape of things to come, hopefully they will be better (than systems like the one Gloria endured) at finding ways of exposing any who cause harm to children, and committed to identifying and supporting those who really care.

With Thanks to Barbara Dockar-Drysdale

from Mill Grove

I first came across the life and work of Barbara Dockar-Drysdale while I was researching residential child care at Edinburgh University from 1969 to 1973. Some of what I gleaned was through her own writings, but also from the work of Richard Balbernie and others who admired her pioneering initiatives. This period was seminal in my own life and work, as I was consciously seeking out models for what was to become my life's work at Mill Grove. I met John Bowlby, and his work together with much else, including that of R.D. Laing, D.W. Winnicott, seeped deep into my subconscious. As far as I can recall I did not meet Barbara Dockar-Drysdale, and it was only many years later that I finally visited Mulberry Bush.

Like the most formative influences, I cannot recall many specific nostra or cases but, looking back with their writings beside me, I discover just how significant their combined influence has been. Some years ago I was asked to distil my own thinking and practice into book-form, and I did this in *The Growth of Love*, with its two supporting volumes, *Reflections on Living with Children*. With these in mind, I revisited the contribution of Dockar-Drysdale and immediately realised that the five fundamental principles of my understanding of therapeutic child care were completely congruent with her overall thinking and practice: Security; Boundaries; Significance; Community; and Creativity. It doesn't take much imagination to find the equivalents in her writings.

What is more, on reflection the fact that Mill Grove still exists may be said to owe something to her. It is an individual residential home requiring intense, unconditional commitment, where the rhythms and minutiae of daily living and the quality of the personal relationships between carers and children are the key to healing and growth. Mulberry Bush was one of those places that encouraged and inspired us to carry on whatever the fashions and pressures of subsequent periods of professional practice. This is a point that was made (I discovered after writing this) by Chris Beedell in his obituary in the Independent. In the light of emerging beliefs about family support and therapy, and community-based care for all client groups, residential establishments were often seen as unfortunate anachronisms, reactionary last resorts. There were times when it seemed as if the whole professional world, including social work, was determined to erase them from the earth. But she and others had listened more carefully to the expressed and unarticulated realities and feelings of particular children and young people, who needed a form of primary care that was not available through counselling or community support.

One of the terms common at the time was "maladjusted". It is now seen as unfortunate and politically incorrect, but then it was an attempt to move on from the labelling and connotations of "delinquent" and "criminal". My sense is that Barbara Dockar-Drysdale realised that society in general, and education in particular, were maladjusted in their relation to some children and young people. There had to be another, alternative, radical way of seeking to understand, relate to and help them. Those, like her, who knew of the traumas caused to children by wartime experiences, were all too aware that society is not always wholly sensitive and benevolent in its dealings with those deemed to be out of the mainstream.

A term that has proved consistently apt throughout my life alongside hurting children and young people is the word "frozen". It is chillingly indicative of one of the main ways in which they seek to deal with terrifying traumas and the accompanying psychological and emotional pain. Recently one of those who lived at Mill Grove over 50 years ago wrote an autobiography and, when we discussed his reflections, he and I saw that in essence this is how he coped with his lack of attachment for most of his life. When the thaw comes it is potentially very difficult and painful, and this is where the presence, empathy, insight and consistency of those who offer unconditional presence and love are critically important.

Creative and supported regression is vital in restoring the emotional blood flow, and that requires a complete world or "containment". The latter word has become associated unfortunately with the term "pin down", but one of the most important experiences for children is that of "being held". For those who have not experienced a close parent-child attachment, residential care offers the possibility of a place (literal and symbolic) where the distress and pain of controlled and supported regression can be managed over time, and through many different aspects and phases of discovery.

Mill Grove is not a school and therefore does not function as such a total living environment as Mulberry Bush, but when the formal education system fails individual children and young people, it becomes the place that continues to "hold" the child. I recall one boy who was expelled from every school he attended, including a special school. From that point on, and until he attended a residential school during week-days (returning to us at weekends and holidays), he was with me for much of each day. We learned and explored together. There was no doubt in my mind that the educational system was maladjusted to his unique combination of experiences, gifts, abilities and needs.

The strains that such children place on themselves, their carers and their peers are, of course, predictably considerable. And this means that the residential setting needs to be robust enough to acknowledge (rather than deny or suppress) the volcanic, primal eruptions of feelings including those of shame, guilt, despair, annihilation. From the time that Ruth and I started living at Mill Grove as leaders of the community we have been supported continuously by a consultant psychotherapist. There have been just three in over 40 years. It is only with such consistent support, objectivity and challenge that it would have been at all possible to hold on to the reality and discomfort of the childrens' raw emotions and feelings without developing unconscious mechanisms for coping with them (freezing, for example!). Barbara Dockar-Drysdale described children who had not experienced primary affection and holding as having "caretaker selves". One of our consultant therapists introduced us to the term "co-habitee". It is, in my view, a variation on exactly this theme: seeking to make some order out of the emotional fears and chaos by shielding the embryonic ego from the harsh truths of the inner and outer worlds.

Though not a school, or possibly because Mill Grove is not a school, we have been able in the lives of some of the children and young people who have come to us to provide an environment of unconditional acceptance and love that lasts throughout their lives. It is a primary experience in touch with the natural world, seasons, rhythms of life and celebration. And crucially, analysis and daily living, inner and the outer worlds, are connected. It is this connection that Barbara Dockar-Drysdale saw as the key to everything, if only the healthy relationship could be maintained, strong enough to withstand the storms and eruptions that must come if a sense of unity and identity are to be experienced.

Times move on, and our understanding of the experiences, gifts and needs of children thankfully deepen. Some of what Barbara Dockar-Drysdale stood for and described would now be put in different ways and appreciated in new contexts. Attachment theory and resilience have developed since her time. In my view one of her natural successors is Dan Hughes, and I would be interested to hear from others about who they see as the people carrying the torch that she handed on. Meanwhile I am thankful that I came to know of her work and Mulberry Bush at that early stage in my own journey of discovery. I would be surprised if there are not many others like me, who never met her but who have been profoundly influenced by her life and work. Just a pity that I was not able to tell her to her face.

A Finchden Experience

Alan Wendelken
(Lulu.Com: 2019)

Introduction

England was uniquely blessed in the twentieth century with radical experiments in, and models of, therapeutic residential settings for children. There have been similar ventures in other parts of the world, but that is to go beyond the scope of this introduction.

They have in common the fact that they were established, and/or run, by formidable characters who had the interests of children at heart; that they sought to draw from the best theory and practice available at the time; that they knew what a philosophy of life/care was when they saw it; that they wrote up their experiences and discoveries, and inspired others to do the same; that they had the means and wherewithal to purchase or acquire substantial buildings in which to live with their charges; that there were creative connections and links between the places and people; and that they were untroubled by bureaucracy, employment law, health and safety concerns, children's rights and political correctness.

The pioneers and places with which they are associated include, Barbara Dockar-Drysdale and Mulberry Bush; Leila Rendel and the Caldecott Community; Richard Balbernie and the Cotswold Community; A.S. Neill and Summerhill; David Wills and Bodenham Manor School; George Lyward and Finchden Manor.

Having been responsible for the residential community, Mill Grove, since 1986, I count myself richly blessed to have on my shelves books by, or about, all of these influential giants of the past, and to have known the work and writings of several of those whose work influenced and encouraged them (including D.W. Winnicott; John Bowlby; Homer Lane). Like Mr. Lyward, we too shared our family home with those children who came to live with us.

We are unlikely to see the like of these remarkable adventurers again, and this is why anything that furthers our knowledge and understanding of one of them is to be welcomed and treasured.

Hence why it is such an event to have this memoir of Finchden Manor. I was thrilled when Alan's widow, Claire Wendelken Ross, who has been a longstanding friend and social work colleague of mine, first showed it to me, and delighted to be able to commend it to the board of *The Therapeutic Care Journal*. As readers will quickly discover for themselves, this is writing of the highest order, meticulous in its detail and sensitive in its observations and reading of feelings, intentions and relationships. We are indebted not only to Alan for the original text, but to Claire for editing the material following Alan's sudden and untimely death in 1996.

What is so remarkable about this narrative is that Alan was both a boy, and then later a member of staff, at Finchden. This means that there is a richness to his insights, due not least to the different coordinates and perspectives that these two standpoints provided. It is part autobiography and, as such, palpably honest and open. The feel, the odours, the architecture, the residents, the grounds, the seasons, the history of rustic, Spartan Finchden are described with accuracy, and set within the historical context of the times (the late, post-war 1940s). The war had changed Alan's father for good: he had been blinded and his last words were "When I last saw you, you were a boy and now you're a man". And given his mother's own psychological hang-ups and lack of insight, Alan was the emotional scapegoat of the family.

What Mr. Lyward offered was a place in his own home, "unlabelled living" and "stern love". It was an adventure in living based on acceptance, security and inter-dependence. Alan was there in its heyday as a resident teenager and then in its twilight days as a member of staff. He recalls movingly the death and memorial service for George Lyward, and then the day that the place closed. From start to finish his account is laden with observations and comments that will enlighten and often delight those who are committed to providing therapeutic care over 50 years later. It could well take its place among some of the classics of this genre. I certainly hope so.

· ·

Exclusion and Embrace

Miroslav Volf
(Nashville: Abingdon Press, 1996)

These words form the title of a remarkable book by Miroslav Volf, a Croat whose family and people were among the victims of the Serbian atrocities in Srebrenica, and written when the traumas were still raw. After a lecture that he gave, he was asked whether, as a follower of Jesus, he could embrace one of his enemies. The question haunted him, and his book is the story of how he wrestled with it.

The plot thickened for me when I was re-telling the story of "The Prodigal Son" (actually the story of the loving father and his two sons) a few days ago in a school assembly. At that moment I realised that this was the story that Professor Volf saw as the trigger for his "theology of embrace". And then, in a flash, that his analysis of the nature of embrace might be what therapeutic interventions, relationships and communities are all about. It has certainly thrown new light on my life at Mill Grove.

You may find it helpful to have the picture by Rembrandt beside you as you read this anatomy of embrace (it's called *The Return of the Prodigal*). It's a fascinating feature of the story as recorded by Luke (15:11-32), that there is no record of the father saying anything directly to his younger son: everything is communicated by body language and actions. Quite apart from any other insights, this may be something well worth pondering in the field of therapeutic care, when so often words seem blunt or inadequate.

Embrace stripped to its essentials is a drama in four acts.

Opening the Arms

I care about you, and you matter to me more than you may know. I am not content with being merely myself, without you. You are already in my heart, though you have been away from me. I am making space ready to receive you. There is room for you in my heart and life. I am not so cluttered, or so full of myself that every part of me is already occupied. I am not here to do something to you or for you. Rather I open myself to you and invite you to respond. You could imagine the open arms as a symbol of an open door: there is no need to knock; you are welcome. And it doesn't need me to point out that this is all very risky, not least if the other has a machine gun in his hands. But therapeutic interventions are always risky.

Waiting

Embrace is not a taking hold, arresting, pinning down, invasive or a one-way initiative. It's not even a caress. Before the embrace can proceed, it needs the arms of the other to open. By opening our arms, we have conveyed a message: you are welcome, and I am here for you. But another part of the message is that we will not force our way. It is the very opposite of insistence or violence. If embrace starts with the initiative of one person, it can never reach its fulfilment without reciprocity. Of its essence is the movement and response of the other. And there are all sorts of reasons, experiences, traumas, fears, that require patient, hopeful waiting. And in the waiting messages will be conveyed and decoded by each person.

Closing the Arms

We have reached the heart of the drama of embrace. This is where, although there will not be equality, there is complete reciprocity. Each is holding the other; and each is held by the other. They are both active, and both passive. It takes two pairs of arms for one embrace. In an embrace the host is a guest, and the guest is a host. And this means a soft touch is necessary. Rembrandt gets this perfectly (worth looking at the picture again!). Not a bear-hug either way. An attuned response to each other, so that both feels comfortable, and understands that the other is comfortable too. And this requires the recognition that neither understands the other fully. There is an otherness about the person we close our arms around, a mystery. This is the beginning of a process of understanding and knowing that starts with the realisation that I do not fully know the other. I have much I don't know and much more to learn. This may be my enemy, but do I know her story?

Opening the Arms Again

We cannot live in permanent embrace. We have not become one entity. This is not about the welding of two others, so that they have become indissolubly one, and can never be free of each other. Each is still "I" and "You" in relationship. Neither has ceased to be as a person, and so each retains their own agency. This is where the real dance is in the relationship: we are not the same person, we are different, but we have begun to be open to each other. And the truth is that none of us is an island entire of itself: our identity is made up of our experiences and relationships with others. If I am to have an identity then others will be part of that, sometimes for painful reasons.

Conclusion

I have been deliberately concise to stay as close to the insights of Volf as possible, but also to avoid filling in with extraneous material or examples.

My intuition suggests that embrace, understood in this way, is instructive for those of us engaged in therapeutic relationships and communities. If we (that is self and others) are to be, and to develop, we need to be open to others, to realise we are strangers among our family and community, at home with "others" who we thought were our enemies. In embracing an Other, outside can become part of our inside. Hospitality may not be something one offers to the other, but something shared and mutually enriching. Home and away are re-imagined. This is a journey of adventure, and who knows the outcome? If broken relationships are to be restored, then the identities of each must be rethought and reshaped.

No insightful parent or teacher wants a child or pupil to remain forever tied to her apron strings, or sitting in the classroom. There is always the desire to see the other explore in her own way. We know that this is risky, and safety or success are never assured.

All this is in the story, and much more. Not least the chilling self-exclusion of the older son, who misses out on the whole embrace. A total stranger, though he has never left home. The silence of his response is perhaps the most deafening in recorded history. "All I have is yours … Come and celebrate the return of your brother, who was lost and is found, who was dead, but is alive again." These tender and loving words of his father echo in the stony silence which forms the end of the story.

Which is a sober reminder that our proffered welcome may not be accepted by all. The wait-ing may be long, and the offer refused in any variety of ways. So why do we keep our arms open? Isn't it because we have discovered that ultimately there is no other way to discover self and others than through some form of embrace, however tentative or reluctant?

Reflections on Two Films About Children as Agents of Change

Goodbye, Christopher Robin
Eric Clapton: Life in 12 Bars

Over many years I have tuned in regularly to certain BBC radio programmes such as *Desert Island Discs*, *The Life Scientific*, and *Private Passions*, each of which uses a framework in which an invited guest is encouraged to share something of their life story. Among other ways in which I engage with them is to search for any clues into what had caused their lives and behaviour to change, by listening to their accounts of this change. A dramatic example, during the Covid 19 lock-down in the UK, was that of Jane Goodall, an acknowledged world expert on chimpanzees, who subsequently became heavily committed to the cause of preserving planet earth. She said that people asked her how she made that decision, but she replied that she didn't "make a decision": it was made for her. She was changed. She went to an international conference "as a scientist" and left "as an activist". The shift and widening of her agenda arose naturally out of her discovery that human individual and social behaviour had to change. Because she was a changed person there was no option but to live and act in a different way.

A rather more common feature of the stories of those featured is that a teacher or parent enthused and inspired them by way of example, and then taking a personal interest in their questions and discoveries as children.

Both Jane Goodall's story and this element of the stories of many others, are, of course, encouraging for those of us engaged in therapeutic care. It may not be apparent at the time, but by sharing compelling evidence on the one hand, and leading by example on the other, we can contribute to a positive turning point in a young person's life. Often, we will never know this, but those of us engaged long-term in a person's life are sometimes blessed to hear of occasions when this has happened.

But to see things in this way assumes something of a one-way process: a resourceful adult (teacher or parent) proving to be a catalyst or spur to a child's development.

What, I wondered, about the role of children as agents of change in the adults who teach and care for them? An example I recall is of a teacher writing in the school report of one of my offspring, that she had learnt more from my daughter than she had ever taught her. The idea that education, care or therapy leaves only one of the parties changed is surely suspect. Integral to the dynamics and processes in each are the relationships involved between adult, child and subject matter.

Covid 19 has been an agent of all sorts of changes, positive and negative, and one of these in my life has been more opportunity to watch programmes and films with my wife, Ruth. There were two films shown in close succession that at other times I would almost certainly have been too busy to see. One was *Goodbye, Christopher Robin*; the other *Eric Clapton: Life in 12 Bars*. If you don't know them, then I commend them warmly, but with a health warning: each film could seriously affect your mental health.

Goodbye, Christopher Robin

A.A. Milne, the father of Christopher Robin, suffered from what is now called Post-Traumatic-Stress Syndrome following the First World War. As a husband and parent, he was anxious and depressed, suffering unpredictable and harrowing flashbacks. As a writer, he had a complete block, unable to produce anything creative. His (only) child, Christopher Robin, was therefore born into a dysfunctional household, with a strained relationship between his mother and father, and where his nanny (known as "Alice" in one of the poems) was his only consistently attuned and securely attached significant adult.

Things reached a pitch when Milne's wife left for a period, as did the nanny (due to the illness, and then death, of her mother). Suddenly A.A. Milne had become a single parent. Given his psychological condition, and his almost complete lack of experience of childcare and housework, he found himself struggling on a huge learning curve. But the young Christopher proved to be the agent of major positive change. He absorbed some of his father's strange and inappropriate behaviour; they played together; and through this unusual relationship, a whole new imaginary world was brought into being. It included a growing family of characters including Winnie the Pooh, Eeyore, Piglet, Kanga and Ru, Tigger and Owl, and places like the Hundred Acre Wood, Pooh Sticks Bridge, and the North Pole. A.A. Milne started to write the poems and stories in books such as *Now we are Six* and *The House at Pooh Corner*. Almost overnight he became a world-famous author. His wife returned, and Christopher became a celebrity.

Unfortunately, the positive change in his father's life and circumstances cost Christopher Robin nearly everything. He felt that his personal relationship with his father and their imaginary world had been taken away from him. There was chronic bullying at school, and eventually he chose, against his parents' wishes, to serve in the Second World. He explained to his father that this was in large measure not only to get away, but to repair the damage that he had suffered. He survived and his relationship with his nanny was restored. But the emotional scars were with him for life.

Eric Clapton: Life in 12 Bars

Eric Clapton was the world renowned, brilliant guitarist who had everything humanly speaking seemed to have the world at his feet. Musically speaking he was one of the most successful artists ever known. But due to emotional abuse throughout his childhood he was never able to establish, let alone sustain, genuine relationships in adult life. This was as true of professional groups, personal friends or the women in his life. Somehow, he survived a period on cocaine and heroin, only to jump out of the frying pan and into the fire by becoming alcohol dependent. He reflected later that no one had told him that alcohol could be a more serious problem than Grade A drugs.

At this point tragedy struck. Due to his fame, it has been etched in the hearts and minds of a goodly proportion of the world, through one of the best-known songs of all time: *Tears in Heaven*. His son, Conor, fell out of a window of a high-rise apartment block in New York. It could have been the final straw that broke Clapton's back. But it wasn't. And the agent of change was a little child.

Some time after the tragedy, Clapton was in his own house alone, unsurprisingly unable to face anything. After a time, he started going through the thousands of cards and condolences that had been sent to him. Among them, he was shocked to discover a note from his son that had been posted in Milan weeks earlier and before he had set off to meet his father in New York. It read: "I love you. I want to see you again. A Kiss. Love, Conor Clapton." Clapton commented: "Then I realised that if I could go through this and stay sober, then anyone can. Then I suddenly realised that there was a way to turn this dreadful tragedy into something positive. That I would consider living my life from this point on to honour the memory of my son. I got hold of a little Spanish guitar that I had with me at that time. From the minute I got up and for the rest of that year I just played and played to stop from facing the situation."

It was in this period that *Tears in Heaven* was born. One of the most famous songs of all time, it begins with the words, "Would you know my name if I saw you in heaven? Would it be the same if I saw you in heaven? I must be strong and carry on because I know I don't belong in heaven ...."

A single card with words, the simplest of messages from a child to his father, proved to be the decisive turning point of that father's life. The account that Clapton gives is an example of a decision that resulted from a changed life. The change was so profound that he was eventually able to relate to others for the first time, a wife, children, friends, and music groups. And he founded Crossroads, a therapeutic addiction treatment centre in Antigua.

Closing Reflections

Perhaps there are times when we might appropriately share stories of how children have been agents of change in our lives. It occurs to me that over the years I have written this column I have told of some of those who have helped to shape the way I have come to see and value things differently. One of the regular

themes in these cases has been my realisation that they were resilient, both beyond my comprehension and beyond my capability. The more deeply I got to know their stories the more I knew that had it been me in their shoes, I would have been tempted to give up, and most probably would have done. Their determination to "carry on" and "be strong", to use Clapton's words, has been my inspiration.

During Covid 19, one of these has at last received something of her reward. Against all odds, she is a survivor of serial rejection and chronic abuse. She is now full-time in a maternity unit of an NHS hospital. She has been feted in shops, on social media, and by the public at large. Most are thanking her for risking her life for the sake of others. Meanwhile I am thanking her for proving to me that when all the odds are stacked against you, it is possible to absorb any number of setbacks and still carry on, and to channel the hurt and resentment into caring for others.

It is just possible, I suppose, that when she looks back, in some small way I may have been an agent of change in her life. Therapy works both ways. But what I do know is that my life has been inspired and enriched by hers.

The Only Story

Julian Barnes
(London: Jonathan Cape, 2019)

We have come a long way from the time when it was said that everything a child said about abuse and abusers was to be believed. While a child's well-being and interests are paramount, and everything a child says is listened to and taken seriously, things are more complex than that. But it is well to recall that this used to be a mantra of professionals and specialists in the emerging field of child protection and safeguarding. Perhaps it would have been wiser to have listened to the poets and writers. No one who has read Marcel Proust's *A La Recherche de Temps Perdu*, or Anthony Powell's *Dance to the*

Music of Time, for example, is likely to be remotely inclined to accept memories of childhood as non-problematical or clear cut. There is simply too much filtering going on, conscious and unconscious, and there is too much at stake. To retrace one's life story requires imagination and self-awareness, not merely a recall and collation of the hard or indisputable facts.

For much of my life at Mill Grove, time and again, I have been forced to try to fathom how and why it is that some of the children and young people in our care have resorted to lying: against all the odds and all the evidence. Intuitively I have sensed that it is more than a matter of choice or an instinct for survival. And it seems to go beyond issues of ethics and morality. It is as if fabrication and lying are part of a child's being, their (primal?) character. When they are in lying mode, to challenge them with incontrovertible evidence makes not a whiff of difference. They can do none other than deny what stares them, and you, in the face. So it is that I have tried to understand the nature and possible origins of this character trait.

Recently, it was Julian Barnes in his novel, *The Only Story*, who provided a spark of insight. The book is a life-story focusing on the anatomy of love between a late teenager and an older married woman. As their relationship deteriorates the woman turns to drink and a routine increasingly peppered with excuses and lies. But their life-stories are, of course, inextricably intertwined. So, over time, her lies lead to his lies. He reacts by condoning her lies and becoming a "liar by proxy". But it is not long before he finds himself lying, out of weariness, a desire for peace, and also, surprisingly and controversially, out of love. The genesis of lying is set out like this ....

First you tell lies to protect the one you love, and your love. Then you begin lying to her. (This is where the crucial insight occurs). Barnes puts it like this:

"Why? Something to do with the need to create some internal space which you could keep intact – and where you could yourself remain intact." (Page 137)

This is where the light came on for me. Yes, lying in some cases, perhaps in more life-stories than we care to imagine, has its origins, its genesis, in the need to create some internal space that you can keep intact. An imaginary world where it is hoped that safe space can be found, set in the context of a real world which is unpredictable, hostile, confusing, oppressive, overwhelming and sometimes abusive. If such a fantasy world has been under construction from very early childhood, then no wonder that it should be part of the warp and woof of the person's personality and way of living: crucial to their way of coping.

This made sense of those puzzling times when the truth was so solid, so simple, so transparent, so mutually shared, as to be undeniable ... but when the other person still denied it insistently to my face while the evidence was

in front of both our eyes. For a moment I had glimpsed what had been and was going on in the other person's inner world. It was not just a survival technique to get out of a difficult situation, but the surfacing or eruption of the way their life was lived, experienced, organised and processed at the deepest of levels.

There was a time when I might have pursued or contested things to the bitter end in the interests of establishing a foundation of shared truth, but over the years it has become apparent that this course of action, however laudable, risks serious collateral damage. One psychoanalyst responded in this way, when I declared my determination to get to the bottom of things: "And have you thought through what damage might be caused in the process; whether there will be anything left after this forthright quest for what you see as healing and truth?"

The present encounter or incident is just the tip of an iceberg, who knows how vast, and it is not only memories that might unravel, but also the inner world of the person whom you are trying to help. The current example is a warning about the fragility of the truth denier's personality.

But it goes deeper than this. For to construct things in this way is to assume that the other person is a liar, while you always consistently see and tell the truth. And the writers have already questioned how is it possible for any person to know, let alone tell, their life-story with complete accuracy and truth? So, what might be the process by which each of our inner worlds has been constructed?

This leads me to the work of those who like Freud, Jung, Klein, Erikson, Winnicott, among many others, have sought to conceive and reconstruct the development of personality, of a person's self, identity, ego. Professor James Loder, whose work I have mentioned before, sums up a critical, and what he suggests is a universal, moment or stage in ego development, when a young child discovers that the reliable presence, smiling face and succour of the mother or significant other is absent, and that no amount of crying can bring her back. She is outside the child's control. And here the primal fear of "the Void", that is the total absence of security, safe space, is exposed most cruelly and frighteningly. The reaction is to begin to create your own inner world, by setting up an alternative scenario in which you deny help when it is eventually offered (creating "no-win" situations), by pre-empting the "No" of the other, with your own "No": here, he argues, can be seen the very first inklings of an independent, untouchable inner world in its most rudimentary form.

All through life this false ego, a survival strategy, is resorted to whenever in the real world, things threaten to overwhelm the self. Where there is no secure attachment or bonding with another person, this imaginary ego assumes huge, possibly pre-eminent, significance. And over time a person will do almost anything to keep the inner world intact however far it deviates from the truth. The stakes are simply too high. To let go of this lifelong "friend" is to risk losing everything.

So, assuming that Julian Barnes is right, it is not hard to see that whenever we find ourselves confronted by another person who reveals their sense of horror and fear that confrontation with the truth might annihilate them as a being, we do well to bear in mind that within each of us there lies buried a false ego, and that though it is largely unconscious, its needs to be fed and nurtured have been met in any number of alternative ways to barefaced lying. Achievements, success, acclaim, status, possessions can all disguise the underlying primal fact that each of us is frightened of the Void.

In fact, one of the ways in which child development theories tend to deny this truth is by presenting growth in developmental stages from birth to maturity, rather than as the palpably more accurate bell curve that acknowledges the ultimate stage or destiny of all human beings is death.

Whatever the truth, when we ponder life-stories and lying, the stakes are high: for all of us.

- -

The Uses of Enchantment

Bruno Bettelheim
(London: Penguin, 1976)

Recently my wife and I made a trip to the Victoria and Albert Museum in South Kensington, and in the process erased childhood memories of an unattractive place that I had always associated with dark, dingy staircases and large, inscrutable Chinese urns. This encounter with the place in later life effected such a transformation that within a couple of weeks we explored it with our grandchildren (who were really in their element there). Before leaving I decided to purchase a memento to record the visit that revealed just what a remarkable, richly varied, beautifully displayed and inexhaustible treasure trove it was. I hit upon Bruno Bettelheim's *The Uses of Enchantment*, his classic on the psychological meaning and importance of fairy tales.

Of course, at this stage of life, I was not coming to it without a history. I assumed he had chosen the title with reference to Richard Hoggart's book, *The Uses of Literacy*, published nearly 20 years earlier. I have often referred to the significance of stories in general in the development of children's imaginations, self-awareness and the fundamental concepts that are necessary to conceive of their lives as having coherence and meaning. I have written and produced traditional pantomimes performed by children and young people. And having studied English Language and Literature within the course designed by J.R.R. Tolkien and C.S. Lewis, I was not only aware of *The Chronicles of Narnia* and *The Lord of the Rings*, but crucially of Tolkien's timeless and masterly essay, *On Fairy-stories*. I was also familiar with other writings and the work of Bettelheim. Perhaps this "previous" coalesced unconsciously to confirm that this book should be chosen in preference to several other worthy candidates invitingly displayed.

When I began to read and study it, I wondered why it had taken almost as long for its importance to dawn on me as it had to realise the astonishing treasures and worth of the V&A. I commend it warmly to all who are alongside children and seeking to understand and support them, including parents, grandparents and those who operate within a therapeutic milieu. His basic argument is that the greatest and most difficult task confronting human beings is to find meaning in our lives. In the case of the severely disturbed children that Bettelheim was seeking to help as an educator and therapist, it was often a task of trying to restore meaning that had been undermined by trauma and loss. Such meaning (or its restoration) does not come fully packaged at a single point in a person's life, but rather develops throughout our lives beginning with childhood. And for this reason, resources are needed that are appropriate to the stage of understanding that a child has reached. Ideally these resources should be lifelong companions that are always available for re-acquaintance.

Bettelheim believes that fairy stories are ideal and possibly uniquely so for this purpose. They entertain, arouse curiosity, enrich life, stimulate the imagination; help to develop the intellect, clarify emotions, are attuned to anxieties and aspirations; give full recognition to difficulties, while at the same time suggesting solutions to the problems that perturb a child (p.5). Life is bewildering to all children and involves a turmoil of feelings, fears, anger, violence, desires and fantasies that lack both form and a name. Their bewildering and mysterious, sometimes frightening, inner world needs to come into awareness, so that in time order can be brought to the child's own life and story. The way this can happen is the substance of the book, with detailed analyses of individual stories, along with the drawing out of themes that they have in common.

Bettelheim discovered through his long experience of seeking to help children (normal and abnormal, as he calls them) that not only did the children find them more satisfying than other stories, but that fairy stories started where children really were in their psychological and emotional being. Most have had a very long period of gestation, and somehow they speak about a child's inner pressures in ways that she understands unconsciously, while at the same time offering examples of both temporary and permanent solutions to the pressing difficulties.

They do this (among other things) by offering ways in which unconscious feelings, desires and fears can be dealt with by means of engagement with the conscious fantasies of which fairy stories comprise. The stories offer new dimensions to the child's imagination that would not be discovered without them, and the simple form of the stories suggests images to the child so that she can structure daydreams with a sense of direction.

Rather than being overwhelmed by unconscious pressures, this connection to fairy stories allows some awareness of them that can be worked through in the imagination. Vital in the process is that a child is not aware of the psychological processes involved, and that they are not revealed to the child by the therapist or parent. In my view, to those of us operating within therapeutic milieu, this is one of the most important contributions of the book. Perhaps one of our besetting sins, or a default mode, is that we tend to want to make connections and even help to explain them. Bettelheim has no hesitation in warning against this in the case of fairy stories. Referring to a key word in the title of his book, Bettelheim says that fairy stories delight children particularly because they are unaware of the unconscious reasons for their enchantment. Explanations will tend not only to dispel this enchantment, but also deprive the child of struggling to find solutions and meanings of her own.

He continues his warning by stating that fairy stories are not neurotic symptoms, something one is better off understanding rationally in order to rid oneself of them! Rather the child's life is enriched precisely because she does not know how a story has worked its wonder (cast its spell?) on her.

The book is a deep mine or treasure trove of insights which are best discovered directly from within an encounter of its pages (just like a fairy story, which Bettelheim argues is a work of art that defies a definitive summary or explanation).

So, I will bring this commendation to a close, but before doing so, there are two related musings on it that I would like to share. Bettelheim distinguishes fairy stories from other contemporary stories on offer to children, from myths, and from biblical stories. This is inevitable given the focus and limits of his book. What, I wondered, would he have made, had he taken biblical stories as his subject, and would they have had the same potential for psychological growth and well-being? And does his warning hold true, that explanations of them should be kept out of the equation until later in their lives? If so, we need to recognise that Jerome Berryman in his development of the philosophy and methodology of Godly Play has something genuine to offer to those who do tell and re-tell these stories to children.

Bettelheim is aware, of course, that many children grow up in a post-religious, sometimes called secular, age. And many of today's adults do not derive their understandings of their outer and inner worlds, personal and human history, from these stories. This has for some considerable time led me to wonder what such people do with the dark parts of both personal and human history. Bettelheim writes (towards the end of the twentieth century) that there is a tendency to want children to believe that they are inherently good, that everyone is good. But children know that they are not good. So, they find themselves potentially bereft of assistance when neither their own lives, not what they discover of human history and contemporary reality, is not only not good, but sometimes depressingly far short of the mark.

I am one of a minority in Western Europe who still tells and re-tells biblical stories to children and delights to listen to their musings on them. For those who are uncomfortable in doing this, perhaps fairy stories are even more important. Unless that is you believe that Philip Pullman's *His Dark Materials* provides a possible way forward. What we cannot do, I believe, is to pedal a hollow myth that all humans are unequivocally good, and that history is a story of uninterrupted human progress. Any wise parent or sensitive therapist knows, like Bettelheim, that this simply will not do. In the face of truth, it is ultimately a recipe for despair.

As a matter of fact, Tolkien wrote his famous stories, notably *Lord of the Rings*, as a warning against totalitarian government and the disastrous belief that unbridled power in the hands of any human person or group would produce utopia. And he wrote his essay, *On Fairy Stories*, with an epilogue sharing his belief that the Gospel story was where all true fairy stories find their embodiment: "Art has been verified … Legend and History have met and fused" (page 63, Faber 1966 edition).

This edition of *TTCJ* is being published in the month during which Christians celebrate Easter. It would be sad if the therapeutic potential of both fairy stories and biblical stories lay unrealised and undisturbed.

The Windermere Children

Film directed by Michael Samuels
Warner Brothers: 2020

I am not sure whether the 2020 film *The Windermere Children*, directed by Michael Samuels, written by Simon Block, and based on The Windermere Project, has become one of the resources for those seeking to help children who have experienced trauma. But while watching it recently, it was a powerful reminder that all children who are placed in some form of alternative or substitute care have suffered trauma, not least loss of, and separation from, kith and kin. We can conceive of some sort of scale of trauma with the likes of the children who suffered in the holocaust, and of children from war zones suffering most, but watching the film for the first time reminded me that it is only a matter of degree: the essential dynamics and challenges are the same.

After 40 years of seeking to help children and young people at Mill Grove there were several aspects of the Project represented by certain scenes in the film that struck home.

For those who are new to the Project, it began in 1945 immediately after World War Two, was intended to last two years, and sought to care for and rehabilitate 300 children and young people who had just been liberated from concentration camps in Poland. It was supported by the Central British Fund for Jewish Relief. Spearheaded by Leonard Montefiore, who had also been involved in the Kindertransport initiative, it was an act of charity, underpinned by genuine empathy and love. Montefiore was a gifted organiser who, having arranged for a coalition of nations and bodies to make the Windermere Project possible in the first place, then chose with consummate care a team to head it up. He wanted gifted professionals who would understand the challenging and radical nature of a venture that would test them individually and collectively beyond reasonable or predictable limits.

Dr. Oscar Friedman, the leader chosen was a psychiatrist and teacher from Berlin. He was an orphan who had himself escaped Nazi persecution, during which time he lived in a concentration camp and was beaten up. In time the children discovered that he was in some ways like one of them. They later recalled that he never raised his voice. And he always listened to what a child or young person was trying to say. The aim he set for the Project was that each child should be seen as an individual and be encouraged to develop their own character. They needed to learn to stand on their own two feet, and to be prepared to take their place in society. He saw that the time would come when they could no longer rely on charity or pity.

To achieve this, what children needed was genuine experience of choice and freedom. After the brutal regimentation of the concentration camps, there were boundaries such as shared mealtimes, but otherwise there were as few rules at Windermere as possible. Each had a bed with sheets! One former child commented: "I started living". As a psychiatrist Friedman found that he never engaged in formal one-to-one sessions with the children and young people. They weren't at that stage,

and so he didn't attempt it. He did not encourage his team to attempt conventional counselling either, sensing that insight and healing would come by other means.

Though not engaging in conventional psychiatry, he was able to use his experience, wisdom and knowledge to build a team and establish boundaries, not only within the life of the newly formed community, but in relation to the surrounding villages, farms and neighbours. This meant helping his team to understand the extent of the traumas the children had experienced and were going through. He encouraged one of the children to leave the camp without explanation and without conditions knowing that would be the child's first experience of freedom. In the film this is depicted dramatically as he waves on a boy furtively trying to get out of the camp. Difficult to encapsulate the significance of that moment when the boy realised a newfound trust and freedom to explore the natural world by himself.

Mediated relationships with the surrounding community required all his psychological insight and ability. Had these relationships soured seriously the healing process would have been set back. He managed to retrieve a stolen dog; to find a way of acknowledging stolen goods, including eggs, without reprisals or punishment. He knew that the children were nowhere near the stage of taking responsibility for such actions: they were in a different mode. He handled a group of teenagers mocking the Windermere children with Nazi salutes in a masterly way. It was a brilliant example of applied group psychology.

He inspired and supported a team of volunteers that pioneered innovative ways of responding to trauma that were being developed in Germany. There was interaction with Anna Freud and her colleagues in Hampstead, particularly in relation to the six youngest children.

Marie Paneth, the art therapist, was a friend of Anna Freud, and she was allowed to operate without prescriptions or restrictions, complete freedom. It was crucial that the children only came when they wanted to do so, and that there was no comment on what they painted. The examples of their paintings given in the film were horrific in their symbolism and implications. This was a pioneering approach because there was no art therapy to speak of in the UK at this stage. She was guided by her own intuition in responding to exceptional grief and repressed anger; holding the face of one child, and allowing another to rest her head on her shoulder. Such actions are the quintessence of sensitive and professional responses and decision-making. They are about gut reactions. Significantly no word was spoken, so the boundaries of the art therapy sessions were maintained despite these deviations from standard practice.

Windermere was selected, not only because there happened to be a disused War Factory available, but because the initiators of the Project believed in the restorative quality of the beautiful world. Somehow some of the deepest emotional and spiritual healing would be enabled through direct contact with nature. Looking back, the survivors described Windermere as "The Promised Land". Interactions with the natural world were the setting of some of the most insightful and emotional interactions and discoveries. The lake. They loved being together beside it, and often swimming in it. And exploring the mountains. Who can explain why running through woods, diving into water, rowing across a lake, climbing a crag, is so full of potential for healing, self-knowledge and relationships?

The sports teacher, Jock Lawrence, was in some ways out of his depth, but his genuine desire to help and inspire the boys came through. And he was, like his colleagues, ready to learn with and from the young people: to admit his mistakes and apologise. His use of the term "son" in relating to the boys was obviously gauche and inappropriate in this situation, but they found a way of communicating this to him, and he was ready and willing to adjust and move on. He helped them to develop physically and in confidence. Winning football matches against local teams was hugely significant to them. In the process he became very close to them, and helped to shape some of their lives and careers.

A special education with its own curriculum was developed. Most of the youngsters had not known any formal education for six years. And they were keen to learn. Speaking and writing English was what they wanted to do more than anything. They were encouraged to learn what they wanted to do, for example playing the piano. They worked hard outside of school hours, working at books under trees. They knew that they had to learn to stand on their own two feet and that this started in the present, not at some later date.

The rabbi was a crucial figure in a community where Montefiore wanted there to be a Jewish context for the children. Some had lost any faith or trust in God, but open discussion, as in the rabbinical tradition, was encouraged, with no holds barred.

But now we come to the heart of the matter. Despite the exemplary boundary-keeping and facilitation of Dr. Friedman, the expertise and commitment of his team, the real action took place in the relationships between the children. It was through their conversations, their silences, their shared experiences, their anger, despair, the way in which their resentment was expressed, and in some way absorbed or deflected, that a process of healing developed. They could say what they really felt on occasions to each other. They had all, without exception, lost their closest relatives, and when the news of this arrived officially in the post things took a darker turn. But their shared grief was somehow held by the place/community and by their bonds and bonding.

The indication of how far they had come was indicated by the arrival of the brother of one of the boys, Salek. He was the only surviving relative of the children who appeared in Windermere. How would the others react, given that this reunion was a powerful and poignant reminder of their own loss? The film showed several of them smiling in empathy. That was a pivotal moment, a tipping point. The long-lost brother, the one who was feared dead, was alive again, and he was welcomed to the party, as it were, by those whose brothers and sisters would never return.

The group of six young children were the subject of a study by Anna Freud and a colleague. The children functioned as a tight-knit family. They felt for each other, cared for each other. If, for example, they had a nightmare, they didn't go to grown-ups but helped each other out. Because of the loss of their families, they had to be in a group. This group was some sort of safety net. Through careful recording, notes were shared with Anna Freud. And psycho-therapeutic meanings of behaviour were identified.

This reading of where the true healing lay is not simply that of a professional intuiting what might be going on: the reflections of the significant players in the story in their later lives confirmed this. Having lost their blood relatives, this group became their family. For many of the children who were part of the Windermere Project, it was something that worked, and for which they have been truly thankful.

And this is what we need all those responsible for responding to the needs of traumatised children (that is all children who have suffered some significant loss of attachments), whether directly or as policy makers, to learn to hear. Sadly, despite the testimony of so many children that they have found acceptance and healing in groups such as this, the myth continues: residential care is the last resort. If family rehabilitation is not possible for whatever reason, then the best alternatives are always adoption or foster care. There are no ifs and buts: this is a binary way of characterising the choices.

All my professional life I have listened to children, and to adults reflecting on their childhoods in different forms of care. The fact is that some have had positive experiences in each form (family, adoption, foster and residential care) and some have had horrendous experiences in each of these forms of care. The evidence is robust. So why is it that we cannot listen carefully enough to ask which they feel is most appropriate and why?

"It was like a family: a family affair" reflected one of the children much later in life. The choice of words is significant. For some reason professionals are resistant to the application of a label such as "family" being applied to settings very different from conventional nuclear families or households. I still meet those who tell me their stories of being part of the family of a large UK children's charity decades after one of its CEOs had explained to me that this was not appropriate. And I have virtually daily reminders of the bonds that have been established between those who have lived at Mill Grove. It is not a case of one size fits all.

You may find it hard to believe, but when I reached this point of the draft of this article, I received the following email from a retired teacher who had lived at Mill Grove as a child:

"I hear that you celebrated a special wedding anniversary last year. Congratulations! I'm so sorry that I wasn't able to be at your celebration, although [N] filled me in and told me how she met up with so many of our contemporaries while she was there. I was so happy when she contacted me to tell me that she had met up with a bunch of people who we hadn't seen for a very long time. For me, since I was 13, a long time ago!! I have since been able to swap numbers with them all and am hopefully going to be able to meet up later this year. I can tell you: this has been one of the best things to have happened to me in a long time. When I left Mill Grove … at the age of 13, I put on a huge amount of teenage bravado and pretended that I was happy to leave. But actually the wrench away was enormous and so I'm so thrilled to have made contact with so many friends/siblings? (How do you describe the relationship which we shared?) and really can't wait to see them all."

For whatever reason or combination of reasons, her words will never begin to disturb the myths and ideologies of those professionals and policy makers that know better than her, and all like her. My sense is that a Eurocentric pride still prevents well-meaning professionals from listening to the voices from the margins (the professionals see themselves as at the centre), seemingly completely unaware that in many countries and situations there is no way in which adoption or foster care is possible or appropriate. For the avoidance of doubt, I am not an advocate of one form of care over another. Rather, that we should seek to listen to and understand children in responding to their situations and needs without doctrinaire commitments and be willing to unlearn accrued dogma when the evidence contradicts them.

Why then can we not see that what happened at Windermere was not only one of the only options available, but also possibly the very best setting that there could have been, given the tragic backgrounds of the children? Had they all been adopted or separated into different foster care settings, then wouldn't the very heart of the healing process would have been destroyed? And yet we seem incapable of learning.

I have pondered this long and hard, as you can probably imagine. My conclusion is that there seems to be a myth in every society that family is best, and that therefore any alternatives that seem to be better for whatever reasons, are treated consciously or unconsciously as unthinkably subversive. And that what was in vogue a decade or so ago, labelled "evidence-based practice", is itself a myth.

But for those who can listen, the Windermere Project has not only much to teach, but much to inspire and enjoy.

INDEX

Lightning Source UK Ltd.
Milton Keynes UK
UKHW050918141122
412172UK00010B/503